THE UNFIN SH D
SOCIAL ENTREPRENEUR

BY JONATHAN C. LEWIS

red press

PRAISE FOR THE UNFINISHED SOCIAL ENTREPRENEUR

"This book is fucking incredible. What a pleasure to read. Required reading. I think this will be one of the most important books in social entrepreneurship. I don't actually know how Jonathan managed to capture this much nuance, wisdom, leadership and other things and never let it get boring. I read the whole thing in a day. I couldn't put it down."

—Saul Garlick, Founder and Chairman, ThinkImpact

"A book for our times. A witty, must-read primer for every social entrepreneur and every changemaker. Practical, hard-hitting advice coupled to important ethical questions confronting our field. A refreshing, unique look at the field of social entrepreneurship. Jonathan gives us the pragmatic guideposts we all need. The book I wish I had read in college."

—Premal Shah, President and Co-Founder, KIVA

"Buckle up! From the Bolivian Andes to the California lowlands, Jonathan takes you for a ride that will shake your inner radical free. By turns erudite and irreverent, angry and inspiring, this riveting, remarkable book nails what it means to be a social entrepreneur. On Lewis's rollicking road to enlightenment, you'll laugh out loud and be moved to tears. You'll meet an unforgettable cast of characters who have shaped one self-proclaimed "unfinished" social entrepreneur in his life's quest to right all that's wrong in the world. Read this book to rekindle your passion, re-right your compass, and restore your belief in what human beings can achieve. Read this book to renew your soul."

—Sally Osberg, President and CEO, Skoll Foundation

"*The Unfinished Social Entrepreneur* is certainly a call to action, but it is equally a call to reflection, to celebration, to accountability. Jonathan's voice is exuberant; ebullient; authentic. He is irreverent toward the current orthodoxies of social entrepreneurship and unapologetically seeks to reorient his reader to root motivations—

to be honestly engaged in demanding work that aligns our own needs with the core social and environmental challenges of our times. His is a wide-ranging, eclectic, inclusive mind. His vision is both grand and gritty, inspirational and everyday, inviting us to bridge and meld lofty ambition with practical reality."

–Tony Sheldon, Executive Director, Program on
Social Enterprise, Yale School of Management

"Lewis will make you laugh, cry or get angry, and then act! An impassioned plea to do change-making: citizen-get-off-your-ass. This is a good book! Saul Alinsky meets Dave Barry. Mandela meets Chris Rock."

– Michael Gordon, Arthur F. Thurnau Professor of Social
Entrepreneurial Studies; Faculty Director, Center for Social
Impact, Ross School of Business, University of Michigan

"Jonathan humanizes social entrepreneurship. He talks to us in a straightforward way, illustrating with personal experience the ups and downs of a social change career. He reminds seasoned social entrepreneurs of the importance of a moral compass, of remembering whose side we're on, and of deciding which enemies are worth making. Funny; engaging; deep. The book I wish I'd read when I was 18."

–Martin Burt, Founder and CEO, Fundación Paraguaya

"You had me at the book jacket... I don't even need to read this book to know that it's amazing. I mean, its Jonathan Lewis writing about social entrepreneurship. There will be hot dogs, bad puns and sage advice. And you won't be able to put it down..."

–Randall Kempner, Executive Director,
Aspen Network of Development Entrepreneurs (ANDE)

"Jonathan's chapter on whiteness and privilege is stunning. It is one of the best pieces written by a white person I've ever read. He is humble, thoughtful and brave as he describes his lived experience of navigating the delicate dynamics of race. Beautifully written; deeply heartfelt."

–Akaya Windwood, President, Rockwood Leadership Institute

"I love the line: 'What is social entrepreneurship if not a love affair with justice?' Well-said."

–Roshan Paul, Co-Founder and CEO, Amani Institute,
(Brazil and Kenya)

"Jonathan captures the feelings we don't dare share openly. Stunning and engaging. I found myself nodding, laughing and at times tearful."

–Chingwell Mutombu, Managing Director, Women Rising

"I am going buy a copy for my daughter to read when she turns 18. She is 12 now and repeatedly tells me she wants to be an activist when she grows up. We live in Lagos, Nigeria, a case study in inequality! From Jonathan's book, I can see my daughter at 18 finding the bearings she needs to chart her cause."

–Amara Kyna Agbim, Founder/CEO, The Nanny Academy (Nigeria)

"Jonathan Lewis has risked trying and learning changemaking, and shares that journey in a light-footed style that treats the reader like a family member."

–Bill Drayton, CEO, Ashoka: Everyone a Changemaker

"I want to underscore just how valuable this book is. There's a wealth of experience, insight, and wisdom in these pages. There are some lines that hit you in the gut, others that stab you in the heart, and others that blow your mind. It's a visceral experience, an emotional read, and a thought-provoking analysis."

–Alexandra McGee, Community Power Organizer, MCE

"Jonathan pairs honest, vulnerable experiences with incredible proven insight. A great read and guide for anyone wanting to be a social entrepreneur."

–Sara Minkara, Founder and CEO, Empowerment
through Integration (Lebanon)

"Required reading for anyone developing the head and the heart necessary to run a game-changing social enterprise."

–Chid Liberty, Founder and CEO, Liberty & Justice (Liberia)

"Jonathan's blend of stories, wisdom and poetic prose stirs emotions. His words invite deep reflection about this complicated, beautiful journey. I'm reminded that I am not alone."
–Amy Paulson, Co-Founder and CEO, Global Gratitude Alliance

"I love this book. Jonathan includes us on his life journey – and joins us on ours. He seems to know that we will ignore him at times, but our motives (more or less) are pure and our devotion inevitable. Through story-telling, witty delivery and Socratic questioning, Jonathan shows us how to turn self-doubt into an asset. This book is approachable, welcoming, soulful, truthful and personal."
–Rosalinda Sanquiche, Founder and CEO, Well Written Consulting; Former Executive Director, Ethical Markets Media

"Jonathan humanizes the bold journey of the social entrepreneur and empowers us to find mastery in being vulnerable, authentic and powerfully imperfect."
–Tiffany Persons, Founder and CEO, Shine On Sierra Leone

"Just about the best explanation of social entrepreneurship that I have ever read. Honestly."
–Sam Vaghar, Executive Director, Millennium Campus Network

"With honesty and delightful wit, Jonathan shares the inside picture of how he started and maintained his social entrepreneurship. We are learning from the master."
–Babita Patel, Founder and CEO, KIOO Project

"Jonathan's writing is beautiful, important and unique, vulnerable and honest, thought-provoking and funny, encouraging and realistic. Urgently important and universally inspirational. Made my insides say *Yes!* or giggle."
–Holly McKenna, Poet and Cacao Social Entrepreneur

In the way he lived his life, my father Louis A. Lewis showed me that kindness is strength.

California State Senator Nicholas C. Petris, my first employer, taught me to make justice a verb.

ABOUT JONATHAN C. LEWIS

Jonathan C. Lewis is a life-long social justice activist and an accomplished social entrepreneur. He founded MCE Social Capital, an innovative social venture that leverages millions of dollars of private capital to finance tiny business loans to deeply-impoverished people, mostly women, throughout the developing world. MCE, a rarity in the nonprofit sector, is entirely self-financing without donations, government grants or direct impact investments.

He is Founder and President of the Opportunity Collaboration, an annual strategic business retreat for 450 senior-level anti-poverty leaders from around the globe. Tagged an *un-conference conference*, the event is self-sustaining without corporate underwriting or other external financing.

Jonathan also co-founded Copia Global, an Amazon-like consumer catalog serving the base of the economic pyramid in Kenya. Jonathan serves as a General Partner of Dev Equity, a social impact investment fund in Latin America.

Jonathan has taught courses on social entrepreneurship at New York University, the University of California (Berkeley), and has lectured at universities around the world. He is a recipient of the Social Venture Network Innovation Award. He is a Trustee of the Swift Foundation.

During his eclectic career, Jonathan has served as the Founder and CEO of a global business knowledge company in the healthcare sector; Chief Budget Adviser to the President of the California State Senate (who, in public debate in the Senate, said to his colleagues, "if the Senate has a resident genius, it's Jonathan Lewis"); Founder and CEO of an urban real estate development company; and owner of a contemporary art gallery.

Jonathan is on a search to find the tastiest hot dog at the wackiest hot dog stand in the world. He lives near San Francisco with his wife of 45 years. His son Aaron and daughter-in-law Michaela are the parents of Miles Lewis which, by all accounts, makes Jonathan a new grandfather.

ABOUT THE COMMUNITY CONVERSATION GUIDE

What can you expect from the *Community Conversation Guide* that accompanies this book? Well, let's start off with what it's not. Much like the book itself, it is *not* riddled with sector-specific language that requires a Google search just to sift through each sentence. It's not tied to academic benchmarks, designed to test your knowledge of the material. And it's not a how-to guide that tees things up step-by-step.

The *Community Conversation Guide* is a tool that friends, clubs, classmates, and colleagues can use to bring their own experiences and perspectives into the fold, digging deeper into the ideas presented in the book. We want you to transform the written words in *The Unfinished Social Entrepreneur* into something that means something to you, that helps move important conversations from the shadows to the center. The guide is designed to support social entrepreneurs in taking ownership over and applying the ideas presented in *The Unfinished Social Entrepreneur* to the daily practice of change-making.

Whether you've read the book in its entirety or not, the Guide will provide key insights from each essay. We've teased apart each essay and crafted a handful of questions for your group to get things rolling, designed simple activities to that keep things engaging, and compiled reading lists for those of you who want more of the good stuff. We've also pulled Jonathan's most interesting excerpts for sharing on social media, because who doesn't love a shout out? (And, if you haven't read the book, you can at least pretend like you have.)

All that we ask is that you have fun with it. Wherever you are on your social justice journey, we hope that the Guide proves useful. We highly recommend that you pair it with snacks and beverages, and that you post yourself on a cushy sofa or swaying hammock.

Head to www.jonathanclewis.com to download the Guide.

TABLE OF CONTENTS

WELCOME

Welcome to The Unfinished Social Entrepreneur. My name is Jonathan Lewis.

This book is about powering up your social justice career. Maybe you've already found your social justice job. Maybe you haven't. Either way—in the pages ahead, know that we are colleagues, and friends. At this moment in your life, maybe a job in social entrepreneurship isn't for you, and that's totally cool. You alone will decide when you're ready for the serious, soaring work of improving the world.

Regardless of when and where you start—we are kindred spirits. We belong to a global community of ordinary citizens, activists, social entrepreneurs, businesspeople, students, artists, philanthropists, scholars, scientists and policy-makers. We all work in concert, in our own way, and at our own pace, to combat the disgrace of grinding poverty, social injustice and environmental pollution.

Before I forget, I want to mention that I'm using the word 'you' in the first-person singular. I didn't write this book for your roommate, your best friend, your hair stylist, the other members of your book club or, for that matter, anyone else. Just you. Social entrepreneurship is a collection of individuals, of ones—of you and of me. Social change starts with one person.

Even when our all-too-human imperfections are evident, social entrepreneurs possess a calming strength that flows from understanding our life purpose. On most days, we are empowered, empowering and powerful in our professional lives.

That's not all. We also tell better jokes; make more friends; get the best tables in restaurants. At movies, our popcorn is fluffier and more buttery. When we travel, our flights are always on time, and the pilot personally shows us to our seats. When we overeat, we don't gain weight. Our lottery tickets always pay off. (Okay, *okay*. The part about the fluffier popcorn isn't true.)

Social entrepreneurship is a career of mind-blowing satisfactions and mind-boggling self-doubt. At some point in our social entrepreneurship – actually, at many points – we each wonder if we fit in, if we are doing enough, if we are worthy. No matter how small or insignificant you might feel on any given day; even if you are just getting your career underway; even if a hurtful defeat has set you back—your unique life perspective matters, but not uniquely. Everyone matters.

ABOUT ME

It's human nature to group people, to make assumptions based on appearances and first impressions. When we agree with the characterization, we speak of tribes and identities. When we don't, we speak of prejudice and bias. If it helps you unpack my writing, you might want to know the following about me.

I'm writing this book in my 68th year. I am a Caucasian male born in the United States, the only child of two working-class parents. My parents married during the Depression; on their wedding day, they had $15 between them. I grew up in liberal San Francisco during the tumultuous Sixties, where I gravitated towards antiwar and civil rights activism. All my life, I've lived in Northern California. It was here that I met my wife of 44 years, and helped raise my son (now a 32 year-old public interest lawyer). Here too, I'm a new grandfather.

My social sector biography is a collage of governmental service, nonprofit work and social impact investing. About a decade ago, I founded MCE Social Capital, a nonprofit social venture that has leveraged private capital to finance over 400,000 microloans for deeply-impoverished businesswomen in 33 countries throughout the developing world. I am the Founder and President of the Opportunity Collaboration, an annual strategic business retreat for 450 senior-level anti-poverty leaders from around the globe. I'm also am the Co-Founder of Copia Global, an Amazon-like consumer catalog company serving the base of the economic pyramid in Kenya.

Having no other choice than to be me, the book is framed (and limited) by my personal experience, and my particular perspective, as an American social entrepreneur. I wish I could have written about social entrepreneurship as the global phenomenon it is becoming, or from the point of view of indigenous activists, but I can only write what I've lived.

Depending on your viewpoint, the book is further informed, or distorted, by my lifelong Type A entrepreneurial problem-solving approach. Knowing this, you should moderate my take on things to fit your own personality, talents and life history.

I do want you to know that I've written the best book that I can. It might not be the book you deserve, but it's the best that I can do. In these pages, I've been as honest as my inhibitions allowed me to be. I've tried to be a truth-teller, sharing what I'm thinking and questioning.

At times, especially late into the night, alone with my qualms, I felt vulnerable in the certain knowledge that, no matter how carefully I crafted a sentence, no matter how thoughtfully I chose my words, the received wisdom of the cynical and the self-righteous would critique and judge me. Perhaps even harshly. I had to resist the cowardly urge to self-censor.

As I wrote, I tightly embraced the thinking of journalist Bill Moyers (quoted in *The 100 Greatest Americans of the 20th Century*). He states: "When I left the White House, I had to learn that what matters in journalism is not how close you are to power, but how close you are to the truth." While writing, I discovered my own jarring inconsistencies, infirmities, contradictions and hypocrisies—as well as amazing optimisms. I decided to trust that what mattered most was not how firmly I held on to my convictions, but how much I was willing to doubt them.

TIPS FOR USING THE BOOK

Let's talk about the heart-mending, heart-ripping, heart-happy joy of social entrepreneurship, social change and social justice. Let's talk about the issues, the challenges, the topics of greatest concern to us.

Read the essays in any order you like. I wrote them as stand-alone pieces. Read them as and when they are relevant to your social entrepreneurship, and read them again when you need to. Some are about getting your social justice career started. Others raise questions and challenges that, together as colleagues, we face throughout our careers.

Each essay tees up a canard or challenge—a provocation, if you will. Each is a reflection, almost a meditation, on a topic of disquiet for me. In many parts of this book, I'm unable to offer answers. You might find that frustrating; unsatisfying; alarming. No one has all the answers, so at the end of the day, no social entrepreneur is released from the responsibility (and the fun) of independent exploration and critical thinking. Some days, I'm not even asking the right questions. It's a cause for humility, not for halting.

This book is neither a comprehensive overview of the social sector, nor a compendium of all the operational advice that a social entrepreneur should know. It's also not yet another well-researched book about the deplorable disgrace of global poverty, or the stupidity of environmental desecration. I will die happy if I never read another numbing policy analysis detailing a heart-breaking, and solvable, societal disgrace.

This is not a how-to manual, because the written word is an intrinsically stingy medium for teaching good judgment, leadership and wisdom—or for explaining the character, compassion, commitment and courage that every social entrepreneur needs by the bucketful. In apprenticeship, and in solidarity, with the communities we serve, the life-essential qualities of the social entrepreneur are acquired over time. Like kissing and like cooking, we master the mechanics of social change work with practice.

If I missed talking about something important, if I speak of a subject in a way that aggravates you, or if you find yourself sputtering out a rebuttal—I hope you will share your views, openly and widely, in a public forum so that other changemakers can learn from you. Maybe you will write your own book, post a blog, or tweet your opinion. I'd love to read what you think. Really. Let's make each other better.

Because *social* entrepreneurship is not called *solo* entrepreneurship, I asked colleagues to supplement my words:

1. At the close of every essay, under the title *Take Two,* you will read a commentary from a change agent whose life experience differs fundamentally from my own. These commentaries were curated and edited by the Co-Founder of Strength of Doves, Lissa Piercy. Each individual was selected because they are a fierce and fearless defender of their community or cause—and more importantly, willing to express themselves without kowtowing to my sensibilities. In fact, to create more space for their candor, I promised not to read or edit any of their commentaries; I'm reading them for the first time along with you. I've come to think of them as small gems of insight, much like a late-into-the-night email from a thoughtful colleague; a fleeting moment of intellectual intimacy in a taxi ride; or the good friend who calls out your bullshit but still has your back.

2. On my website, check out the *Community Conversation Guide.* It's written by Jen Gurecki, the Co-Founder of Kenya-based Zawadisha. This is your free companion guide to the book. Essay by essay—the guide includes questions and activities to help you take the book's insights to the next level; it also includes short and accessible readings for further exploration. Educators, book clubs, student groups, and community activists alike will find it a helpful time-saver. As long as you credit *The Unfinished Social Entrepreneur,* download and distribute the *Community Conversation Guide* as much as you like.

ABOUT LANGUAGE CHOICES

In this book, I use the terms *social entrepreneur, changemaker, change agent, political activist, community organizer and social innovator* almost as virtual synonyms. A tight definition of social entrepreneurship is not, by any measure, the most significant challenge confronting the world, or our social justice careers. We can get started doing good work before we define our terms.

Some manuscript reviewers urged me to simplify my terminology. They argued that, if I know a word that you don't, you might be too lazy to look it up on your smartphone dictionary app. As colleagues who respect each other, I argued that, if I dumbed down my vocabulary, you would resent it.

One essay – entitled *White* – is meant to spark a conversation among changemakers with melanin deficits. Everyone is welcome to read it, but bear in mind that I wrote it for a very narrow audience of Caucasian social entrepreneurs. This essay is me, being the white person that I am, asking other white people to take action to make certain that our sector is as diverse as our inclusive rhetoric calls for.

In a linguistically-perfect world, we would all appreciate that the term 'American' applies to every single person living in both North, Central and South America. Following the common custom, I use 'American' to mean citizens of the United States of America.

Also, around the edges of an in-person conversation, you and I may have different shades of meaning for certain nouns, pronouns, words and phrases. In person, a smile or a concerned look helps to smooth over these minor miscommunications. The printed page can't smile, so the choice is yours: we can arm wrestle over the perfect way to say something, or we can roll up our sleeves and attack the problem itself.

When I write about social justice, I'm prone to sanctimony. And why not? The world feels so screwed up, so unfair, so unnecessarily mean, so *Trumpian*. It makes me livid. Sometimes, my anger sounds preachy. I don't see why I should apologize, but I also hope you're not put off.

You should also know that I am on a quest to find the tastiest hot dog at the silliest hot dog stand in the world. As a result, I scatter frivolous hot dog references throughout the book. Vegans and vegetarians: stand aside.

Some of my closest friends and colleagues have questioned my sense of humor and, in particular, my cringe-worthy puns and snarky quips. These critics, obviously lacking in comic judgment, are manifestly mistaken.

AN UNFINISHED WORD

The decision to write a book unfolds slowly. This book took me a lifetime to start. Often, I thought it would take me a lifetime to finish. Throughout my social change career, well-wishers flattered me by saying 'you should write a book' or insisting that 'I had a book in me'. This latter point frequently brought to mind those science-fiction movies in which an otherwise perfectly-normal person is host to an alien life-form (an apprehension I can now, with hindsight, confirm). In any case, flattery doesn't write a book any more than good intentions create social change.

I was also assured that authorship defines you as a person of consequence. A book bestows *gravitas*. It might even get you invited to speak at an important conference, or interviewed by Oprah. I was unmoved by all of this. To me, 'gravitas' sounds like paving material.

For most of my life, the idea of *writing* about social entrepreneurship has paled in comparison to *doing* social entrepreneurship. Then, while I was reading *Essays in Love* by the social philosopher Alain de Botton, one sentence pushed me towards my computer: "Certain things are said, not because they will be heard, but because it is important to speak them." He was writing about romantic relationships, but what is social entrepreneurship if not a love affair with justice?

In any case, after years of protestations and procrastination, I started this book as an untidy, private journey to explain to myself what it means to be a change agent. I wanted to better understand my place in the world. I discovered writing as one way to think harder about social entrepreneurship and social justice, to catalog my reflections and missteps, to collect my joys and concerns.

This book is a book of conviction, but I did not write it to lecture you about our global humanity or shared challenges. If your conscience doesn't move you to action—nothing else can or will. Even so, 'social entrepreneurship' is a career term proudly owned by changemakers with progressive views. In the places where I hang out—the verb 'to social entrepreneur' means fighting sexism, homophobia, xenophobia, racism, militarism, environmental degradation and economic exploitation. And, it means building social ventures that both serve communities and create jobs. It means inclusiveness and diversity. It means human dignity, civil liberties and human rights. It means participatory democracy, transparent government and freedom of thought. It means peace and prosperity. That's certainly what it means to me.

Writing allowed me to imagine the world as I would like it to be. The more I wrote, the closer I stood to my moral imagination; to my life's unfinished mission; to the unfinished work of social justice.

JUSTICE

When you and I really think about it, when we burrow into our souls, we both know that, at its core, social entrepreneurship is a love affair. Our life partner is justice.

At the age of 22, I dropped out of my senior year of college to begin work as the top legislative assistant and *aide-de-camp* for a California state senator. I had only learned about the job opening by accident while interning at the State Capitol. At the time, I was an unpaid grunt worker in an office cubicle, answering constituent mail about potholes and lost Social Security checks. Two months into my part-time internship, mundane letter-writing was about all I was good for.

Future historians will doubtless scratch their heads as they wonder why a state senator with approximately one million constituents (in addition to being a ranking member of the health, tax and judiciary committees; a seasoned lawyer; a trained journalist; an acknowledged policy expert and a celebrated orator) troubled himself to hire me. Even I knew that I was utterly unqualified. No doubt a footnote will also record that it took me three whole months to discover that the second door in my office was, in fact, a private passageway connecting his office and mine (and not, as I had assumed, a storage closet).

For elementary school students visiting the State Capitol, the Senator's office distributed *How a Bill Becomes Law*: a simple, cartoonish flowchart explaining the legislative process. This was the kind of rudimentary information that a legislative aide was expected to already know by heart. I, on the other hand, secretly taped a copy behind my office door and studied it frantically before each appointment.

To compensate for my incontrovertible shortcomings, I worked in a fevered state—a work ethic that (for better or worse) I follow to this day. I was at my desk at 7am, took 30 minutes for lunch, and worked until 7pm. Then, I walked two blocks to the Country Maid Diner for a 'rotunda hamburger' on an oval platter mounded with french fries. A double-thick chocolate milkshake served as both drink and dessert. I ended my workday around 11pm. On weekends, my recreational reading consisted of government reports.

I was the Senator's only legislative aide, sole press secretary, one policy researcher, lone speechwriter, chief clerk for constituent mail (before emailing, faxing, or texting) and prime surrogate for policy meetings with constituents, lobbyists, journalists and anyone else who happened by the office. In the fullness of time, the Senator and I also became a book club of two. In a contest to read the eleven-volume *History of Civilization* by Will and Ariel Durant, he won.

State Senator Nicholas C. Petris is the very soul of the social entrepreneur that I am today. When I write and speak about my social entrepreneurship, it is his voice that you hear—his clear sense of right and wrong; his bold embrace of new and controversial ideas; his courageous use of power; his principled instinct to fight alongside those without privilege or advantage.

—∞—

Across the street from the Capitol was the Senator Hotel—the hub of social life among the political class, the scene of lobbyist-financed banquets and smarmy political plots. And, in the hotel's elegant Empire room, my first public event as the Senator's aide.

The night that the Senator was scheduled to receive the legal profession's 'Legislator of the Year' award also happened to be the first time I had worn a suit since my high school graduation. I found myself in a ballroom bursting with banquet tables adorned with crisp white linen, fine china and floral centerpieces. Like preening peacocks with law degrees, the legal profession was in full strut. As many as 500 trial lawyers (all men, as I recall) were wining and dining, laughing and talking over each other. The speeches went largely ignored—because they were less profitable and less entertaining than network-ing and deal-making. As a result, the Head Table dignitaries, Senator

Petris included, seemed little more than table decorations. Following standard protocol, after dinner, the Senator approached the microphone to accept his award. The din was raucous; unrelenting. At the back of the hall, straining my ears, I leaned forward to listen to my new boss.

"Ladies and Gentlemen, fellow members of the Bar, honored guests," he began. "Thank you so much. I am proud and honored to join you this evening. I know we are at a party, gathered here to celebrate with friends and colleagues, but, if you would indulge me, I want to take a few minutes to talk with you about our profession and our special responsibility, as lawyers, in building a better California."

A gradual hush befell the room as more and more heads turned to listen. The Senator's voice rose above the waning clamor—serious and sober, commanding attention. These many years later, his words remain the markings on my moral compass. I can repeat them almost verbatim.

"California is a wonderful place to practice law. Blessed with abundant resources and unlimited human talent, California's economy is growing and vibrant—and in need of lots more lawyers." Laughter swept the room. "But all is not perfect in our state or in our profession," he continued, falling into a speech cadence I would come to love, and make my own. "As attorneys, as officers of the court, sworn to uphold the law, here's what I want to talk with you about.

"Who are the corporate attorneys who told their clients that it is perfectly acceptable to dump poison in our rivers?

"Who are the school district attorneys who advised their school board clients that it is legal to shutter schools during the harvest season so young children could be forced into the fields to pick our fruit?

"Who are the attorneys who looked the other way when their clients exploited our glorious coastline for private gain? Who are the attorneys who allowed their bank clients to discriminate against women and minority customers?

"Who are the attorneys who wrote the legal memoranda sanctioning racial discrimination by their housing developer clients?"

By that point, the audience was rapt with attention. No talking. No whispering. No clanking food service. Not even a cough.

"My fellow lawyers, we are officers of the court. We did not take an oath to practice the law. We took an oath to practice justice."

— ∞ —

Senator Petris wasn't just talking to a room full of lawyers. He was talking to me. He was talking to you. He was challenging us to activate our moral authority—as professionals, parents, voters, students, workers, writers, business leaders and ordinary individuals. He was calling us to be social entrepreneurs for justice.

If social entrepreneurship exists, it exists only because you and I swoon for justice. Our social entrepreneurial careers depend on a sustained reverence for fairness, decency, kindness and justice.

When you and I really think about it, when we burrow into our souls, we both know that at its core, social entrepreneurship is a love affair. Our life partner is justice.

Like any love affair, justice awakens an insatiable yearning. The more we embrace it, the more we are fulfilled by it. The more justice we get, the more we want—and the more it demands of us. Just like in any dynamic relationship, my mind focuses on what I can give, not what I can take. Thus, my happiness is fused with the happiness of others. As the old adage reminds us: giving is receiving.

I don't have a precise definition for social justice. I also don't have a precise definition for freedom of speech, or human dignity or, for that matter, the perfect romance. What I can confirm is that fairness, decency and kindness come naturally to social entrepreneurs, and from there, our hearts build our vision for a just world.

The nature of justice is elusive: a sea of shifting circumstances and expanding horizons. Each generation enlarges our working definition of justice to reflect a more generous, more inclusive understanding of the human experience. Consequently, we can never finish our social justice work, any more than we can ever achieve absolute perfection in playing a musical instrument, leading a life of virtue, or cooking the yummiest hot dog. The *pursuit* of a more perfect world is the euphoric part of our social justice work.

— ∞ —

If you were down on your luck, if you lived on the edges of society, Senator Petris was never too busy to hear your petition. Never too high and mighty (or too calculating) to spend his political capital on your behalf; to be on your side; to walk with you. In my mind's eye, I still see the Senator walking to the nearest mailbox, licking a stamp as he went, refusing taxpayer-funded postage. He always kept a few stamps in his wallet, smashed between his business cards. If he had saved himself a few minutes by leaving that one single letter with the outgoing Senate mail, honestly no real harm would have been done. But if you lick your own postage stamps—it's a reasonable bet that you haven't lost the common touch, that all-important capacity to hear and understand the lives of ordinary people.

As social entrepreneurs, you and I reject the impulse to distance ourselves from others, to objectify others, to make others invisible for our own comfort, to walk past human suffering, or to deny our own. We don't do social entrepreneurship because people need us. We do it because we need people. And, because everyone needs justice.

Like most social entrepreneurs, Senator Petris was an ardent, zealous, hot-blooded advocate for social, environmental, economic, racial and gender justice. Even if our individual personalities are quiet, reflective, introspective changemakers are fierce in their committed values.

We don't do social entrepreneurship because people need us. We do it because we need people. And, because everyone needs justice.

A life of social entrepreneurship means passing judgment. We are opinionated bastards. Judge and jury. I've heard some people in this sector claim to be non-judgmental. I have no idea what they're talking about. Maybe they're in a coma.

For instance, you and I don't accept that our human species is, by fouling our own nest, committing suicide. We don't accept a world in which half of us survive on $2 per day—roughly $700 a year. We don't accept a world where cruelty, racism, sexism, aggression, exploitation and war are routine.

Social entrepreneurs are aggrieved—and those grievances, collectively and individually, identify and bind us as a tribe. Talk to any nearby change agent: the gripes and grumbles about the world's vulgarities come gushing out. In polite, polished conversations, our grievances are sometimes called 'policy concerns'.

A fearless dealer in disruptive ideas, Senator Petris intentionally proposed controversial legislation to spark public debate and, thereby, challenged Californians with a vision that none of us had yet imagined. To call attention to air pollution, he introduced legislation to completely outlaw the internal combustion engine (in car-crazy California, no less). To safeguard farm workers against the ravages of pesticide poisoning, he proposed putting public health doctors in charge of farming practices. To protect the mentally ill from *de facto* incarceration, he proposed a patient bill of civil rights. To spotlight prison reform, he proposed law libraries in every penal institution. Petris wielded his legislative power like a bullhorn, highlighting societal problems and pushing public awareness in new directions.

By watching Senator Petris in action, I learned that the highest and best use of power is empowering the unpowerful. Each of his legislative initiatives had a working theory about who had power, who lacked it, *and why*. A dogged truth of social entrepreneurship is that we stand, persistently and indefatigably, with the underdog. When a complicated policy problem arises, and if I'm confused, uncertain or unclear about what to do, I side with the outsider and the outcast, the different and the despairing—because even if I turn out to be wrong on the merits, I'm usually right on the morality.

Inside every changemaker, a bit of the missionary gene lurks—a crusader complex on behalf of our causes and concerns. We feel a compulsion to leave our compassionate, disruptive, transformative, creative mark on the world. It's messianic, but so what? I don't see how we can believe in social justice and not proselytize for it.

As it happens, there are plenty of terrific ways to make the world better, but being a purist isn't one of them. In the trenches of social change, every day is a compromise. Every day, our vision of perfection is imperfectly implemented. Social entrepreneurs tarnish our ideals through hard use. In our pragmatism, we are happy to get our hands in the muck and mire of changing the world. We settle for the victories we can win. We make real choices. We negotiate with the malevolent and the malicious. Everything else is wishful thinking, a good-hearted hallucination.

Because the social sector routinely appropriates words from the business sector, social entrepreneurs often describe their next career opportunity or social venture using terms such as 'risk-taking'. That makes sense because what you and I do is risky. Risky in every way but one. We never risk our convictions. In fact, the only time our convictions are at risk is when we don't use them.

—∞—

The crusty work of social entrepreneurship is as much fun as I'm permitted to have in public. It's joyous, fulfilling and happy-making. Whenever I take my place in the public square, life is more challenging, more rewarding, more engaging and more entertaining. Tackling big challenges is heady stuff. Fighting the good fight is utterly gratifying—completing and comforting. I'm a happier person because I'm a social entrepreneur.

In elemental ways, social justice work is the most selfish thing I do. Every time I work in partnership, in community, in solidarity – whether working on a political campaign in the United States or a social business venture in the developing world – I learn something important about myself. Of course, that's not the self-centered endpoint of my social entrepreneurship, but it is an excellent side benefit.

Service, sacrifice and surrender to our deepest principles is the private pride of every social entrepreneur.

Social entrepreneurs are humbled, and made happy, by the privilege of service. It's a sentimental, old-fashioned value, but it's central to who we are and what we do. When President Kennedy famously challenged an entire generation to "ask not what your country can do for you; ask what you can do for your country," he did not qualify it by adding: 'if there are financial returns at market rates' or 'if it's a smart career move' or 'if you can find the time in your otherwise busy life'. Service, sacrifice and surrender to our deepest principles is the private pride of every social entrepreneur.

In all the years that I observed Senator Petris, I never once saw him agonize over questions of 'good public policy' versus 'political expediency'. Like the best social entrepreneurs, he was always 'on principle' because, existentially, it was his only option. He didn't know how to be any other way.

7

You and I make a conscious choice to stand up for social justice not because we should, but because it's who we are. It's how I want to live my life. That's pretty much all there is to say about a social entrepreneur's job.

One of our secrets (I'm sure you've discovered this already) is that there's nothing quite so thrilling, so satisfying, as doing the decent or kind thing, the right and just thing, *and not getting credit for it*. No financial return. No social impact metrics. No 'doing well by doing good'. No bragging annual report. No media story. Just a personal moment of profound paradise.

Social entrepreneurs are a club of conscience: a community of concerned citizens for whom social change work is a personal awakening, a way to contribute, a way to belong, a way to make life worthwhile. Membership means that, not only do we think good thoughts, we also take a spirited stab at turning a few of those good thoughts into good deeds. There are no armchair social entrepreneurs.

Is social entrepreneurship a toolkit, a methodology, an industry, or an asset class? All of the above. Now is a challenging and important time for anyone to launch a changemaker career. A hundred times I've tried, and failed, to write a few paragraphs about the world's troubles, a few lines to summarize the world's heartaches. I finally gave up, instead agreeing with Charles Blow in *Fire Shut Up in My Bones*: "I don't know how to describe the sound of a world crashing." To your credit, you already know that the world needs repairing. You already know that it's a hot mess.

Because our battles are with the interconnected monstrosities of racism, sexism, ageism, classism and eco-terrorism, it can be really tough figuring out where to start and what to do. You might feel as I once did, as I stood lost and befuddled on a narrow, twisty street in the 9th-century walled city of Fez, Morocco. Unsure of my next turn, unable to spot a familiar landmark—I was still wildly ecstatic to be there. Social entrepreneurship is like that: an exciting, enriching journey of discovery, marked by moments of total bewilderment.

In classrooms and at conferences, people variously describe social entrepreneurship as a profession, a toolkit, a methodology, an industry, or an asset class. It's all of those, of course. But we are called to it for subterranean reasons that form the very foundations of who we are as individuals, and as global citizens. We measure ourselves against the fulfillment of our majestic hopes for social and environmental justice.

Some people think that if you want to fundamentally and comprehensively understand social entrepreneurship, you need to read separate books: a book about business, a book about public policy, a book about economics, a book about management and a book about justice.

Read the book on justice first.

STARTING

Enroll in the university-without-walls around you. It's hard to invent a more lifelike, more poignant, classroom for understanding inequality than inequality itself.

On a typical day between 1963 and 1967, you would have found me slouched down low at my high school desk, staring at the wall clock as it ticked indifferently towards my freedom. With my body language set to 'invisible', my purpose in life was to avoid the dreaded 'Mr. Lewis, would you like to answer the question?' My daily routine was stashing half-done homework in my school locker, showing up unprepared for exams, and screwing around in the precious few minutes between classes. My study habits (if they can be called that) sucked. My grades hovered in the 'not-living-up-to-his-potential' category.

Wedged between an eight-lane freeway and a blue-collar shopping district—my private, all-boy, mostly-white, prep school was a geographic trespasser. Acquiring a habit of mind common to ruling elites the world over, the students didn't hang out in the less-affluent neighborhood surrounding our school; in fact, we pretended that it simply didn't exist. After all, and by design, we were being groomed for the professions; for the best universities; for success among the privileged; for life among the upper echelons of society.

After school, instead of doing homework, I traipsed up and down the fog-bound hills of San Francisco, discovering gleaming mansions in the posh Pacific Heights, and cardboard houses in the troubled Tenderloin. I wandered Chinatown to savor the scent of roasted ducks hanging in restaurant windows. After pawing through the used books at Green Apple Bookstore, if I had any extra money, I planted myself in an aromatic Russian bakery in front of a hot meat-filled *piroshki*. On Sunday afternoons, I explored Golden Gate Park hoping (and failing) to meet girls.

According to the social metrics of youth, I didn't measure up. When I thought about it, which was most of the time, I was keenly aware of my status as an outsider. When I forced myself to join the football team (for one single bruising season), the cool kids reluctantly invited me to sit at their lunch table. While my classmates summered at Lake Tahoe, I worked minimum-wage jobs to afford extra clothes. I was unathletic; ungraceful; ungainly; unhandsome.

Some afternoons (probably fewer than my memory recollects), I volunteered to do grunt work for the Congress of Racial Equality and the Student Nonviolent Coordinating Committee. There, I learned that everyone, even a hapless high school kid, can do their part.

Judged fairly, these extracurricular activities in social activism were nothing more than youthful R&D into my emerging identity. Nothing noble. Just a teenager's developmental urge to belong to something, to carry a membership card, to find himself. It's the underlying motivation for my social entrepreneurship even to this day.

I'm grateful that those teenage years in San Francisco occurred during a time of protests and poets. Of standing against appalling racial injustice. Of opposing an immoral war in Vietnam. Of freedom marches and a presidential war on poverty. On street corners, I nodded in lifestyle kinship to hippies wearing love beads and smelling of pot. Drugs, sex and rock 'n roll were in the news. In smoky coffee houses, I listened to Beat Generation folk singers strum secondhand guitars and sing about peace. Within this landscape, I found my moral compass.

Thanks to my up-from-poverty, hard-working parents, each night I returned home to a safe, conventional American zip code. I didn't know it at the time, but I was luckier than hundreds of thousands of American students whose poor schools, race, gender, economic class and family circumstances amounted to a perverse, upside-down, reverse affirmative-action program. Learning to see and understand this privileged distinction became the journey of a lifetime.

If empathetic solidarity originates, in part, from experiencing the isolation of the outsider, then in some ways, the ache of feeling like a misfit in high school seasoned me for social justice work. If the tendency to rebel against authority in youth in any way foreshadows a tendency to challenge the status quo in adulthood—then my teenage years definitely equipped me for a social change career. Either that, or for a life of crime.

— ∞ —

As social entrepreneurs, you and I take two kinds of risks: social venture risk and personal career risk. To take a risk on yourself, you might first need to fend off loving, well-intentioned resistance from parents, friends and professors. That's okay. If your decision works out, there will be accolades; if not, a rousing chorus of 'I told you so'. That's okay too. To quote one anonymous sage: "In the end, we only regret the chances we didn't take."

Once I realized that saving the planet, stopping wars, ending hunger, promoting equality and upholding justice was urgent, then starting my social change career felt urgent too. So is starting yours.

Starting a social justice journey is like starting one of those aggravating jigsaw puzzles without a picture on the box. If you and I want to make any progress at all, we have to start somewhere, taking a leap of faith that, with perseverance, we will find what we need when we need it. As you and I observe the pieces scattered helter-skelter before us, patterns emerge, and the path forwards clarifies itself.

Your social justice career started yesterday. It's underway now. "There is no roadmap. There is no textbook. There is no teaching assistant. Make your own way. Take action. Take a risk. Go make a mistake. You are going to anyway. When you do, go fix it. We are not flirting. This is no quickie. We are in it for the long-term," prods Shawn Humphrey, Associate Professor of Economics at the University of Mary Washington. Wanjiru Kamau-Rutenberg, Founder and former CEO of Kenya's Akili Dada adds: "Don't wait for permission. No one is going to come along and say 'Here's your permission.'"

In biographic puff pieces about social entrepreneurs, you can read *ad nauseum* about a change agent's social venture and vision, but usually not about the requisite and unrelenting requirements of learned leadership. No evidence of hard work; no zigzagging path to greatness.

Speaking for myself, I have had moments of deflating, paralyzing self-doubt, cemented and reinforced with blocking questions: *Am I good enough? Can I measure up? Will I embarrass myself with failure? Should I be doing something else? Why do I have to work so hard at what others make look so easy? If I can't configure a new, supercharged startup led by a brilliant, supercharged team, is there any role for me? If I 'settle' for being second in command, or third, or lower, will my career be satisfying?* When I was 20 years old, I asked myself these questions all the time. In my sixties, I'm still asking them.

When your inner voices and insecurities are in an uproar, tell them to shut the fuck up. You are not alone. Even when hiding behind protective professional jargon, most everyone is just 'faking it until they make it'. During some point of every day, we are all insecure about something. Despite my social venture track record (some successes, some failures), I still have gut-tightening moments when I feel like the impostor I that know I am.

I'm not a natural at social entrepreneurship. I'm too quick to rely on my gut instincts before studying the numbers or field-testing the options. Too quick to make a significant decision without taking a measured pause to listen and learn in collaboration with community, clients and colleagues. Too cocky. I'm getting better at it, but good social entrepreneurship is hard work. Bad social entrepreneurship comes easy. I've spent a lifetime trying to improve.

> *When your inner voices and insecurities are in an uproar, tell them to shut the fuck up.*

Indeed, Meg Jay assures us that "for the most part, naturals are myths. People who are especially good at something may have some innate inclination or some particular talent, but they have also spent about 10,000 hours practicing or doing that thing," as she writes in *The Defining Decade: Why Your Twenties Matter and How to Make the Most of Them Now.* "Confidence is trusting yourself to get the job done... and that trust only comes from having gotten the job done many times before."

In reality, you and I develop the baseline proficiencies of social entrepreneurship through school, internships and on-the-job experience—a triad of learning and doing, and then redoing and learning more. Social justice work is not a compare-and-contrast exam question. Indeed, there is no final exam. No grading on the curve. Life *is* the exam.

The hurdle is knowing what to do, how to do it, where to do it and – if we are busy in school, or raising a family, or starting up a new business – finding the time to do it. It's confusing, because social entrepreneurship is both an end and a means.

If you are new to social change work, you might feel unsure of your capacity to make a difference. You might be uncertain of where you fit in, worry about repaying your student loans, or otherwise don't believe you've earned the right to call yourself a social activist, social entrepreneur or change agent. That's normal. Millions of us feel the same way.

Social entrepreneurship is like first-time sex. Fumbling, urgent, often messy. Sometimes a little scary. It's hard to know how to get started or where to begin. A dose of care, collaboration and calculated risk-taking is essential. Shared desire and shared permission keep it ethical, interesting and dynamic. Practice makes it better. Listening makes it better. Giving, not taking, makes it better. And, sometimes when least expected, it produces a result.

—∞—

Social entrepreneurship isn't learned in a cave, a closet or a cocoon. All kinds of opportunities exist for us to unpack the world's truths. If we can't find them, we aren't looking very hard. Often, indeed very often, if we simply open our empathetic selves to what's right in front of us, the world teaches us what we need to know.

As Sally Osberg and Roger Martin write in *Getting Beyond Better: How Social Entrepreneurship Works*: "It's tempting to think that [social entrepreneurs] are extraordinary individuals who are capable of connecting all the dots in a flash of insight or a killer strategy, people who were born with a talent for solutions and the perseverance to see them through. But in real life, it's not as straightforward as that. Each story involves a journey. Often these [journeys] begin with the recognition of injustice or suffering."

Enroll in the university-without-walls around you. It's hard to invent a more lifelike, more poignant, classroom for understanding inequality than inequality itself. Follow the lead of famed community organizer Saul Alinsky in *Rules for Radicals*, and make "a determination not to detour around reality." Let your heart be sickened by the injustice it meets. Here are a few examples from my own learning-by-exploration (some recent, some long before my changemaker career was officially underway):

Soon after the collapse of apartheid in the mid-1990s, as a tourist, I visited the black township of Soweto on the outskirts of Johannesburg, South Africa. Before that, as a student activist, I had unsuccessfully pushed US companies and pension funds to divest their assets in protest against the ruling white government. So, I was gratified to learn that, while our efforts often felt futile at the time, they were seen by black South Africans as an act of solidarity. Today, when activists agitate to impose economic sanctions on human rights violators or petition universities and foundations to divest from fossil fuels, I support the tactics because, as I learned, they are movement-building steps towards justice.

One college summer break, under a searing Mediterranean sun, I worked on an archaeological dig excavating a 5th-century BC Phoenician city along the coast of Israel. At the top of our hierarchical summer work team: Israeli archaeologists. At the bottom: Israeli Arabs who shoveled sand and dirt from dawn until dusk. I was somewhere in the middle, but functionally closer to the diggers. It was achingly difficult manual work. I can't confirm the causation, but today I never fail to leave a tip for the hotel maid, or side with blue collar workers striking for a living wage.

When I journeyed up a minor tributary of the Amazon River, a rising pale moon illuminated the low mudflats stretching hundreds of yards on either side of our slow-moving boat. Here and there in the mudflats, rickety shacks tottered on stilts like inverted cubes of cheese on slender toothpicks. As I watched, a man stepped away from dry land and into the knee-deep muck to trudge towards his home. Even at a distance, I could see his leg muscles straining as they punched staple marks into the mud, and the water that filled the holes in his wake. This and similar moments come to mind when I hear talk about preserving local customs. Before my knee jerks in agreement, I'm moved to wonder if we are preserving lives lived in perpetual discomfort. I wonder if anyone has bothered to ask that man if he wants his tradition of living on the Amazonian mudflats preserved for posterity. For me, it was an enjoyable boat ride to see a diverse ecosystem; for him, well, let's ask him what he thinks.

At home in California, I live in the epicenter of the richest farmland in the world. Tomato fields stretch to the horizon; nut trees stand in orderly rows. Grapes, hay, rice, almonds, livestock can be seen from every country road. The 5,300-acre University of California Davis campus ranks first in the nation for its agricultural research. If you work in the university fields tending the research crops, your health insurance is paid for. But, if you harvest real crops, you probably get hand-me-down health care at free clinics. As I discovered at a community open house, the local Yolo County health clinic survives on constant fundraising: donations, volunteer medical staff and government grants. The clinic's very existence is an advertisement for health justice. For why universal health care, financed and guaranteed by a democratic government in service to all of its residents, is the necessary and moral choice.

In the Kibera slums of Nairobi, as our little van headed towards an innovative, fee-for-service, for-profit private school, the guide warned us to keep the car windows rolled up to ward off the dust and the dirty fingers of beggars. Arriving at a one-story school compound, we took in the sight of classrooms with windows open to both breezes and bugs. Outdoor latrines lining one side of a dirt playground; a hand pump for potable water. Students at their wooden desks on hard benches. Uniforms clean. Faces eager and curious. At recess, the less-reluctant students practiced their grade-school English on us. A few of the younger children clung shyly to the skirts of the American women, grasping for the human contact that both the kids and the donors both seemed to want. Based on that single trip, I'm unable to draw any conclusions about the school, either educationally or as a sustainable social venture. But this I know: each day without school is another day lost for each one of those children. And, for them and us, that's inexcusable.

—∞—

Let's talk about where you fit in. Let's talk about social sector diversity and the contours of your life. Let's talk about your cultural norms and habits: what you like to eat and how you dress; the skin color your parents bequeathed you; the streets you've walked; what you know about surviving life's grisly parts; what lifts you up or what makes you cry; the scars you hide; the fears you never share; whatever makes you angry enough to take action. These are the fixed attributes that make you distinctive and in-demand for social justice work.

Ever wonder why some job applicants tout extracurricular interests like traveling, music or windsurfing as assets on their résumés, but seldom include the lived experience of an unprivileged childhood—even though that hard-won knowledge has probative and inarguable value for social justice work? Call me skeptical, but I don't think a leading indicator for a kickass social change career is whether or not you can windsurf.

"You talk to kids today applying [for a job] and they invariably say, 'I cured cancer, I brought peace to the Mideast.' Spare me. How about, 'My father never existed, my mother is a convicted drug dealer. I work three shifts at McDonald's.' That's the kind of kid I want – with an ethic of taking care of his family – because then he'll take care of others," advocates Michael Bloomberg, former New York City Mayor and Founder of Bloomberg News.

If you've experienced the stigma of needing charity; if you've shopped with food stamps; if you've feared for your daily safety; if you've been bullied; or if in some other way you've lived up-close-and-personal with hardship, discrimination or violence— your life résumé is more relevant than the candidate who plays chess, cooks or windsurfs. One: with any luck, you might empathetically relate to the tribulations of others. Two: with a bit more luck, your life trials might have produced a person of character, conviction and compassion. Three: with even more luck, you will fill in a perspective or sensitivity deficit in your future team of colleagues.

All kinds of human capital are required to energize the field of social entrepreneurship and build out a broad ecosystem for change. That means a porous, dynamic employment market awaits you. Critically, if the social sector is going to avoid the stupidities of paternalism, colonialism, cultural incompetence and ideological hegemony, we need people who can relate to a huge variety of local norms, embedded traditions and unspoken customs.

We need social entrepreneurs who speak the world's 6,000 languages; who practice the world's 4,000 religions; who belong to the world's 30 racial subgroups; who were born in at least one of the world's 196 countries. Chances are your life résumé reflects a few of these usable assets.

If you're an aspiring change agent with a unique personal history, push open a door for yourself. Of course, this advice might seem easy for me to hand out from position of relative privilege, but surely we can agree that social entrepreneurship needs *you* more than it needs, for example, more windsurfers?

Also, don't be put off when social venture competitions, philanthropists, impact investors, grant-makers and magazine articles lionize the social enterprise founder or chief executive officer. Social entrepreneurs are routinely glamorized as visionaries—tenaciously overcoming groupthink and charismatically building their scaled, impactful social ventures. In truth, that's a cramped and miserly distortion of the social sector job market.

Social entrepreneurs don't arrive in the world by immaculate conception. Social sector prima donnas and 'cults of personality' might sell books, and might even get a Hollywood movie deal—but marquee billing obscures the multitude of job descriptions required to drive social change. For sure, innovators and leaders deserve their standing ovations—but while all the world might be a stage, not all of us are suited to play the leading lady.

Graphic designers, political operatives, accountants, business people, human resources professionals, faith leaders, scholars, horticulturists, researchers, IT geeks, artists, office administrators, lobbyists, fundraisers, grant writers, social media whizzes, policy experts, scientists, healthcare workers, grassroots organizers, editors, teachers, hydraulics specialists, conference planners, librarians, journalists, publishers and playwrights—we are all needed. Unless you are a kleptomaniac or an arsonist (in which case your career is probably up in flames anyway), there's a rewarding and necessary job waiting for you in the social sector.

—∞—

Social entrepreneurs are made, not born. Social entrepreneurs don't arrive in the world by immaculate conception, their birth attended by angels bearing the heavenly gift of social change competency.

Your first changemaker job is you. "We must not only give what we have; we must also give what we are," urges Cardinal Désiré-Joseph Mercier. And, before we can give what we are, we need to know what that is.

"Be prepared to transform yourself without attempting to transform others to be like you," advises Tiffany Persons, Founder of Shine On Sierra Leone. "Be prepared to grow yourself. Don't get into the [social sector] thinking that you know everything and you are coming to transform someone's life. Into what? *Into being you!?*" Well said, Tiffany.

The secret reason that so many job openings require prior experience is not the promise that you will *know something*, but rather the hope that you will have already figured out *what you don't know*. No one in social entrepreneurship – from public sector activist to private sector analyst, and all of us in between – knows absolutely, really, completely, *entirely* what we are doing. I suspect this is true for most occupations and most professionals, but social entrepreneurs are less embarrassed and less frightened by our ignorance. We know, almost instinctively, that old problems require innovative solutions, and that we are on a learning quest to find them.

Even the best social entrepreneurs cannot anticipate every problem, every obstacle, every unintended consequence, every new opportunity or unexpected challenge. As we have long suspected, change agents are not clairvoyant. The very nature of a social entrepreneurship career requires nimbly and creatively responding to market unknowns, the changing needs of populations, unexpected external events and the ups and downs in human and financial resources. The social philosopher Eric Hoffer slams home the point: "In times of profound change, the learners inherit the earth, while the learned find themselves beautifully equipped to deal with a world that no longer exists." That's just the way it is. For change agents like you and me, it's what makes the work challenging and (let's be honest) fun.

The variations for how you use your skills and talents are nearly infinite—and perpetually subject to change without notice. In social change work, "there is very little precedent for the roles that people are taking on," says Jessamyn Shams-Lau, CEO of the Peery Foundation. "Essentially, we're all making it up as we go along. Hopefully, we're all smart enough and self-aware enough to learn from our mistakes."

As a young man, I observed how decisions were made by volunteering in the anti-war and civil rights movements, interning with anyone who would take me, apprenticing in political campaigns, and working in boring entry-level positions. I learned civic character by rehearsing it. Like operating a flight simulator for social entrepreneurs, the benefit of starting our social change careers by making coffee and copies is the opportunity to practice using our moral compass, advocacy skills and implementation abilities without crashing our social justice career or putting at risk the causes and people you and I care about.

A social justice journey is a trial-by-doing-good experience. It's exciting, challenging, terrifying and totally worth it. My 10,000 hours of social entrepreneurship practice started in high school. Your 10,000 hours can start whenever and wherever you like. You can even start today.

Take Two: Starting

Holly McKenna, 23, is a nomadic connector journeying through Latin America to study complex barriers to health. Hometown: Palo Alto, California. Favorite pastime: running up mountains. Guilty pleasure: raw cookie dough.

"*Starting* spoke to the contradictions in the development sector that have been spinning me around over the past few years. There's this strong pull to just do it, push open doors for yourself, don't wait for permission, go feel something deep and start something incredible. And at the same time, there's a pull for listening more, taking time and deepening empathy. This simultaneous push and pull has recently brought me to a place of 'analysis paralysis', allowing me to reflect on some of the mistakes I've made:

"*Mistake 1:* I said yes to everything. Because I didn't have any requirements, I had no way to vet whether opportunities made sense. I ended up in two environments where there was a drought of feedback, collaboration and leadership. I know now that job opportunities are a two-way street.

"*Mistake 2:* I took everyone's advice to heart. People will tell you things. Quickly, you realize the underlying biases, self-interest and randomness of feedback. If you talk to enough people, you will soon get the exact opposite advice on almost all levels. Learn from those who inspire you, and then listen to your intuition.

"*Mistake 3:* I jumped in without developing my skills in a context where I didn't have the mentorship needed. Working in the nonprofit sector in another country, language and culture is especially difficult if you don't know what you can offer. I know now to keep my needs and expectations aligned with the opportunities I pursue.

"*Mistake 4:* Jumping in too far. Don't feel like you have to quit your job and move to another country, or start the newest social enterprise, or change your job (at least for now). But do something, at any level, now. It's this initiative, motivated by a place of human connectedness, that's going to create the just world we want to live in."

TOUCH

Powering up my social justice career means powering down my laptop. Experiential learning replaces someone else's filter with our own.

For social entrepreneurs, there is little emotional distance, no protective wall, between the world as it is and the world we seek to build with our human hearts. We can't, and don't, stand apart from the people whose lives matter to us.

Some years ago, while in Rome, after a multi-course lunch, I endeavored to stave off a 'pasta coma' by meandering opportunistically down an ancient winding cobblestone street. Heavy wooden doors and shuttered windows lined my path like sentinels. At one point, to escape the heat, I stepped into a local museum.

Inside a gallery of Renaissance sculptures, a poem on a wall, by Michael Glover, caught my eye. It was called *Touch is the Truth of the World at the Finger's End.* I was transported. Museum-goers fell silent. Street traffic faded from consciousness. Museum staff froze *in situ*. Alone amongst the statues, the poetic heart-beating of my social entrepreneurship pulsed through me:

> *You come alive at the touch of my finger's end.*
> *All of a sudden, there you are,*
> *In your shape and your weight and your size,*
> *Perfectly given to me in all your yielding softness.*
> *Touch makes me love you...*

For the activist and the social entrepreneur, for you and me—
our lofty, principled and heartfelt commitments are grounded in a
reality, a vibrancy, and an urgency that comes from seeing, smelling,
and *feeling* the world. It's like the difference between looking at a
sculpture in an art book and the tactile, gritty thrill of touching it.

My capacity for sadness, outrage and blistering anger over an act
of cruelty, neglect or injustice is possible because, in the instant of
discovering it, I'm *touched* by it—sometimes like a punch to the gut.
My capacity for empathy, compassion and respect is possible because
people touch me with their life stories.

Social entrepreneurs, change agents and community activists are
schooled *in* the real world; *by* the real world; *for* the real world. We
usually learn about the broader tactics and strategies of social change
work in school, on television, in books; we vicariously experience
it online via blogs, photo essays, videos and news reports. As our
knowledge and empathy deepen, we soon realize that we can't win
the world we want without directly engaging in that world. Without
touching it.

Change agents train for their careers by working in communities for the same reason doctors put their hands inside cadavers, and
human rights lawyers stand watch on death row. "We need to have
field experience, especially in economic justice work. We need to
experience what economic *injustice* looks like," says Rajasvini
Bhansali, Executive Director of Thousand Currents.

When I'm out and about doing social action work, it's my time
for intense discovery. My connectedness to the world deepens, my
compassion expands and my self-awareness is on steroids. As I sculpt
and chisel my social justice career; when I'm outside my comfort zone;
when I am learning within a community—that's when I find myself
falling ever deeper in love with my life purpose.

— ∞ —

Social entrepreneurs carry two different 'résumés of reality'. First:
you and I grow up within a particular community and tribe. Possibly
(because of skin color, economic hardship, gender, religion or other
comparable outsider status), you have known the isolation and sting
of being the *Other*. Your history, naturally and invaluably, will inform

your social justice work. Or, maybe your life experience has been easier and more protected. Either way, we each have an inherited résumé.

The other résumé is earned in apprenticeship. We volunteer, train, intern and work to soften the jagged edges of life on behalf of the discarded and the left out—whether at home, abroad, or both. Without sharing in the world's suffering, without feeling the sharp jabs of injustice, without witnessing the torching rage caused by inequality, without sensing the frustration of the impossible, our social entrepreneurship – like a fire waiting for a match – lacks the heat of conviction.

Both of these résumés are revealed when we do social justice work. When it comes to your core identity as an agent of change, I can't learn all that's truly important about you by reading the paper epidermis of your life (aka your résumé). Perhaps I can learn where you went to school, but I can't learn about your moral fiber. I can't know the extent or depth of your courage, compassion or character.

Closeness to community catalyzes two essential qualities for the social entrepreneur: the angered impatience to take on the most egregious injustices, and the resolute patience to persevere in the face of setbacks. On the days when I'm most discouraged, real people with real names and real lives, with real hardships and real hopes, give me strength.

Our work is personal. Try as we might to abstract and conceptualize the fight for social, environmental, economic, racial and gender justice—for social entrepreneurs, the very notion of professional detachment (even if appealing on an intellectual or academic level) is viscerally anathema. Social entrepreneurship thrives on empathetic connection, trust and respect.

At a distance, it's hard to hear the faint whisper of a person without agency.

—∞—

You and I need opportunities to learn about the world. Equally, we need opportunities to develop and test our social entrepreneurial talents and ideas. Even more critically, we need opportunities to learn from communities and constituents; to grow our souls; to have our stereotypes crushed; to partake in what the *Other* have to teach us; to earn our self-respect as agents of change.

When I was in college, stirred to protest pretty much everything, I took courses on American slavery, Native-American history, Latino studies, feminism, colonialism, imperialism and more. Before I owned a passport, the campus bookstore was my window to the world. Predictably, I ended up with a cardboard-cutout view of people living without power, and a static understanding of a dynamic world.

For a modest example, in the sixties and seventies, I pretty much automatically embraced what was then called the women's liberation movement. Equality of the sexes fit my abstract understanding of what a just society should look like. Back then, we optimistically assumed that one day, the United States would adopt the Equal Rights Amendment. After leaving college and entering the workplace, I became part a loosely-structured community of young professionals working at the State Capitol.

One night, as the check arrived after dinner at a local sushi restaurant, the married women seated around the table shared their annoyance (to put it mildly) that banks refused to issue them credit cards without their husband's signature (read: approval). *Gasp.* In an instant, an intangible principle shifted to an actionable problem with a solution. The next day I began drafting corrective legislation. Engaging the real world had touched me in a way that simply reading about gender issues could not.

We need both angered impatience to take on egregious injustices, and the resolute patience to persevere in the face of setbacks.

Optimally, we start our social sector careers with an innate sense of humility—but humility also comes from listening to other people's stories. I'm a slacker in comparison to a single mom in Ecuador working to feed her kids. A Kenyan shopkeeper's cash flow challenge reminds me that my small business achievements are commonplace. My activism feels easy when compared to that of a public interest lawyer working to reform my country's apartheid-like prison system.

Field experience mitigates the risk of glamorizing, romanticizing or objectifying the oppressed (or glorifying ourselves or our social entrepreneurship). Increased proximity to the real problems of real people decreases the chance I will spit-ball solutions. Once I have listened, laughed, cried, built friendships and made allies in a community different to my own, it's nearly impossible for me to blithely impose arrogant, top-down, simplistic, shortcut answers.

At a practical level, community engagement is how we learn to operate the machinery of social entrepreneurship; how we test the heft of it in our own lives. From trained medical professionals to unskilled religious congregants, from high school clubs to the Peace Corps, "social involvement helps us enter new worlds. We may build on our existing values and knowledge, but we also develop new priorities, gain new skills, meet new people, hear and heed new stories," notes Paul Loeb in *Soul of a Citizen: Living with Conviction in Challenging Times*. By preference and good practice, social entrepreneurs don't live in gated communities.

Experiential learning replaces someone else's filter with our own. However robust our search engine, the realities of time and selection bias mean that the information sources we study, we study through the filter of someone else's eyes. Powering up my social justice career means powering down my laptop.

Yet before we move out into the world to be touched by it, you and I will be given a triptych of cautionary advice. First: we are warned that we are naïve, unprepared and lack cultural competency. Second: we are advised to start our international development careers by working or volunteering domestically where, presumably, we are more entitled to do. Third: we are cautioned to 'Do No Harm' and (even more unnerving) that whatever privileged position or status we enjoy is a virtual guarantee that we will insensitively mess up.

—∞—

As you prepare to get out there in the world, you will read mocking critiques and disparagements. You might be asked to imagine a make-believe Nepalese college student or fictional Egyptian social entrepreneur who, upon learning about an American social deficit (say, gun violence or poorly-performing schools), invents a solution without any direct experience of American life, politics, culture or sociology. Notably, this presumptuous problem-solver speaks halting high school-level English. They hop on a plane, armed with good intentions, affability, smiles and a suitcase full of delusional aspirations. They arrive in the US, intent on sparking bold, transformational change—somewhere, somehow. For sure, neither of us wants to be that person.

The practical dilemma: wherever I am, I am a stranger. Even in my own hometown – a college town encircled by agricultural prosperity and farmworker poverty – I'm a foreigner. I'm not an academic; I'm not a student. I'm not a farm owner; I'm not farmhand. I'm also not a member of a census-designated minority group, a woman or a church-goer. Every human grouping – village, community, marriage, classroom, sports team, corporation, book club, secret society, hair salon and men's circle – is a complex micro-culture. You and I will never, ever, belong to most of the world's communities and sub-communities.

On the other hand, in the world that we care about, endlessly preparing for social change work without actually doing it produces the exact same results as endless procrastination. As a matter of simple priority-setting and time management, the dilemma is that by the time I properly ready myself by (a) apprenticing myself in one or more field placements; (b) becoming proficient in a foreign language; (c) getting up to speed about my identity and my privilege; (d) studying the structural causes of social and economic injustice; (e) figuring out the complex drivers holding back a marginalized population; (f) mapping institutional racism and sexism; (g) upping my cultural competency; (h) fine-tuning my emotional IQ; and, (i) sorting through the hurdles of political correctness— I could be dead.

The fact is: nothing even comes close to going out to touch, and be touched by, social injustice. No one doubts that moving through the world is fraught with anxiety, both for us and for the communities with whom we intersect. After all, we are asking strangers to help us be our best selves. Listen to these three voices, each one chronicling the inherent complexities that come with stranger status:

1. After college, John Anner (now CEO of The Dream
   Corps) joined the Peace Corps. "I was sent to a village
   in Mauritania where most people had never seen a

white person before. No running water, electricity, newspapers, nothing," he recalls. "You can approach the Peace Corps as a two-year camping trip, or you can get serious. The best thing about the Peace Corps is that volunteers don't have enough money or time to do any real damage." Manifestly, John's insight could only come from his own real-world engagement.

2. After college, Holly McKenna started building her social sector skills and deepening her Spanish fluency by finding paid internships in Latin America. A few months into her journey, she chronicled her feelings: "Sending *abrazos* from Guanajuato! Life has been crazy in a wonderful way. Feeling simultaneously under- and over-qualified; alone and not alone." To my ears, that's what learning and respecting community sound like.

3. "When education is prioritized over impact, it can really suck for people you thought you were going to help. Whether homeless, incarcerated or hungry—yes, these people have needs. And it's nice that students want to better understand those needs," challenges Kriss Deiglmeier, CEO of the Tides Foundation. "But these people are not guinea pigs for your learning pleasure." Turns out that the words 'exploitive' and 'extractive' describe more than just pulling natural resources out of the ground.

Ideally, in every situation where I show up with my social entrepreneurship, I'm an invited colleague, as welcome as a dinner guest with an exceptionally good bottle of wine. But that's not often realistic. First, it's hard to be invited if no one actually knows that I exist. Second, in the beginning, we are all strangers to each other. In my case: my nationality, skin color and gender make me the stereotypical face of Western colonialism. As a result, even before I arrive, I'm unwelcome in some conversations, and in some communities. I can't wish away this maddening legacy, but I'm only complicit if I sit comfortably on my ass. The only thing we know for certain is that privilege will never disappear if the people *with* it segregate themselves from the people *without* it. In the long run, it only matters if we *remain* strangers.

Naturally, you and I fear becoming social change window-dressing, the clueless outsider. In truth, at the start of our social sector careers, that's precisely what we are. And, that's precisely why we let the world, and its people, touch our hearts. That's why we accept, without pretension, our learner's place in every new community and on every new job assignment. "It doesn't matter what you don't know. The only thing that matters is what you do with what you find out," challenges Jerr Boschee, Founder of the Institute for Social Entrepreneurs. It's the learning curve that every social entrepreneur climbs.

—∞—

Voluntourism is an unregulated $2 billion cottage industry mobilizing more than 1.6 million volunteer-tourists each year (mostly women and young adults). However, industry standards don't exist. There is no ethical code of conduct, and little transparency. Unless you are in favor of wasting your time and money—vet potential programs for educational integrity, development rigor and community solidarity. These five questions will get you started:

> *Privilege will never disappear if the people with it segregate themselves from the people without it.*

1. Is the program a community-based partnership, or does it import paternalistic, top-down solutions to local problems? Is it collaborative, or closed-off to local input? Are local citizens actively involved in planning, or are they treated as passive beneficiaries?

2. Will the in-country host organization, and your host family, be financially compensated for their troubles? Educating visitors about local customs, mores, language, cuisine, etc. takes time and effort.

3. Will you be learning from your peers as well as from your field experiences? Will your classmates, church mission group or team members represent the diversity of America? Does the program's price make it prohibitively restrictive such that you will be traveling in an echo chamber of homogeneity?

4. Is the program literature honest in acknowledging that your contribution may be none at all? Don't trivialize your commitment to social justice by succumbing to frivolous websites with exaggerated claims promising that your untalented, untrained wonderfulness is going to make a real difference in an impoverished community. If you go—you're there to learn, listen, absorb, grow and become a better-informed, more empathetic change agent. Later, you can decide how you will repay the life indebtedness that each of us owes the teachers, mentors, role models and communities who have nurtured our careers, shared their time and opened their lives to us.

5. Does the program address the root causes of social and economic injustice? Just by asking the question, you and I can get an insight into the core values of the program and its leadership.

One form of faux community service learning – trashy, cheap and avoidable – is some version of the economic development one-night stand. A particularly dreadful example is reported in a *New York Times* article entitled: 'A 7-Night, $250 Cruise? Yes, and You Might Also Do Some Good'. To attract idealistic tourists, cruise ships organize "on the ground projects with local nongovernmental organizations, and encourage passengers to take part in activities like teaching English in schools, sorting cacao beans at a cooperative or helping to install concrete floors."

"I met the girl I would tutor for roughly the next 90 minutes, a shy eleven-year-old named Racieli," explains the journalist Lucas Peterson. "I was given a binder with a basic English curriculum.

I wasn't given much instruction or time to review it, but soon Racieli and I were reciting the alphabet and beginning to learn numbers." The news article is silent on what Racieli thought of this tutorial revolving door, her need for English proficiency, how many tutors she had babysat or why, after all this cruise-by instruction, she was not reciting Shakespeare.

I wonder if, one day in the future, a Japanese travel agency will offer social impact tour buses to low-income areas in London to tutor local cockney-speakers in remedial Japanese? Or, will there be New York Broadway theater tours for European or African tourists with pre- and post-show stops in Times Square to pick up litter?

In 'To Get to Harvard, Go to Haiti?', Frank Bruni of the *New York Times* reports about a kind of volunteerism that seems tailor-made for future gun manufacturers, cigarette makers, war profiteers and corporate polluters. For those career paths, I presume that it's important to gain early experience in profiting off the woes of others. As Bruni reports, some high school students seeking admission to top-ranked universities are ginning up community service experiences to pad their résumés. "After as little as a week helping to repair some village's crumbling school or library, [they] return to their comfortable homes, and quite possibly write a college application essay about how transformed they are."

The bragging rights are, of course, documented with a Facebook photo of the college applicant surrounded by, or playing with, a bunch of young brown or black children. Everyone is smiling—although in fairness, we don't know if the kids are smiling because they are happy, or because they are glad that their drop-in helper is about to leave.

Is it necessary to say that drive-by empathy and posturing charity work is nothing more than a game of charades? Is it necessary to distinguish between genuine service learning versus manipulating the college admissions process? You and I know the difference.

—∞—

In the practice of medicine, the admonition 'Do No Harm' encourages doctors to avoid making the patient worse. Applied to the social sector, it brings to mind a myriad of cockamamie economic development interventions, harebrained social enterprises, unsophisticated volunteerism and unintended consequences that have left communities, and entire nations, worse off. The literature of economic development is filled with horror stories about people who, waving a 'do good' banner, acted clumsily, insensitively and stupidly. These cautionary tales are important, but let's not forget that there are countless *more* horror stories caused by people who looked the other way or who substituted excuses for engagement. What's the greater shame: Up-and-coming social entrepreneurs who take a risk and screw up? Or, social entrepreneurs who turn inward and isolationist?

'Do No Harm' is easy to say, important to remember, and impossible to follow. In my life experience, 'Do No Harm' is nearly unusable advice; a soul-sucking denial of common sense.

Maybe you and I already feel naïve. That's because we probably are. Change agents are supposed to be. We are dreaming the impossible dream. Cynicism and jaded sophistication have no place in the world of social entrepreneurship. Every sacred value that we now hold as inviolable was first promulgated by some naïve visionary.

When a Bangladeshi economics professor (and future Nobel Laureate) named Muhammad Yunus ventured out of the academic ivory tower (a place of privilege) to lead his students on a field trip to a nearby poor village, he talked with impoverished women making bamboo stools. He learned firsthand about the economics of local furniture-making, including the deplorable reality of loan sharks and banking discrimination. From there, he innovated the initial idea for modern microcredit. Of course, this is a streamlined version of the microcredit story; over time, it required countless iterations to refine and scale. The essential point is that Yunus was willing to venture out into the world, let his heart be touched (and saddened) by what he witnessed, and take a chance on creating a solution to an economic injustice that he witnessed with his own eyes.

I wonder if, at the time, Yunus anticipated every one of the unintended consequences and trade-offs that would arise as a result of his social entrepreneurship. I wonder if he met doubters who told him to 'Do No Harm'. I wonder if he was warned not to steal a job from a local loan shark. I wonder if, some days, Professor Yunus self-deprecatingly chuckled, along with the poet Carl Sandburg, "I'm an idealist. I don't know where I'm going, but I'm on my way."

When I hear the phrase 'Do No Harm', I hear the lackadaisical voice of comfy privilege. Who in their right mind thinks that the status quo, anywhere in the world, is harm-free? *Doing nothing* does harm. For sure, before we act, we can be more thoughtful listeners and learners. For sure, our baseline instinct should always be to co-create in respectful partnership with clients and communities. For sure, I want to check that my volunteerism is not displacing a qualified local worker. But, I also want to factor in 'the harm' done by sitting at home, safely and ignorantly, not learning firsthand about our wonderful world. An apprentice change agent has to start their career *somewhere*.

'Do No Harm' is a high-minded caution worth contemplating, but if carried to its logical extreme, becomes a prison of our own making. In the real world, social entrepreneurship is an endless series of hard choices and troubled trade-offs, forced on us by the great divide between the haves and the have-nots. I have to accept that, to be of some use in the world, I will occasionally, even frequently, find myself the outsider, the *Other*, the stranger—maybe welcome, maybe not. It's the chance every global citizen takes.

Defeating paternalism, racism, sexism, economic exploitation, and the forces behind the destruction of the environment requires that I take a risk. It's the same kind of risk required of every new friendship; every new romance; every new partnership; every new collaboration. Someone needs to make the first move.

Risk-taking, by the way, is multi-directional. Perhaps you are an African-American woman working with Latina teenagers headed to college; or a Kenyan-born American doing impact analysis on Southeast Asian social ventures; or a Bolivian working in a Syrian refugee camp; or a Native-American Peace Corps volunteer stationed in Thailand; or a Congolese woman working with young at-risk girls in the United States. The so-called white savior comes in many colors, many combinations.

—∞—

Of course, I don't have the right to impose myself on another community. At the same time, the notion that you or I need to pass some imaginary qualifying exam, get our passports stamped by a social change customs officer, or justify to anyone why we care about other people – even people we don't yet know – is pin-headed.

What's profound, and profoundly worth knowing, is the truth of the world at our fingertips. Transformational experiences, filled with humanizing insights and defining moments of character, are really tough to have while we are designing minimum viable products, poring over evaluation reports or hiding out in the attics of our minds. If you have not personally experienced oppression or inequality, observing it firsthand is the next best option. What I experience, I cannot un-experience. What you see, you cannot un-see.

You and I can't understand our place in the world until we're participating in it. Perhaps an over-simplification, but I don't think so. Community service is a constructive act of self-improvement. You envision your future career as it actually might be. You learn practical, durable skills. You discover how to respect people with different views; different traditions; different community values. You are mentored by the marketplace. Most of all, you decide whose side you will fight on in the timeless struggle for social, gender, racial, environmental and economic justice.

Take Two: Touch

Jessica Loman, 31, is Director of Special Projects at Toniic, the global action community for impact investors, and convener of movers for peace. Hometown: US, Brazil, Indonesia. Favorite pastime: capoeira. Guilty pleasure: whiskey and coffee ice cream.

"I remember when I first realized that social change agents approach new communities in different ways. During the US Fulbright Teaching Program in my motherland (Indonesia), I gathered for orientation with 30 fellow Americans; we were all jet-lagged and excited for the one-year program ahead. As the weeks went by, many became frustrated with the plastic trash all over the streets, the teachers who would not show us the corruption, economic disparity, etc. Meanwhile, there was a smaller group of us curious to understand more and motivated to support (and possibly create) solutions.

"I approach 'life in the shoes of others' slightly differently than Jonathan. I recognize that some people need anger to motivate them— yet aggravation can also breed hate. Instead of 'angered impatience', what if it we approached difference with *curiosity*? With anger out of the equation, we can more objectively observe, receive more unguarded responses, keep a bird's eye view from outside the cage, and take the quality time to get to know ourselves, our allies, and the *Other*. For some, the *Other* may mean marginalized communities, but in my case, there are situations where I also need to take time to understand the perspective of the majority, the government, system creators, policyholders and fellow entrepreneurs.

"I believe that everyone makes judgments, but are you open to changing that judgment? How quickly can you adapt and empathize? Six months into my Fulbright program, all of my fellow teachers reconvened. It was a refreshing reconnection. We had heartwarming discussions about what we had learned, including discussions about our roles as individuals, as a group, and as US citizens. We were touched to see with new perspective and to join in a global effort to address shared concerns. Touch does not end there. Touch informs our ability to learn, empower and act consciously with ever-evolving communities."

PASSION

Whose side are we on? What enemies are we willing to make?

In life, in love and in social entrepreneurship, the question nags at us: *How do I find my passion?* Throughout our changemaker careers; in moments of doubt; in the still quiet when our concerns speak to us—we will ask ourselves some variation of this question many times over.

In actuality, the passion quest means different things at different points in our careers. There's passion for power, passion for profits, passion for fame, passionate idealism, passion to serve, patriotic passion, passion to grow our social enterprises, passion for a cause, artistic passion, passion for people and passion for a community. And, of course, there is passion fruit.

There are passionate people on all sides of every question. Passionate people who have succeeded. Passionate people who have failed. People who are passionate about trivial things. People who are passionate about important things. And, passionate people who seem indiscriminately passionate about almost everything.

Being dispassionate is, presumably, a bad thing: indicative of cold detachment from one's true self; a callous indifference towards a world overflowing with human suffering. Even when a hardened remoteness is justified as impartiality, we like to believe that everyone is passionate about something. Otherwise, it rattles our sense of human connection.

If we believe the oft-repeated social entrepreneur's fairytale, we know that we are destined to one day find our passionate purpose. Perhaps we will find it during an eye-opening internship or rainbow-filled gap year; perhaps after a soulless career spent plundering the planet or in rampant profiteering. We find our one true passion, and we are transformed; energized; forever focused on a mission larger than ourselves. A passion that is less picturesque (but certainly no less authentic) is found amongst the rubble of our personal hardships, setbacks or melancholies. Either way, we imagine our passion welling up from some deep, heretofore undiscovered corner of ourselves—much in the way that an *El Niño* shifts the oceans, or falling in love rocks our world.

At the start of a social justice career, it's common for us to define ourselves as 'searching for our passion', but frankly—that's ass-backwards. Your passion will find *you*. When you're ready for it, your cause will emerge in the same way that an enticing pastry in a bakery window, or a sizzling bit of skewered meat on a sidewalk food cart, calls to you. Part serendipity. Part accessibility. Part opportunity.

When presented with a social venture opportunity or career choice, or when social justice calls, to test myself, I fill in the blanks on this handy 'Passion-o-Meter':

> *The animating principle of my life is_____ .*
> *Deep in my core, _____ lights me up.*
> *I stand for _____ .*
> *I stand against _____ .*
> *For _____ , I'm ready to ignore the skeptics.*
> *For _____ , I'm willing to sacrifice (money? romance?).*
> *When I'm not fighting for _____ , a part of me feels missing.*
> *Fighting for _____ makes me feel like a better person.*

In the interim, instead of passively waiting around for our passion to materialize, social entrepreneurs have an unswerving, instinctive disposition towards social justice action. As Paul Loeb explains in *The Impossible Will Take a Little While*, "we gain something profound when we stand up for our beliefs, just as part of us dies when we know that something is wrong, yet do nothing... We don't have to tackle every issue, but if we avoid them all, if we remain silent in the face of cruelty, injustice and oppression, we sacrifice part of our soul."

If day after day, week after week, either of us is endlessly postponing our social sector careers, or indulging our fantasies about tomorrow's imaginary, transformative social venture, we need to recalibrate how badly we want the world that we say we want. "An activist is someone who cannot help but fight for something," praises Eve Ensler, playwright of *The Vagina Monologues*. "That person is not usually motivated by a need for power, or money, or fame, but in fact driven slightly mad by some injustice, some cruelty, some unfairness." Passion is not a passive thing.

—∞—

Insofar as you and I think the status quo is unacceptable, we have a crucial choice to make, an anchoring decision: *Whose side are we on? What enemies are we willing to make?* These questions – more than anything else – define our social entrepreneurial character and street cred. Social entrepreneurship is not a popularity contest. Social entrepreneurs grow thick skins, steel spines and bionic hearts.

Changemakers are outsiders. Status quo circuit-breakers. Revolutionaries without rockets.

Social entrepreneurship is unavoidably partisan. At the fulcrum of our souls, changemakers are outsiders: questioning; challenging; agitating. We are status quo circuit-breakers. Warriors for economic and social justice. Revolutionaries without rockets. When we work to create a world with dignity, agency, environmental sanity and economic opportunity for all— passion has found us. It's that simple. Really.

Taking sides confirms what we stand for, and who we are. "Find a way to get in the way. Find a way to get in trouble; good trouble; necessary trouble; be prepared to speak up and speak out. Be bold, be courageous. If you see something that is not right, that is not fair, that is not just, you have a moral obligation, a mission and a mandate to get in the way and make some noise," urges Congressman and civil rights leader John Lewis (unfortunately, no relation).

Outwardly, making enemies sounds wholly impolitic, and an affront to cordiality, but change doesn't occur without a compelling moral narrative backed up by the willingness and the will to make enemies (more politely, to challenge the status quo). Only the naïve or weak-minded think that social injustice is willing to go down without a fight. "All new ideas arise from conflict. Every new idea has been a challenge to sacred ideas… inevitably a conflict has raged," notes Saul Alinsky in *Rules for Radicals*. Unless we are making a few first-class enemies, what are we doing?

If social entrepreneurship were a color, that color would be passion red. Or maybe blood red. "For many cultures, red is both death and life—a beautiful and terrible paradox," reports Victoria Finlay in *Color: A Natural History of the Palette*. "In our modern language of metaphors, red is anger, it is fire, it is the stormy feelings of the heart, it is love, it is the god of war, and it is power." Adds labor organizer Eugene Debs in *The Crimson Standard*: "The red flag, since time immemorial, has symbolized the discontent of the downtrodden, the revolt of the rabble." Indeed.

— ∞ —

My lifelong passion for economic justice found me unexpectedly, but not accidentally. As you know from the essay *Justice*, I was a student intern in a California legislator's office when I landed my first full-time job as an aide to a state senator. Within a few short weeks of starting work, my boss was

If social entrepreneurship were a color, that color would be passion red.

selected as the chief negotiator on a major overhaul of the state's tax system. When I heard the news, I was in my office arranging some personal items in the cluttered lower drawer of my desk. I certainly wasn't thinking (passionately or otherwise) about macroeconomic tax policy. In fact, to that point in my life, I'd never earned enough money to even justify filing an income tax return.

In the months ahead, I found myself explaining the Senator's progressive tax positions to constituents; handling media inquiries; negotiating tax policy with opposition legislative staffers; fending off corporate lobbyists and conferring with public interest allies. Every night, after the work day wrapped up, I grabbed a sandwich and headed to a private briefing with the real tax experts. Late into the evening, they patiently taught me tax policy—answering my beginner's questions and preparing me for the next day's legislative negotiations.

By cramming every night, I was I able to stay a few hours ahead of what I needed to know.

It was grueling, scary, electrifying, thrilling, unnerving and (let's just say it) taxing. I felt overwhelmed because I *was* overwhelmed. I'm sure that the wafer-thin veil hiding my ignorance was apparent to just about everyone.

In any case, as I was force-fed more and more facts and figures about taxation, I was offended to discover the insidious ways that the tax system redistributes income and wealth from the bottom of the economic ladder upwards into the most privileged tax brackets. In a short time, I went from knowing nothing to knowing what tax justice could look like, from unconcerned ignorance to eventually founding the California Tax Reform Association. While revenue and taxation debate is arcane and complicated, at every turn in the negotiations, I discovered that my job performance improved when I asked: *How does this tax proposal affect the unemployed, the low-income family, the single mom or the small business owner?* I had chosen sides.

And, as I explain in *Bruised*, the battle for tax reform was buffeting. I was on the side of the tax-disadvantaged over the tax-privileged. To this day, my heart beats for tax justice, passionately.

Tax policy, like religion and politics, is one of those issues that quickly turns into an argument. However, if tax justice interests you, give me a shout. And, if you are an apologist for corporate tax welfare, in favor of tax loopholes or of shifting your taxes legally (but selfishly) onto other people (especially people with lower incomes)— then shame on you.

The point of my story: your cause finds you, not the other way around. You don't have to design it, invent it or search inside yourself for it. Instead, use this amazingly simple crisscrossing, overlapping, paralleling, Venn-diagraming trick to help a social justice cause find your heart. First, hang out in a community of conscience. Then, as you're waiting around for passion to show up, take sides and do something!

—∞—

Passion, contrary to the saccharine mush that we read on motivational posters, is not a shining North Star, magically and magnetically pointing us towards a blissful life of social entrepreneurship precisely customized to our talents and interests. C'mon, who believes that?

Instead, listen to these seven passionate voices talk about their experience with passion, purpose and meaning:

1. Meaning is something you build into your life. You
    build it out of your own past, out of your affections and
    loyalties, out of the experience of humankind as
    it is passed on to you, out of your own talent and
    understanding, out of the things you believe in, out of
    the things and people you love, out of the values for
    which you are willing to sacrifice something."
    –Former Secretary of Health, Education and Welfare
    John Gardner in 'The Road to Self-Renewal'

2. "A calling doesn't come in the form of a checklist," says
    Sara Hall, author of *Drawn to the Rhythm: A Passionate
    Life Reclaimed* and eight-time World Masters Sculling
    Champion. A calling is the "irrational, irrepressible and
    elemental... the opportunity to experience a stronger
    self, more vibrantly alive, more intensively focused
    than that of our everyday lives, self-armed to take on
    the darkest forces in our own, inner territory."

3. "Your passion finds you. When I set out to help others,
    I succeeded in helping myself. It makes me feel
    accomplished as a human being. This is actually the
    purpose of humanity. Every human being is
    expected to come to the world, acquire enough skills
    and knowledge to add to his or her given talent and
    leave the world a better place." –Grace Mofoluwake
    Anike Omolara, Executive Director of Nigeria-based
    Independent Living for People with Disabilities, and
    author of *Willing on Wheels*

4. "Commencement speakers are always telling young people to follow their passions. Be true to yourself. This is a vision of life that begins with self and ends with self. But people on the road to inner light do not find their vocations by asking, what do I want from life? They ask, what is life asking of me? How can I match my intrinsic talent with one of the world's deep needs?" –David Brooks in *The Moral Bucket List*

5. "I receive an email every day from an amazing person who is pouring their heart out about being unhappy about where they are in their life and wanting to do something with meaning. It's not about you getting into the social sector so you can feel good about helping people. If you don't find happiness where you are right now, you are going to be unhappy in the social sector too." –Tiffany Persons, Founder and CEO of Shine On Sierra Leone

6. "What you take out of the world... is much less important than what you put into the world. Follow your contribution instead. Find the thing you're great at, put that into the world, contribute to others, help the world be better." –Ben Horowitz, author of *The Hard Thing About Hard Things*, in his popular Columbia University commencement speech

7. "Many [social entrepreneurs] are indeed exceptional human beings driven to make change where others either give up or despair... but they are also people—women and men who hit walls in their personal and professional lives, who struggle to balance their commitments, who have egos, failings, and bad days," observe Osberg and Martin in *Getting Beyond Better*. "The difference is their *willingness to take direct action* [emphasis added] to achieve such outcomes."

Social entrepreneurship passion is about you, but not *all* about you. Because we are human, social change work starts with us: our values, our cultural lens, our hope for a better world, our desire for a consequential career. That's an excellent place to begin, but social entrepreneurship faces towards community; towards humanity; towards justice.

Passion is not a speculation for finding inner meaning. It may offer meditative peace and calm, it may center and focus us, but that is not the passion of this book nor, I dare say, the passion that makes us colleagues. When I describe accomplished colleagues, I prefer tougher, more demanding words like courage and conviction. Courage and conviction are the qualities that you and I need to attack social problems *with* passion. They are also the qualities that we need when our values, mission and organization are under siege.

Our passion for social justice work is also, in part, framed by our communal inheritance. By accident of birth, Americans enjoy the benefits of living in a country that is gobbling up the world's natural resources. We luxuriate in the benefits from industries we did not build; wars we did not win; political freedoms we have not earned. "We can deny our heritage and our history, but we cannot escape responsibility for the result," noted crusading journalist Edward R. Murrow. There is something obscene, selfish and ignorant about the entitled person who declines to pay down the social debt bequeathed to each one of us by our ancestors.

Yet blistering indignation, by itself, is not social change passion. What creates a successful social entrepreneur is converting our righteous anger into a focused career strategy: picking one issue at a time and then working really hard on it. In a school of management, we might call that setting our passion priorities.

Knowledge is important – even vital – but it's also not the passionate energy of the social entrepreneur. It's not for lack of programs and proposals, studies and strategic reorganizations, that bad things persist. We are awash in reports, ideas, data, pro-poor gadgets, social ventures, impact investment funds, creative synergies, collaborations and schemes. Indeed, you might occasionally suspect, if you were the suspicious sort, that the relentless documentation of intractable global problems and the production of egg-headed evaluations is nothing more than a very sophisticated, foundation-funded procrastination scheme. After all, saying 'let's study it' is safer (and cheaper) than saying 'let's do something about it'.

Our personal or hobby interests, however entertaining and fun, also aren't a social change passion. For example, I collect folk art made with recycled or repurposed materials. From Haiti: colorful toy buses made from plastic milk containers. From Zimbabwe: papier-mâché bowls crafted from green olive jar labels. From Mali: a mother and son statuette made from insecticide cans. As passionate as I am about my collection (except when it comes to dusting it), it's still just a hobby.

If, one day, I decided to turn my pastime into legitimate grassroots economic development, I could adopt the BeadforLife model. This Ugandan nonprofit trains impoverished women to make handmade jewelry using recycled paper. Along the way, the women get business classes and, with their earned profits, accumulate the capital needed to start local businesses serving local needs, thus liberating themselves from dependency on American consumers. That's social entrepreneurship.

—∞—

The pluck and passion of a social justice career are in showing up. When you and I double down on our beliefs, commit to social innovation, take action against injustice, volunteer, campaign, fundraise, march, picket or petition—we are trusting ourselves to figure out what comes next and to handle it when it does. We are also making a commitment (to ourselves) to stay involved; to not quit.

Not once did I see passion coming before it arrived in my life. Not once did I go looking for it. I can also tell you that my satisfaction as a changemaker did not come from pursuing some grandly-worded, grandiose mission statement.

The absence of structure and scaffolding is part of the excitement of the journey. We take comfort and draw strength from remembering that, since the beginning of history, every explorer, mapmaker, inventor, statesperson, changemaker and social justice advocate has operated in uncharted territory.

You and I don't need a first-class miracle to qualify as being passionate about justice. Life-changing work is what we are doing today; every day; right now. Sure, social entrepreneurship careers have pauses and inflection points, red lights and green lights, but fundamentally there is no beginning and no ending—and no waiting to find our passion.

"As you get up in the morning, as you make decisions, as you spend money, make friends, make commitments, you are creating a piece of art called your life," notes Mary Catherine Bateson in *Composing a Life Story*. "Wisdom comes not from anticipation, but from action. And that's true whether we're tackling issues that affect the whole world or just our neighborhoods." *Boom.*

Social entrepreneurs dream in the active tense. For us, passion propels action. Otherwise, what's the point? Our origin stories, narrated with a touch of pride, explain, justify and inspire our good deeds. Our passion plays are performed to move us from apathy to action; from ennui to inspiration; from dilettante to dynamic change agent.

Our first notion of social sector passion comes, credibly, when you and I realize that it is a dangerous obsession. Passionate social justice work is a benevolent dictator of our own making, temporarily destroying our work-life balance. It channels our energies, consumes our best thoughts, turns us inside out, drains us, and then asks more of us.

When I'm social entrepreneuring, I feel energized. My heart races. My pace quickens. My smile brightens. I feel closer to the person who I want to be. Honestly, I can't decide if I'm passionate about social entrepreneurship or social entrepreneurship impassions me. Either way, it's a great feeling.

I have yet to meet a change agent making change *in absentia*. Like watching a magnificent ballet, savoring a scrumptious meal or enjoying great sex, some things are best done in person, passionately. Social entrepreneurship is one of them.

Take Two: Passion

Babita Patel, 38, is a freelance humanitarian photographer and Executive Director of KIOO Project, a nonprofit that changes gender dynamics in economically-challenged communities by teaching photography to girls who, in turn, teach photography to boys. Hometown: NYC. Favorite pastime: sleeping. Guilty pleasure: watching the movie instead of reading the book for book club.

"I was on the cusp of my 30th birthday, and my life sucked. My career as an art director wasn't the rainbows and pixie dust I had imagined. I was struggling financially. My love life was covered in cobwebs.

"And that's when the panic attacks started. Scary ones where I couldn't breathe. Where my insides heaved themselves out of my body. Where my mind mushroomed into gray muck. When I was in the middle of one, there was no end in sight.

"Travel was the only remedy I could think of. If I was going to have a meltdown, I might as well do it on the other side of the world without any witnesses. Which is how I found myself trekking to 19,500 feet up a holy Tibetan mountain frantically looking for divine intervention. Someone who would miraculously fix me. No questions asked.

"I walked off that mountain with jack crap. Apparently God is like love. She doesn't appear when you're searching for her. She smelled the desperation on me and stayed away.

"Weeks later though, I had my moment. Sitting with my feet in the Ganges, eyes closed, hands together, sun on my face, I got it: I needed to get over myself. If I stopped obsessing about me, stopped feeling shitty about myself, stopped hating myself, the panic attacks would stop.

"But my slightly OCD, anal-retentive brain needed *something* to obsess about. If it's not about me, is it about others? I came back to New York to try the 'giving not taking' thing. Somewhere along the way, I threw in things that get me jazzed: travel, international affairs and photography. And that's how my reason for existing smacked me on the head.

"I didn't go looking for my passion. I just wanted my panic attacks to stop."

PREPARED

Compassion and conviction are not the same as competency.

Patrick Awauh steps into a room with the palpable confidence of a person changing lives. Maybe even a whole country. Maybe someday, an entire continent. He carries himself with a quiet intensity and a strength of purpose. Every waking moment, his mission is educational opportunity in Ghana.

As the Founder of Ashesi University, Patrick is garnering international recognition. Some of his honors: a MacArthur Fellowship (nicknamed the 'Genius Award'), the McNulty Prize and Ghana's Order of the Volta. In 2015, *Fortune* magazine tagged him one of the 'World's 50 Greatest Leaders'.

In 2002, Ashesi University consisted of 20 students crammed into a couple of rented buildings on the outskirts of Accra. Since then, student enrollment has swelled to 700—over half on scholarship. Within three months of graduation, nearly 100 per cent of Ashesi alums find jobs or matriculate to graduate-level studies.

Twice, I've interviewed Patrick before a live audience. Twice, I've peered into a mind that epitomizes the social entrepreneur. Twice, I've heard his formula for preparing for a career of conscience. Twice, I've seen the future of social entrepreneurship.

For social entrepreneurs, Ashesi's pedagogical mission is instructive (get it?). You might assume that in a country, like Ghana, its educational lens is tightly focused on technical education for practical occupations: science, engineering, math, chemistry, law or medicine.

Nope.

In Patrick's words, each Ashesi student needs a "deep compassion for society, critical thinking, the ability to solve problems, the ability to create, the process skills to work productively in a team, a strong work ethic, the ability to deal with ambiguity and to tackle unforeseen problems." By infusing the school's applied majors and practical careers with an ethos of collaboration, creativity and moral questioning—he's creating a generation of leaders for an African "renaissance incorporating philosophy, the liberal arts, the humanities, literature, ethics and social theory." Patrick reminds us that "the real privilege of leadership is to serve humanity." He asks us to embrace transformational change that is founded upon honor, ethics, ideals, community service, empathy and a vision for the good society.

Equip yourself with expertise, skills and ethics in equal measure. Acquire moral grounding to weather the tough days ahead. Learn process skills to make yourself powerfully effective. Gather solid domain knowledge to confront whatever injustice pisses you off. In social sector careers, our truest job assignment is not just about building a stronger résumé. It's building a stronger world.

—∞—

Equip yourself with expertise, skills and ethics in equal measure.

At the start of our social change careers, we encounter people with the annoying habit of trying to tell us who we are (or should be); what we should do with our careers; what the 'safe, normal' way to earn a living is; what we should expect out of life. They mean well, they do. Even this book means well. Take every bit of advice into account, and then chart your own course.

It's worth knowing that there are hundreds of pathways leading to your social justice career. Your educational ascent to change agent professional is yours, and yours alone, to customize. Preparing for a social justice career is a non-linear, design-it-yourself project. "There are alternative paths for reaching your social justice dream job," says Jessamyn Shams-Lau. She should know. Jessamyn's changemaker career began by dropping out of high school, enrolling in art school, teaching elementary school in China, earning an MBA—and then networking herself into a plum job as the first program officer for the respected Peery Foundation. Today, she is the CEO.

In the complex world of social change, it's also true that social entrepreneurs with multi-part life experiences and varied backgrounds have a distinct advantage. They tend to be less absolutist, and more nuanced problem-solvers. They are better at adapting to unexpected situations. They are more resilient. They often have stronger listening skills. They anticipate problems with a wider peripheral vision. They have more internal benchmarks against which to measure the potholes and progress on the road to economic and social justice.

Of course, not everyone is destined to launch their own social enterprise, captain a large institution or win a Nobel Prize. In fact, what the social sector really needs most is a myriad of team members and mid-level managers from all walks of life, all races and all genders. Translation? No matter who you are, no matter what your occupational interests and talents, there's a social sector job waiting for you.

None of us is ever completely and totally prepared to succeed on the first day of our first job, or the first day of our last job, or any of the days in between. Over my lifetime, I've cooked up progressive or social entrepreneurial schemes in the private sector, in the social sector and in the halls of government. A good number of these proposals merited the pre-launch rejection they received. Some failed to reach their full potential (often thanks to my shortcomings). Some are a prideful source of accomplishment. Not once was I fully prepared in any common sense meaning of the word.

And while you may never *feel* prepared, you're also never off the hook when it comes to stocking up on basic skills before you start. Indeed, it's an arrogant and wrong-headed privilege to neglect what we can learn before injecting ourselves into other people's lives. To overestimate what we think we already know. To assume our own genius or ingenuity will overcome every problem. Consider the counterfactual: without either of us knowing our ass from a hole in the ground—let's head out into the world and inflict our good-hearted ignorance on vulnerable populations, or mess around with our precious planet. Hasn't the world had enough of that?

Throughout our careers, shrewd social entrepreneurs periodically conduct an inventory of capabilities: a personal SWOT analysis (strengths, weaknesses, opportunities, threats). Ask: Would you hire yourself to work for your favorite charity, cause or social enterprise? What core competencies do you bring to the table, beyond a passion for the cause? Would you delegate a major job assignment to yourself? What about your life history equips you to solve the problem that you care about? A personal SWOT analysis is like tuning up our car before an exciting road trip.

If we hold ourselves to lesser performance standards, we disrespect the people whom we seek to empower. For that, the future that will hold us accountable. Former Aspen Institute President Walter Isaacson, in *The Innovators: How a Group of Hackers, Geniuses, and Geeks Created the Digital Revolution*, bluntly sums it up: "Vision without execution is hallucination."

Compassion and conviction are not the same as competency. Social entrepreneurs need all three. Charm and charisma open doors; they don't sign contracts. If we skimp on proper preparation with amorphous generalities such as 'I enjoy working with people' or 'I want to make a difference'; if we think our social invention, app or gadget will transcend our résumé deficits; or if we believe that the only thing holding back our social venture is more money—then we're probably not ready for a major road trip, not ready for prime time. Sorry to break the bad news.

—∞—

Among the best social activists, there's broad consensus about the indispensable professional prerequisites for social change work. In addition to preparing ourselves with content knowledge and a moral compass, in the beginner years of our social change careers, here are a few learnable skill sets—the lack of which (at one point or another) set my career adrift, disempowered me or sabotaged what I thought was a brilliant social enterprise idea:

Embrace learning. Learning from others, especially victims of injustice, is the highest order personal skill for social entrepreneurs. Focus your social change preparation on understanding the aspirations, assets and needs of the communities you plan to partner with.

As One Acre Fund Founder Andrew Youn writes, "Serving the base of the pyramid requires understanding someone that is probably very different than you. True success comes... from spending hours and months listening to them with an open and eager mind. Learn from the person you wish to serve."

Embrace numbers. "The language of finance is really power-ful. When combined with community organizing skills, training in business is great for figuring out how to make change," advises Jacob Harold, CEO of Guidestar. In my own case, at mid-career, I beefed up my financial management skills by taking inexpensive executive education classes at the local community college on the weekends.

Embrace words. Writing press releases, annual reports, blog posts, policy positions, fundraising appeals and business plans (and job applications!) requires – wait for it – good writing. Take a few online writing workshops or dig out that college composition textbook. To write this book, I needed an editorial coach and lots of tough love from hundreds of other allies whose names are celebrated in *Credits*.

Embrace focus. The potent social entrepreneur is the focused social entrepreneur. It is so tempting – especially if we have an active, curious, social entrepreneurial mind – to see market gaps, community needs and social enterprise opportunities everywhere we turn. Moreover, the enthusiasm and energy of our colleagues are seductive. Our unlimited capacity to sympathize, empathize and strategize means every small and large social injustice catches our attention. Our love of justice is infinite, but our time and energy are not. As the psychologist-philosopher William James called out, "The art of being wise is the art of knowing what to overlook." It all comes down to saying no—another learnable skill.

Tidy up. Be the organized person of conscience the world needs. Social change work happens because of superior organizational skills. The savvy changemaker, the courageous civil rights leader, the principled politician, the successful social venture CEO are all strategic visionaries *and* disciplined self-managers. "You cannot be effective in this work... if your desktop is a shit show. In social entrepreneurship, the most awful details are the most important," says Saul Garlick, Founder of ThinkImpact. If you must, go retro: start a paper filing system; use paper clips; make a sundial. Take it from social activist Mark Albion in *True to Yourself*: "When you are values-based, when your style of leadership isn't the norm, attention to detail is even more important for building trust and confidence."

Show up. Be the punctual person of conscience the world needs. Showing up late or unprepared to a meeting disrespects our over-worked colleagues. It drags mission and morale down. Even if people say they understand, they don't really mean it. When they think about it weeks later, they will resent me for frittering away their most valuable resource: time on task.

Embrace the slog. Grunt work is the trench warfare of social change. Often, the nature of the work under-utilizes our educational accomplishments and capabilities. "It's challenging for a new employee, fresh out of school, who is full of enthusiasm to make the social impact they have dreamed of, to get assigned grunt work," notes Kari Hayden Pendoley, Director of Social Impact for Rodan + Fields. "Grunt work builds trust internally and teaches the nuances of how an organization works. Everyone has done grunt work. Accept grunt work with grace."

If you suspect that one of these guideposts doesn't apply to you, or to me, or to all of our fellow social entrepreneurs—think again.

—∞—

You and I can be forgiven for secretly craving a global moratorium on more studies, reports, analyses, evaluations, documentaries and investigations about the world's troubles. Since that's not going to happen, we need a way of managing the Information/Disinformation Age.

Social entrepreneurs cultivate easily-practiced habits of mind. In other words: ways of looking at problems. Knowledge frameworks protect us from one particular embarrassment that I have had all too often. You know the one. Despite everyone assuring me that there are no stupid questions, I ask one anyway.

In meetings, to guard against appearing clueless, I lump all factoids, data points and even subjective speculations (including my own) into three decision-making containers. Container One holds technical information. For example, if I'm building a bridge, the amount of required steel, how long construction will take, the number of workers, what will it cost, etc. Container Two holds policy information: Should I build a bridge or should I develop a mass transit system? Will the bridge serve the community equitably or will the transportation poor, those without cars, be left out? Container Three holds strategies and tactics for implementing the project: Who will pay for the bridge? How will various constituencies be enlisted to support the project? What opposition is anticipated? In every meeting, if you don't have on-point information, that's the perfect time to keep quiet. For instance, butting in with a policy or political consideration while the technical people are sorting out how many rivets to order is a great way to guarantee that I won't be invited to the next meeting.

To appear smarter than I actually am, I also use the triad of *What? So What?* and *What Next?* to synthesize almost every situation into manageable decision points. Marshaling agreement around *What?* defines the problem. *So What?* defines the issue, the challenge, and the implications of acting or not acting. *What Next?* defines our assignments and responsibilities.

Here's another habit of mind to cultivate, direct from Groucho Marx: "Learn from the mistakes of others. You can never live long enough to make them all yourself." For example, if your career goal is to import merchandise from the developing world—get experience as a buyer working for a major retailer; apprentice with a grassroots producer at the start of the supply chain; or intern at the headquarters of a fair trade organization. Organizations make plenty of mistakes, all the time. They also do things right an awful lot of the time. Pull up a seat and learn all you can.

Make the most of every opportunity to upgrade your social change skills. "Be patient and proactively seek feedback," advises Andrew Youn in his article 'Want a Fulfilling Career in International Development? Start with Humility'. "Careers are forty years long. If you are an early-career professional, realize that the important thing is not your current job, but rather how fast you are growing. Whatever job is handed to you: destroy it with a smile on your face and ask for how you can do it better next time. Don't see your current job as a stepping stone—focus on it and annihilate it, and eke every lesson you can from it."

Lastly, Mathias Craig, Co-Founder of blueEnergy, offers a habit of mind called 'optimistic realism'. In his commencement address to the 2014 graduating high school class at St. Augustine Preparatory School in Nicaragua, he said:

> "Private victories precede public victories, meaning that personal transformation and personal leadership must come before you can effectively change the world. Science, technology and resources alone don't make the world a better place. We need empathy to make the world a better place. We need love to make the world a better place. We need service to make the world a better place. Good leadership combines realism and optimism. Don't ever be fooled into thinking these are opposites.
>
> "Realism is about acknowledging external facts and circumstances and accepting them as they are without judgment. It is a dispassionate exercise. Optimism is an internal state where you exercise the power to choose your response to external facts and circumstances. Some of the facts and circumstances cannot be changed and should wisely be accepted. Others can and should be changed... Plot a course to get there and then get to work. Optimism is of the heart.
>
> "Pessimists will never lead us to a better world because they don't believe that it is possible. Optimists who fail to acknowledge reality are equally as dangerous, because they plot courses to a better world that are unachievable. Our hope lies with the optimistic realists."

Renowned World War II spymaster Bill Donovan liked to tell new recruits to be "high-minded without being soft-headed". Similarly, social entrepreneurship pursues the loftiest of goals by deploying hard-won practical tools and techniques—tools learned in the marketplace and techniques acquired in apprenticeship.

—∞—

When I unspool my days as a college student, the totality of my learning occurred in two very different classrooms. Whatever was happening in world events consumed my every thought. From unionizing farm workers to supporting civil rights campaigns; from antiwar protests to joining the Democratic Socialist Organizing Committee, my student activism felt big, important and pressingly urgent.

In stark contrast, my formal studies were a grim cycle of droning lectures in cavernous auditoriums; late-night cramming while my roommates slept; and menacing tests filled with long questions to which I only had short answers. I had the distinctive demeanor of a truant. I was not a good student. To be fair, I might be exaggerating a bit because, in spite of my mediocre GPA, occasionally I find something at the back of my brain that I'm sure was put there by a professor. There's no other explanation.

A tiresome trope touted by some wannabe-social entrepreneurs goes like this. A natural entrepreneur (typically a male in a hoodie) drops out of college to pursue a visionary, disruptive business idea that, serendipitously, is discovered and funded by an equally visionary venture capitalist who, motivated by good or by greed (or both), finances disruption at the base of the economic pyramid. It's a nice daydream.

If you have the good fortune to be a polymath with the answer for halting climate change, ending racialized prejudice and religious bigotry, creating universal economic opportunity and masterminding world peace, then, by all means: drop out of school. Otherwise, acknowledge knowledge. "On average, companies founded by college graduates have twice the sales of companies founded by people who haven't gone to college. Founder education reduces business failure rates and increases profits, sales and employment," reports tech entrepreneur Vivek Wadhwa in 'Here's What It Actually Takes to Make It as an Entrepreneur'. No doubt, the same holds for our changemaker careers and social ventures. Besides, even if riches are your aim, according to a *Forbes* survey, "of the world's richest 1,125 billionaires, [only] 73 of them dropped out [of] school." If you're into gambling, a Las Vegas slot machine has better odds.

—∞—

In all probability, in between graduating from college and matriculating to a nursing home, you will want a full-time job. I tried it a few times. It wasn't so bad.

It takes a lifetime to figure out how to lead an honorable life in a dishonorable world, but the job doesn't get any easier by putting it off. Start by amassing your most valuable resource: identity capital. The ideal, of course, is figuring out how to earn a living that also makes life worth living. But that's going to take some trial and error, because there are no safe career choices in the job market.

> *It takes a lifetime to figure out how to lead an honorable life in a dishonorable world.*

Here's an unsettling, reassuring, unnerving, soothing, rattling, comforting thing to know: almost every employment decision is a blind gamble involving two unfolding variables. First: you are betting on yourself to succeed at whatever the hell gets thrown at you. Second: you are betting on your next employer to help you become the best possible version of your social-entrepreneurial self. Despite the odds, most social sector jobs do pay off. Here are a few ways to think about our social sector careers as they get underway:

At some point, "you need to claim something," recommends Meg Jay in *The Defining Decade: Why Your Twenties Matter and How to Make the Most of Them Now.* "Saying yes to one concrete thing feels like saying no to an interesting or limitless life. In fact, it's the other way around. When we make choices, we open ourselves up to hard work and failure and heartbreak, so sometimes it feels easier not to know, not to choose and not to do. The one thing I have learned is that you can't think your way through life." Jay's advice is doubly true for any of us with a conscience because, for us, there are so many damn injustices in the world to pick from.

Be realistic. Before we find our first social sector job, it's easy to imagine ourselves working for a terrific social enterprise where our talents are exercised to the fullest, where we are given broad decision-making authority and where we toil alongside understanding mentors and fun colleagues. Nice fantasy. Most jobs are suboptimal.

Our first job is not our last job. Urban legend tells us to stick with a job for some arbitrary 'professionally-decent' period of time. If you aren't fulfilled and learning; if the mission does not align with your values; if your colleagues and bosses are unethical or badly-behaved—resign. Resign as soon as you can financially afford it, and long before you tarnish your brand or your self-respect. After a thrilling change-the-world first job in politics, my second government job was a disaster; I quit after six months. Towards the end of my career, I again took a job that was a mistake, and felt I had to quit again. In both cases, I lost my pride and a few workplace contacts, but recovered my equilibrium. Your employer deserves your very best effort while you're drawing a salary, but let's face it: indentured servitude is *so yesterday.*

Most social sector jobs are better than social sector unemployment. It's a lot easier to look for a job when you have a job. It's a lot easier to network and show off your talents from a place of employment than from a café, a sofa or a hot dog stand. It's a lot more fun to get a paycheck than to not get a paycheck. And, it's nearly impossible to get a letter of recommendation from an employer if you don't have one.

The location, compensation and benefits package need to work for you. Throughout your social sector career, you'll have multiple chances to choose a smaller paycheck. Do what feels right for your budgetary realities. But remember: no matter how important a job might seem, if it financially exploits us, separates us from those we love, disrupts our work-life balance or jeopardizes our personal safety, then we are going to be unhappy, distracted and lousy change agents. Being despondent is not a badge of honor, it's just stupid and self-destructive. As a little girl growing up in Kenya, Wanjiru Kamau-Rutenberg dreamed of being a pilot, a doctor or (wait for it) Madonna. Today, she is the Director of African Women in Agricultural Research and Development (AWARD) in Nairobi, Kenya. Cautioning us against social sector martyrdom, she notes, "You don't add value to the world by being so miserable that the people who you purport to help would rather you were not in their lives."

—∞—

Social change work is not about us being perfect. It is about making a difference. The truth is: we are all works-in-progress. As you prepare yourself to step onto the most electrifying career path imaginable— if you are feeling overwhelmed, then you are normal. Remember that there was a moment in the career of every Nobel Prize Laureate, every great journalist, every visionary statesperson, every big-shot entrepreneur and every successful inventor *before* they imagined their invention, unleashed their creative spark or latched on to their social justice mission. If you are prepared for it, your moment could be tomorrow. Or, even today.

Our passion for social justice work is a good thing, but it's not the only thing. Well-motivated is not the same as done well.

Our passion for social justice work is a good thing, but it's not the only thing. Most of us want to do good, but at the start of our careers, we aren't all that good at it. Well-motivated is not the same as done well. Social entrepreneurship is an applied discipline. A *doing* profession. Social entrepreneurs are the trial lawyers and surgeons, the pilots and plumbers, of the social sector. We are pragmatists with a heart and a conscience, and ethics, and empathy. It's exacting, tough, tiring work. It's not for the faint- or fickle-hearted.

To change the world, we need to *know* something. Then, we need to know *how to do something* with what we know. The one and the other are super-glued together: to study feminism, and then fight for it. To study rhetoric, and then raise our voice for justice. To study finance, and then balance the budget of a social venture. To study journalism, and then expose the world's corruption and moral cowardice. To study environmental law, and then sue the shit out of some polluter.

When you are ready to get moving on your social justice career, don't worry about finding something to do. There are plenty of social, economic and environmental tragedies, plenty of poor people and loads of racial bigotries to keep all of us busy for a long time to come.

Take Two: Prepared

Roshan Paul, 37, is Co-Founder and CEO of the Amani Institute.
He is also a frequent columnist on social innovation and author of
Such a Lot of World. Hometown: Bangalore. Favorite pastime: cricket.
Guilty pleasure: TV shows about politics.

"I once got a Skype call from a social entrepreneur in Mexico, who asked for help in thinking through life and death choices. Her life and death.

"Her life's work was preventing the trafficking of women and girls. And so she herself lived under constant physical threat. We discussed her limited options to stay safe from the Mexican trafficking mafias. She described the point-blank assassinations of acquaintances in broad daylight, and the attempts on her own life.

"We talked about her choices. For example, should she hide from the mafia or get even more public? If she hides, and they find her, it would be easy to kill her off in secret. If she becomes more public, she'd be easier to find but at least it raised the stakes of going after her.

"'What should I do?' she asked me. I stared at her image on the Skype window, my heart full of dread and my mind utterly empty. *I had no idea what to tell her.* In a 15-year career working in social entrepreneurship across five continents, I have come across this sinking feeling over and over again: my education had not prepared me for the work I have to do.

"The six 'professional prerequisites' Jonathan cites as vital for a social change career aren't learnable in school. Except for perhaps the first one, finance. But the others: learning how to 1) listen; 2) write professionally (not academically); 3) focus; 4) manage an organization; and 5) work hard—you likely won't be fluent in by the time you graduate. At least not fluent enough to prepare you for the challenges you are about to face.

"So if you want to be 'prepared' for a career in social entrepreneurship, realize that your undergrad education is kindergarten, and grad school is first grade. When you get into actual social change work, that's when your education truly begins. Be prepared for that!"

RESCUED

When it dawns on us that our work, and indeed the remainder of our lives, impacts real people—a transcendent sense of responsibility sets in.

California's Interstate 80 is a rush-hour quagmire. Even on a no-accident good day, drivers dejectedly aspire to achieve the speed limit. Stuck in I-80 traffic on the way from San Francisco to my home in Davis, I couldn't avoid reading the bumper strip in front of me. A cartoonish dog's paw print outlined a life question for dog lovers and social entrepreneurs alike: *Who rescued who?*

Much like caring for a pet is a paradoxical version caring for yourself, caring about the world is also self-care. In the words of sages, saints and inspirational posters: "The more you give, the more you get."

To one degree or another, our activism is motivated by three interlocking drivers. Admirably (yes, be proud), we empathize with the agonies and aspirations of others. Rightly (yes, hold our values tight), we are indignant about issues of inequity and inequality, and about environmental contamination. Selfishly (yes, we matter too), we are building a life to be proud of; a legacy of engaged compassion. We want a life that is worthy—a life worthy of our best selves.

Social entrepreneurship and a social conscience create defining moments of motivation, psychic inflection points that cause us to take ourselves seriously. When it dawns on us that our work, and indeed the remainder of our lives, impacts real people—a transcendent sense of responsibility sets in.

From that moment forward, hanging around in a namby-pamby job – wasting our talents and watering down our values – is living a lie, or worse. "Above all, don't lie to yourself," advised Russian novelist Fyodor Dostoyevsky. "The man who... listens to his own lie comes to the point that he cannot distinguish the truth within him, or around him, and so loses all respect for himself and for others."

Truthfully, I can't say that I've always been truthful or self-aware. As you are about to read, during my career, I've lied to myself.

— ∞ —

A news magazine once dubbed Burbank, California the 'entertainment media capital of the world'. The Walt Disney Company, Warner Bros., Nickelodeon, and NBC (to name a few) all have corporate offices or production facilities there. Backlots and movie studios take up full city blocks. Nondescript office buildings with darkly -tinted windows loom like parked tour buses. Inside, the mandarins of Hollywood do deals.

Thirty years before joining the ranks of social entrepreneurship, I was a lobbyist-for-hire, prowling California's State Capitol. My most glamorous client was the American music industry, which is why I found myself in Burbank on a sunny California day.

Dressed in a blue pinstripe suit, creamy white shirt and red silk power tie, I looked like a well-connected lobbyist sent over from central casting. More to the point: that's how you look when your career is out of sync with my conscience. I was acting a part in a political drama; reading lines from someone else's script.

The plot: protecting the music industry's profits by defending a lucrative tax break. The cast: corporate lawyers, chief financial officers, publicists, and me. The script: manufacture a credible public-facing rationale for a tax loophole. The ending: peddling corporate self-interest as furthering the public interest.

In Burbank that day, after the scene wrapped, I was a brooding mess. Until that point in my career, I had ardently declared my allegiance to progressive tax policy and the end of corporate tax breaks—which is why this particular client assignment was mortifying. In a past life, I had even co-founded and led the California Tax Reform Association, a 4,000-person, statewide citizens' group promoting fair taxation.

Returning the next day to my offices near the State Capitol, still profoundly unhappy – without rehearsal, without any future plans, without even forethought – I unceremoniously informed my lobby partners that I was quitting the firm (despite the fact that my name was stenciled on the front door). Following my resignation, I did not vault directly from corporate flackery to social justice work. If I had, this might be an easier story to tell.

Instead (in chronological order), I opened an art gallery (mildly successful); started a small real estate development company (modestly successful); prototyped a retail chain selling high-end artisan merchandise (disastrously unsuccessful); worked as the Chief Executive Officer of the California Association of Health Maintenance Organizations (back then, the health care good guys); and started a consultancy called the Academy for International Health Studies (financially successful). After all that, a full ten years later, I resurrected my Sixties activist soul and rebranded myself as a social entrepreneur.

As I share this story with you, it is incredibly tempting to retrospectively connect all the dots: to explain the ethically inexplicable; to claim failure leading to fame; to narrate the screenplay about my noble choice of meaning over money. But really, there was no soul-shaking enlightenment, no confrontation with my conscience, no Dickensian Ghost of Jonathan Future to help me find my inner goodness.

I never meant to become a lobbyist. Following a successful stint as a senior legislative aide in the California state senate, I launched a consulting firm to sell policy expertise to clients with business before governmental decision-makers. I had imagined that I would be writing authoritative reports to inform sound public policy-making. About that, I was carelessly naïve. It turned out that my real market value was the incremental utility of my insights about individual legislators: how they thought; their policy predilections; and, more importantly, how to win their support (or opposition).

To make the rent, pay my staff and avoid unemployment, I slithered down the greasy slope of rationalization, moving from policy to persuasion. Registering with the Secretary of State as a professional lobbyist, I initially signed clients whose policy views I could unapologetically endorse. Then (because my consultancy's expenditures exceeded revenues) I began accepting clients with whom I neither agreed nor disagreed. Eventually (hitting the nadir of my professional life) I represented clients whose policy viewpoints I had once pugnaciously opposed.

Thus, bit by bit, decision by decision; responding to the marketplace; listening intently to clients and listening even more intently to potential clients—I discovered myself tread-milled on a debasing job without principled boundaries. I was earning a fat paycheck by exploiting political friendships on behalf of policy positions I did not care about or, worse, did not agree with. *Cha-ching!*

There is a tyranny of lost time, a kind self-incarceration that comes from working on things that don't matter to us. A zillion small, insignificant minutes wasted which, when added together, amount to an emptiness of purpose.

There is a tyranny of lost time, a kind of self-incarceration that comes from working on things that don't matter.

My fall was uncomplicated. As my consulting business expenses grew, it seemed obvious to me that I had no choice but to start accepting clients whose values did not match my own. Then, one day, it seemed equally obvious that I had no choice but to stop.

Years later, I'm still shocked to recall my breach of moral will; how seamlessly I switched from singing with the angels to dancing with the devils. Every day, our social ventures and our social sector careers are subject to the exact same financial pressures and, thus, vulnerable to sloppy moral lapses. Be alert.

— ∞ —

It's brightly comforting to assume that social entrepreneurship has a redemptive quality. It doesn't. At least, it didn't for me.

I've never been able to figure out a moral equivalency, if such a thing even exists, for using a good deed to counterbalance a bad one. Does my public opposition to corporate polluters excuse my personal over-consumption of gasoline? Does denouncing a Klansman in a white uniform give me a pass on denouncing a Klansman in a blue uniform? Did fighting to kill an oil industry tax loophole earn me a get-out-of-jail-free card for the time that I defended a recording industry tax break?

Where is the blended value between upholding our core values, and life's compromising and uncompromising realities (paying for college, earning a living, raising a family, growing a career)? If I can't know pleasure until I've known pain, can I know moral joy without knowing moral crisis? Life is complicated.

At public gatherings, people get curious about me. They ask: 'What inspires your commitment?' 'How did you get started?' 'Why do you care about poor women?' Often, by way of opening a conversation, people share their own involvements, whether as volunteers or donors or community leaders.

Does denouncing a Klansman in a white uniform give me a pass on denouncing one in a blue uniform?

For my part, I reference my experience in the Bolivian Andes visiting a microfinance program for the first time. I never mention my short-lived lobbyist days. I'm more than a little embarrassed. After all, I want you to think of me as a much better person than I truly am—as someone who always stands up for their values. Neither of us wants to be remembered for the lousy things that we've done.

My social entrepreneurship, no matter how accomplished, impactful or grand, can't rewrite or erase the imperfections of my past. Large and small mistakes, poor career choices, forgetting to shop ethically, neglecting to call out a misogynistic joke—none of these are my personal best. I suppose you would be justified in deciding that I am a hypocrite. There's plenty in my life story to support your conclusion.

Social justice work, beyond its many honorable purposes, can be a theatrical façade: pancake makeup to hide life's wrinkles, a wardrobe tailored to flatter a waistline of poor choices. A mask to help me look more like the person I want to be.

Yet stumbling is how we learn empathy for the stumbles of others. As a result of my ethical migraine working as a lobbyist, I like to think that maybe I'm more understanding, less contemptuous and more supportive of others who have fallen off their principled perches.

— ∞ —

If a career in social entrepreneurship isn't a corrective for past misdeeds, it's certainly a powerful prophylactic against future blunders. Social entrepreneurship protects us from the selfish and the un-meaningful. By doing things that I'm proud of, I'm rescuing myself long before I need rescuing.

"Though we are often taught to think of ourselves as inherently selfish, the longing to act meaningfully in our work seems just as stubborn," social philosopher Alain de Botton tells us in *The Pleasures and Sorrows of Work.* "It is because we are meaning-focused animals rather than simply materialistic ones that we can reasonably contemplate surrendering security for a career helping to bring drinking water to rural Malawi or might quit a job in consumer goods for one in cardiac nursing..."

A career in social entrepreneurship is formidable, because in many other careers it's simply harder and less common to ponder: *What is our larger social purpose?* For instance, I would guess that a doctor or police officer contemplates morality and ethics more frequently than your standard-issue corporate executive chasing quarterly sales targets. Wall Street bankers who practice savage capitalism are probably not hanging out at the water cooler talking about the environmental externalities caused by rapacious market practices. The executives who work for gun manufacturers, I assume, kick their dogs.

I've never heard a social entrepreneur say that they are confronting one of the world's ailments to cure their own—but it's damn nice job perk. By all accounts, the experience of giving back, of pitching in, volunteering, donating, serving on a nonprofit board and canvassing at election time stimulates our sense of personal happiness and well-being. Science tells us that, biologically, happiness promotes improved physical health right along with emotional health.

Indeed, the impact investing mantra of 'doing well by doing good' may actually have a double meaning. It commonly applies to the notion of generating healthy financial returns *while* doing some good in the world. It may also mean generating a healthy lifestyle *because* we are happy while doing some good in the world.

If either or us, accidentally or otherwise, finds that our pursuit of profit is damaging either our moral sensibility or ethical sanity, we always have the principled power is to raise our hand and quietly say: *No. Halt. Not through me. Not now. Not on my watch.* We have the power to leave a hollowed-out, ethically-empty, heart-deadening job.

Quitting a crap job is often the simplest, most liberating solution. But quitting a job is not for the faint-hearted or cowardly. On the contrary. It's brave. It's powerful. It's a loud megaphone of courage. It's confirming. It's the ultimate accountability to the most important critic in your life: you.

And, while we are talking about savvy career moves, there is no dishonor in working at a 'learning job' to upgrade our skills while we wait for a productive social justice opportunity to materialize. The lawyer acquiring litigation experience in a big law firm is one step closer to working for EarthJustice. The MBA getting budgetary experience at a corporate giant could be the next CFO for the microfinance lender KIVA. The ad agency junior associate perfecting her graphic design skills might be getting ready to do communications work for *Conscious Company* magazine. Only you and I can know our plans, and only you and I can implement them.

Quitting a crap job is accountability to your most important critic: you.

An everyday, add-on benefit of fighting injustice is building trust in ourselves, exercising our moral fiber, and strengthening our moral muscles for the next decision point. Often that means admitting a mistake, revisiting a bad career decision, giving up a nice paycheck or, in the secrecy of our thoughts, apologizing to our conscience.

According to the bulk of empirical research and most anecdotal evidence, social entrepreneurs are fallible. In pursuit of our goals, we make mistakes. Even when we know what's right, we can do what's wrong. If by chance you're infallible, I'd like to recruit you as my life-everything coach. If you're like the rest of us, then you might find that social justice work is a refreshing elixir, an invigorating opportunity to reality-check your principles against your frailties and failings.

Making a lousy ethical decision (and what else is social entrepreneurship if not a series of ethical choices?) is like stepping in a big pile of smelly dog shit. You can't undo it. But, looking forward, you can make a habit to watch where you step.

— ∞ —

Whatever our former or future sins, we all bring our own motivations to the work. No single reason is more or less legitimate than any other. The one exception is guilt, which is pointlessly ineffective (not to mention ridiculously old-fashioned). Wanjiru Kamau-Rutenberg, Founder of Kenya-based Akili Dada, nails it when she says: "The most useless people are people driven by guilt. You are most efficient, most effective, and reach people most deeply when you're acting from a place of self-consciousness and self-awareness. It's about trying to heal the world from what you've experienced."

Guilt firmly in check then, almost anything else that gets you and I off our asses can motivate and sustain our changemaker careers. Here are six to consider:

1. If we want to live life to the fullest, then tackling the biggest, baddest problems is a major endorphin high. If your life is boring (or if you feel like *you* are boring), social entrepreneurship may be the remedy. If you've been copying and pasting someone else's choices into your life, pretending to be someone you aren't, then social justice work will reveal the real you—the first step towards a scintillating, sparkling self.

2. If you have something to prove to yourself, then discovering and demonstrating where and how your life brings value to the world is one way to claim your self-worth. If you're pushing back against overbearing parents, academic rigidity, workplace norms or just want a personal adventure, then social change work is the respectable answer. Who can argue with a choice of conscience? Tell your parents and the doubters to step aside. It's your life now.

3. If either of us are nursing the sting of failure, then losing ourselves in the service of others can be therapeutic. "Our culture has established a kind of officially acceptable style of causal explanation, and it is one that encourages the individual to blame himself for failure," counsels Barry Schwartz in *The Paradox of Choice*. "A crucial vaccine against depression is deep commitment and belonging to social groups and institutions..."

4. If you are in the middle of enduring one of life's travails or traumas, living your life in the social sector can help keep your personal problems in perspective. Your misery, hard and hurtful as it seems, might feel more manageable in comparison to the hardships of others.

5. If you have a psychological, and entirely human, need to be needed, then being needed by a gigantic global cause is as good as it gets. In this age of unknown internet friends and interaction-by-app, the human connection of being a helper or a healer affirms our humanity.

6. If we're feeling unloved, perhaps a job in the social sector will help you to sort through potential life partners. Falling in love with someone who shares your worldview can be enchanting. Also, did I mention that social entrepreneurs are, by reputation, terrific lovers?

—∞—

Some of us become social entrepreneurs for the same reason some people fall in love. To be recognized. To be heard. To be seen. To feel alive. As Dr. Martin Luther King, Jr. preached in his 'Drum Major Instinct' sermon, "Deep down within all of us is an instinct. It's a kind of drum major instinct... this quest for recognition, this desire for attention, this desire for distinction is the basic impulse, the basic drive of human life. We like to do something good. And you know, we like to be praised for it..." For my part, I know that I shimmer with a palpable sense of pride when people in my social circle judge me to be a good-hearted person (even when I realize, objectively, that their judgment is overblown or misplaced).

As social animals, it's natural – actually unavoidable – that we understand ourselves in the context of community, and in relation to the people and planet that we care about. The desire to be accepted, praised, respected (and maybe even to brag about our triumphs) is fundamental to the human experience.

Community service (from classic charity to conscious capitalism) ignites an exhilarating rush. For me, it feels as celebratory as making an important new friend for life, a new BFF. It's the kind of spine-tingling, heart-expanding thrill that keeps us up at night, and gets us moving in the morning.

Committing myself to social entrepreneurship is an act of self-legitimization, a statement about my better self. If I do serious things, then I am a serious person. If you and I tackle adult problems, then we are adults. We are rescued from the infantile and the sybaritic. We're no longer playing with dolls and dinosaurs.

The motivation for our careers of conscience doesn't start with a big idea. It starts with a small voice deep inside us. It's like a gentle breeze rustling a palm tree before a torrential storm. We sense, even before we can explain it, that something profound has entered our life.

When I stop today and realize that, because of something I did yesterday, moms will be feeding their kids tomorrow, I'm rescued. Doing anything else – anything less – with my life is inconceivable, vacant and dishonest. In the end, I may only rescue myself, but it's a start.

Take Two: Rescued

Amanda Rodriguez, 25, is Operations Manager at Rockwood Leadership Institute. She enjoys offering insight to bridge unlikely connections, and deeply values what everyone has to offer. Hometown: Los Angeles. Favorite pastime: singing in the car. Guilty pleasure: playlists and napping.

"It can be very triggering for me to imagine an American life of privilege. I have to unpack the heaviness of entitlement that I've only ever angrily brushed against on my way from one survival event to the next. I cannot understand how being a social activist can be a choice, and how a life worth living in activism can atone for past mistakes or avoid future ones.

"The women in my life live worthy lives—even though they wouldn't consider themselves activists or fighters. I haven't seen their lives 'improve' with giving, and I've yet to see them claim social justice as their *sancho*. And when they've been approved for food stamps, WIC, or free lunch at the park for their children, they don't claim to be rescued or rescuers. I am proud to be able to make this distinction, one that shapes the way that I show up as an activist.

"These same women taught me that you don't save a pet from the shelter. Your pet comes from a long line of strays from the street, and you have to pretend they aren't yours when the city comes around so you don't have to pay a fee. This and many other reasons often make me feel like being a social entrepreneur is not a choice, that what I and others in my community have experienced would be judged and seen as ignorant, rather than a way of life within our systems that is just as worthy as others.

"I often doubt what I have to offer as a queer woman of color. I feel as though there is no way to separate my being and the work I actively engage in when it comes to social justice. My best advice for others that may share similar experiences is to know our histories are important as we shape where we are going together."

LISTENERSHIP

Listening is the industrial spying of social change.

The small breakfast table enforced a crowded intimacy for which I was not prepared. On banquet-quality silver service— a profusion of toasts and rolls, jams and jellies, hot and cold meats, eggs, cereals, juices and coffee were arrayed before us. Sitting a mere thirty-six inches from me, Nobel Laureate Elie Wiesel began to eat.

We were breakfasting, by ourselves, in the palatial penthouse of a luxurious beachfront hotel. As the morning sun glinted off of the Atlantic Ocean, a panoramic view of white beaches, gleaming coastline and luxury living in grand estates unfolded as far as the eye could see. The location was Boca Raton, Florida. The year, 2001.

Wiesel was there to present the keynote speech at a global healthcare conference on public-private partnerships. As Founder and CEO of the host organization, my job was to profile the audience and its expectations.

Of course, I knew Wiesel would speak about whatever he wanted. He would speak about what he always spoke about: the oppressed, the abandoned, the persecuted; about Soviet Jews, Nicaraguan Indians, Cambodians and Kurds; about genocide then and now.

The Nobel Prize Committee called him a 'messenger to mankind'. Presidential Medal of Freedom winner. Holocaust survivor. Professor. Political activist. The author of 57 books; I had read five or six of them.

Wiesel's face was recognizably gaunt; drooping; skeletal. Every wrinkle an etched map of his experience. In a World War II concentration camp, he watched his father die, slowly and in agony, from malnutrition and dysentery. He projected a mournful, contemplative, intense affect—as if all humanity was seated in one person, in one chair.

As we nibbled at the mountains of food, our conversation stayed small, vapid and tame. As I explained the purpose and history of the conference, I missed spotting some conspicuous conversational cues. In my nervousness, I failed to appreciate that Wiesel, a world figure receiving a generous honorarium for a speech he had given hundreds of times, only craved a bit of quiet time to collect his thoughts. I was talking, not listening—not paying attention.

The meeting, scheduled a full year in advance, was convening in the subdued wake of a tragedy. Two months earlier, on September 11th, 3,000 innocents were murdered inside New York City's collapsing World Trade Center. Caught on camera, and then continuously replayed like the trailer for a disaster movie, the attack galvanized a shocked nation into war. Like a frenzied lynch mob incited by a combative hothead, the American people convicted the wrong country (Iraq) and launched a war of retribution—spending $2 trillion to kill an additional 200,000 people. In the end, more Americans died to avenge September 11th than were killed *on* September 11th.

Searching for a conversational connection, I remarked that 29,000 children also died on September 11th. Indeed, 29,000 children die from preventable causes every day, year after year, and largely unnoticed by anyone other than a handful of humanitarian organizations. To reinforce my point, I compared this loss of life to 48 jumbo jets packed with young people crashing every day, killing all passengers. I prattled on about preventable, poverty-related deaths; about the paltry amount of American foreign aid; about obscene levels of US military spending.

Wiesel considered me, his gaze penetrating and unwavering, and then in a solemn, barely-audible voice he whispered, "You're right, of course. Of course, you're right. But you don't criticize at a funeral."

I stopped talking.

His words seized me. I can't remember a time when I felt quite so small, so utterly irrelevant, so detached from who I wanted to be. In that split second, I grasped that flaunting my social conscience to make a favorable impression was tawdry and base; humiliating and self-disgracing. I don't advise it.

Instead of talking that morning, if I had asked my guest a question or two, or invited him to share what was on his mind, perhaps I wouldn't have blown the chance to learn from his wisdom. At the very least, I would have saved myself the embarrassment of talking without listening, without curiosity. Perhaps I would have heard a version of his 'The Perils of Indifference' speech:

> "In a way, to be indifferent to suffering is what makes the human being inhuman. Indifference, after all, is more dangerous than anger and hatred. Anger can at times be creative... But indifference is never creative. Indifference... is always the friend of the enemy, for it benefits the aggressor—never his victim, whose pain is magnified when he or she feels forgotten. The political prisoner in his cell, the hungry children, the homeless refugees—not to respond to their plight, not to relieve their solitude by offering them a spark of hope is to exile them from human memory. And in denying their humanity, we betray our own."

Listenership is the opposite of indifference. Listenership means hearing others: the *Others* who have come before us, the *Others* who walk alongside us, the *Others* who are marginalized. Listenership is a gift we give ourselves. Listenership is social entrepreneurship.

—∞—

Social entrepreneurship valorizes the listening skill because it's so fundamental, so vital, to achieving social impact. It's an indispensable tool – maybe *the* indispensable tool – of the social entrepreneur.

Listenership incites my moral imagination. Listening to unheard voices – sometimes even the quiet and pained voices deep inside ourselves – is the way that you and I identify injustice. Whatever your background, you and I start our social justice journey ignorant about someone's oppression, lack of opportunity, muzzled free speech, misery or misfortune. Before we can problem-solve, you and I have to listen-solve.

Listenership is the prerequisite for community organizing, political mobilization, networking and wooing financial backers. Your ability to listen matters more than a great elevator pitch, a brilliant business plan or your visionary idea. To grow your social venture, listening is operationally the fastest and cheapest feedback loop.

Good listening begins the process of equalizing power. Listenership reverse-engineers the paternalistic instinct to export 'First World' solutions to 'Third World' communities. If we are truly listening to each other, we are – if not entirely equal – certainly less unequal. In a globalized world, that's important.

Good listening begins the process of equalizing power. It underwrites the empathy we need to respect other cultures.

Listening is the industrial spying of social change. When I listen, I collect intelligence, facts, intuitions and perceptions—not only from the communities that I care about, but also about potential adversaries or allies. As I listen, I learn what I need to know: your civic interests, the size of your heart, your tactical vulnerabilities, the range of your intellectual curiosity, the way you approach problems. Yes, there's an undeniable undercurrent of manipulative intent: to persuade you to support my social venture or cause.

Listenership is form of leadership. When I listen, I create space for others to step in and join the solution-creation process. The very act of listening confirms my leadership commitment to support a collective and participatory process. When I listen, the 'entrepreneurial sparks' fly, inventing and reinventing my ideas. While I'm listening, I'm sharpening the tools I need for my social justice career. Listening makes me better than I was yesterday.

—∞—

Listenership underwrites the empathy we need to appreciate and respect other cultures. Because 95 per cent of the world is not American—the smart, seasoned and successful American social entrepreneur is a listening social entrepreneur.

On a scorching and humid New York summer day, when the 193 flags at United Nations Plaza sway listlessly, the crisply air-conditioned UN bookstore is a really 'cool' place to hang out (get it?). It's in the basement, near the UNICEF counter; across from the arts and craft store; close to the international post office.

Circa 2007, poking around the children's section, I picked up a copy of *If the World Were a Village* by David Smith. The book pioneered the now-popular meme of imagining that the world's population had shrunk to a community consisting of only 100 people. In our tiny global village, we find that:

- 17 of us speak Chinese; 6 converse in Spanish; 5 communicate in English; 3 each speak in Hindi, Portuguese and Bengali; 2 in Russian; 2 in Japanese.
- 33 Christians pray in our village. 25 worshipers are Muslims. 15 are Hindus. 7 are Buddhists. 6 people practice other religions. 6 of us claim no religion whatsoever.
- 61 of us are Asian. 15 are African. 13 of us live in the Americas. 10 people are European.

Listenership means turning off the filters that shield us from understanding the world as it is. Philosopher Aldous Huxley (in *The Doors of Perception*) explains that the point of listenership is "to see ourselves as others see us [and] hardly less important... to see others as they see themselves."

Listenership helps us 'hear' and understand these realities in our small global village:

- 26 villagers are overweight. 11 are undernourished. 2 of our children under the age of 5 are stunted from malnourishment.
- 15 of us cannot read or write. Only 7 of us have a college degree.
- 25 of our fellow villagers are unsheltered, exposed to the winds and cold rains.
- 9 of us cannot routinely drink a glass of clean, safe water.
- 32 of our neighbors lack the basic sanitation of a toilet.
- 73 villagers don't have access to essential medications.

- 5 people in our village use up 18 per cent of its total energy.
- 35 of our wives, sisters and daughters have endured physical or sexual violence.
- The 20 richest people in our village eat 45 per cent of all the meat and fish.

Further browsing in the UN bookstore helped me 'listen' to the authors from every country, and appreciate that so-called American exceptionalism is really nothing more than unwarranted bragging. To wit: "Sweden and South Korea have more advanced high-speed internet networks. Japan has the most advanced trains and transportation systems. Norwegians, Swedes, the Dutch and Finns make more money. The biggest and most advanced plane in the world is flown out of Singapore. The tallest buildings in the world are now in Dubai, Shanghai and Saudi Arabia," reports Mark Manson in '10 Things Most Americans Don't Know About America'.

"In the Social Progress Index, the United States excels in access to advanced education but ranks 70th in health, 69th in ecosystem sustainability, 39th in basic education, 34th in access to water and sanitation and 31st in personal safety. Even in access to cellphones and the internet, the United States ranks a disappointing 23rd, partly because one American in five lacks internet access," reports Nicholas Kristof in 'We're Not No. 1! We're Not No. 1!'

In our global village, glorious for its copious complexity and colorful complexions, humble listenership gives me a shot at learning from others. Even if the Secretary-General isn't there to personally bag my purchase, just being in the UN bookstore makes me feel more international, more cosmopolitan, more connected to a diverse world—and more aware of why the social entrepreneur's listening skill is imperative in our interconnected world.

—∞—

The good news is: everybody can be a good listener. There's no pre-certification or special equipment required. It's not as scary as base-jumping.

Personally, I'm a really listener. Okay, sometimes I could be a little bit better. Well, actually, a lot better. So you can become a better listener than I am, here are a few guidelines of particular value for change agents:

Listenership is vulnerability. Listening means vulnerability to new ideas, new ways of thinking; it means realizing that I might be wrong-headed, or headed in the wrong direction. "The learning journey... requires us to truly hear what those around us have to say and to deeply integrate that perspective into who we are and what we do— all the while maintaining a strong sense of our own values, grounding and perspective," recommends Sasha Dichter, Chief Innovation Officer of the Acumen Fund, in 'Listening with Intent To Change'. "We enter each conversation with... a real desire not to reinforce what we brought into the conversation, but instead to have our point of view altered by what we are hearing."

Listenership implies compromise. Even when I think that I am completely right about a policy issue or social venture solution (by the way, if anyone asks, be sure to tell them that I always am), I still need to slow down and listen. Speaking with righteous indignation, bitching about the opposition, and pounding my ideologically-virtuous chest is not listenership. In the moment, you and I may feel triumphant, but we accomplish very little as a result. That's a problem because social entrepreneurship is about getting shit done.

Leveraging silence is an effective listening habit. No instrument in the symphony plays for the entire concert. When I'm in full-listening mode, people can be discomfited by my silences. In those moments, they often feel compelled to say something; to share information; to reveal more of themselves. When they do, I'm all ears.

In-person listening is the gold standard. We humans are hardwired to subconsciously process visual impressions before consciously absorbing verbal content. We see before we hear; the speed of light is faster than the speed of sound. While I'm posting online to publicize my cause or learn about yours, I'm missing out on the all-important, non-verbal signals—your folded arms; your eye movements; your quiet smile; your wrinkled brow; your posture. In short, I'm missing the 'tell'—in poker, the unconscious twitch or emotional mood change that signals the player's inner thoughts.

Pull the conversational ripcord. When I'm trapped by a yakking, yakking, yakking salesperson, rapid-fire elevator pitch or scripted politician, I want to spit them out like a strand of hair stuck to the roof of my mouth. Give yourself permission to leave. Keep in mind that you don't owe me your time. Suggestions for when to listen, and when to run? For that, I'm afraid you're on your own.

Value substance over style. If a speaker's advocacy is rude, bumptious, strident or politically incorrect, I try to remember that injustice is the politically-incorrect thing. Saul Alinsky, in *Rules for Radicals*, declares, "I do not propose to be trapped by tact at the expense of truth." An acrimonious argument may feel inconvenient or even offensive, but the larger and more damaging risk is that we – and the rest of society – don't pay attention at all.

Urgent injustice doesn't deserve an argument about procedure. It's ridiculous to counsel patience to the person who is denied the right to vote; who is helplessly watching their child die; who is destitute without a job; who is forced to shit in an alleyway. More than ridiculous, it's cruel. As the 17th-century politician, François de La Rochefoucauld, chided in *Maxims*, "We all have strength enough to endure the misfortunes of others." Standing up for justice doesn't include putting people off by telling them you agree with their ends, but 'now is not the time' or noting 'how much progress we've made'.

There is no equivalency between actual oppression and hurt feelings. When issues are identified; when bad behavior is called out; when things are said; sometimes our feelings – my feelings – get hurt. For example, I don't particularly enjoy being reminded that some fraction of my success is based not on merit, but on my privileged upbringing, Caucasian-ness and that Y chromosome that I never asked for. But as a social entrepreneur, my responsibility is to stay focused on the injustice at hand, not walk away because of a few dented and damaged feelings.

Hear what people mean, not just what they say. When communicating across the invisible barrier of unequal power, it's respectful and just plain courteous to remember that people without traditional forms of power or education often don't necessarily have the vocabulary to express themselves in ways that you and I are used to. In that case, I work at playing sleuth. As novelist Agatha

Christie says, in the words of fictional detective Poirot, "I listen to what you say, but I hear what you mean."

In her article 'To Listen Much More Closely', Pia Infante (Co-Executive Director of the Whitman Institute) adds these three recommendations that you and I – and especially all the people who control access to money for social change – can put to good use:

1. Refrain from giving unsolicited advice. Listening that
    affirms and acknowledges, without being quick to
    offer solutions, means restraining pen and tongue in
    ways that are atypical in our culture. Sometimes our
    partners just need to talk through a complex situation
    or confidentially vent about a difficult moment.

2. Listen for opportunities. One way to leverage our
    vantage point... is to [listen] for possible opportunities
    and connections, and to be thoughtful advocates for
    our partners. We can make introductions to possible
    donors and new funding sources. We can point
    partners to resources in networks they haven't come
    across already.

3. Be willing to be changed. There's a kind of listening
    that is basically a head nodding while we formulate our
    next brilliant thought. It is rare for any of us to show up
    to a conversation or experience with a willingness to be
    changed by it. One radical way to listen is to be willing
    to question our own cherished beliefs and assumptions.

Fortunately, good listenership is an entirely learnable skill. Learnable, yes—but nearly impossible to learn from reading a book such as, um, this one. We don't learn to swim by reading about the biomechanics of hydraulic propulsion. We get in the water and practice.

—∞—

Alas, what you and I need to hear doesn't always come wrapped in a familiar, easy-to-open package. If I'm the decision-maker, the listener, the voter, the audience member, the impact investor, the grant-maker or the social entrepreneur, my responsibility is to laser-focus on the message while setting aside (as best I can) whatever biases are triggered by the messenger's appearance or delivery.

Assumptions and presumptions sit in every chair at every meeting. We are representations, symbols, totems of what others think they know about us before they know us better. Triaging ideas or ideologies, proposals or people, before they are fully understood is – for the changemaker – a dereliction of duty.

Being a social entrepreneur means listening for the muted sounds of injustice.

Listening skills are not just useful for social entrepreneurship. "It takes two to speak the truth. One to speak and another to hear," reasoned philosopher Henry David Thoreau. Irrefutably, listenership is a life talent that justifies itself over and over again—in friendships, romantic relationships, parenting, business, politics, negotiations, and pretty much everything else that you and I do.

Listening is a sacred trust—a promise to ourselves and to our constituents. Indifferent listening disgracefully denies the human dignity of the people we choose not to hear. To be a social entrepreneur means listening for the muted sounds of injustice, for the dampened voices of the unheard, for the whispered hopes of humanity.

Take Two: Listenership

Britt Yamamoto, 45, is the Founder & Director of iLEAP, and a profes-
sor at both the University of Washington and University of Vermont. He
works to create more social justice and equity in the world and to lift up
and sustain the community-based leaders. Hometown: Seattle. Favorite
pastime: sous vide and eating. Guilty pleasure: tinned meats.

"For the past decade, I have been working with my team at iLEAP to
create developmental experiences for social leaders to get better at
listenership. It is quite ridiculous that deep listening is considered to
be a 'soft skill', because it's actually very difficult to master.

"At the same time, listening may be the most important skill
for the social entrepreneur to cultivate. It's one thing to have words
go into your ears, and an entirely different thing to carefully discern
the depth of what you are hearing. Those of us who work across
cultures know that something as simple as *yes* can often mean *no*,
and the success of a project often hangs on our ability to discern
the difference.

"Listenership, much like social entrepreneurship, should not
be practiced in isolation. It is the rare person who can escape their
own patterns, behaviors, and biases within their own head. For this
reason, I believe that listenership needs to be done in relationship
and in community. This helps us to uncover the very blockages
that inhibit deep listening in the first place."

WORDS

When I fail my cause with crappy communications, I feel the opposite of awesome. I've let myself down and, worst of all, I've let down what and who I care about.

Social change requires compassion. Social change requires community, courage and competency. And, most certainly, social change requires good communication.

Words persuade, inspire, challenge, question, educate, infuriate and inflame. Words motivate colleagues, convince financial backers and win over naysayers. Indispensably, words are how social entrepreneurs appeal to the conscience of the community. Words are how we communicate our beliefs, share our vision and engage others. Yet when it comes to talking about our work, words often fail us.

Plain speaking is not a social sector rule. It's not even a cultural norm. As change agents, we are engulfed in gobbledygook and the poison pills of jargon, acronyms and buzzwords—a fusillade of shopworn words and vocabulary traps. Never in the history of humankind have so many words created so little social justice.

In a utopian world, our ideas, policy knowledge and heartfelt values would be judged on their merits, separate and apart from our communication skills. Our social innovations and moral imaginations would triumph over bad presentations, bad pitches and bad grammar. "It doesn't seem fair that an idea's worth is judged by how well it's communicated, but it happens every day," writes Michael Bungay Stanier in *End Malaria*.

The hard truth is, if you and I communicate poorly, we trivialize and sideline what we stand for. Fuzzy communications sabotage our opportunities to win converts and collaborators. If my dazzling idea is dead on arrival, there is a good chance that I killed it with a bad explanation.

When I fail my cause with crappy communications, I feel the opposite of awesome. I've let myself down and, worst of all, I've let down what and who I care about.

Without good communication, we can't give each other constructive feedback, let alone support each other's work. Everything we care about depends on you and I understanding each other. Former CIA director Michael Hayden sets the bar at the perfect height: "You aren't just responsible for what you say; you're responsible for what people hear."

As social justice advocates, we're also responsible for making damn certain that words aren't an excuse to shut people up, to silence or exclude them, to disrespect them (except in the case, of course, of people who have earned our disrespect, but let's talk about that some other time). We have to remember that, even if someone doesn't express themselves with proper grammatical construction, everyone deserves to be heard.

Clear communication requires fierce honesty and unflinching self-awareness. Lazy writing reveals my lazy thinking. "The process of crafting your message not only helps convince others of your worth, but also can help you clarify your work *for yourself*," says Mark Jordahl, Founder of Conservation Concepts. "If you have trouble communicating why you do things a certain way, maybe it's a sign that you have to look more closely at your model. Maybe you are doing the wrong things!"

For some unknown, deeply-mysterious reason, three particular types of social sector writing attract the murkiest, muddiest use of the English language: social venture business plans, organizational mission statements, and social entrepreneurship definitions.

— ∞ —

If you want to ruin your day, read a social venture business plan. Considering the many excellent business schools and the proliferation of social enterprise incubators, the number of deadly-dull, substandard business plans is really quite astonishing.

"What's wrong with most business plans?" asks Harvard Professor of Business Administration William Sahlman in 'How to Write a Great Business Plan'. "Most waste too much ink on numbers and devote too little to the information that really matters to intelligent investors. As every seasoned investor knows, financial projections for a new company – especially detailed, month-by-month projections that stretch out for more than a year – are an act of imagination. An entrepreneurial venture faces far too many unknowns to predict revenues, let alone profits. Moreover, few if any entrepreneurs correctly anticipate how much capital and time will be required to accomplish their objectives. Typically, they are wildly optimistic, padding their projections. Investors know about the padding effect and therefore discount the figures in business plans."

Famed entrepreneur Steve Blank in *The Startup Owner's Manual* argues, "Business plans rarely survive first contact with customers. No one, besides venture capitalists and the late Soviet Union, requires five-year plans to forecast complete unknowns." Our business plans need projections, but you and I should acknowledge, humbly, that they are speculations and estimations—not ironclad certainties.

A challenge for us, as social business plan writers, is that the words we have at our disposal to 'wow' a potential impact investor or ally are devalued and flabby. There are only so many variations for describing a societal problem and our transformative, disruptive solution for it. It's entirely likely that our reader has read every possible hyperbole about our 'game-changing, transformative social impact'.

Moreover, "a social business plan should not deviate from a traditional business plan. One of the biggest mistakes aspiring social entrepreneurs make is over-emphasizing the social part," charges Tracey Turner, Co-Founder and Board Chair of Copia Global. "Forget you are a social business for a second. Then, once [you have written a pure business plan], add one section that articulates the social value of your business. But don't let that section pervade the whole business plan." With enthusiasm, I agree with her.

In simple, declarative English, our business plans should explain how we intend to raise or earn money by having social impact. State what is known and what is unknown, what will be done next and by whom, and at what cost. If we hide ourselves behind a fortress of fat words, obscure messaging and messy numbers, well, just remember the words of Alain de Botton in *Religion for Atheists*: "There is no justification for delivering world-shaking ideas in a mumble."

As every savvy social impact investor will tell us, the real purpose of a business plan is to assess the quality, capacity and leadership thinking of the management team. Use your plan to demonstrate that you are a pragmatic realist. The heckling advice of American satirist Will Rogers applies: "You never get a second chance to make a good first impression." So, write like the coherent, compelling social entrepreneur that you know you are.

— ∞ —

Here's a quiz: which of the following items is *least* like the others? Diplomatic missions; heroic missions; mission statements; California missions; space missions; mission figs.

Answer: mission statements. All of the others are, for one reason or another, useful.

Has anyone ever made a funding decision or taken a job based on a mission statement? Have either of us ever registered for a conference based on its mission statement? Are consumers reading the mission statements for Boeing, Google or Nike? Any novelty hot dogs named in honor of a mission statement?

To give mission statements their due, debating them is a popular exercise for procrastinating board members whose time might be better spent fundraising. In fact, composition-by-committee is a major reason most mission statements are saccharine to the point of indigestion. Honeyed sentences. Sugared phrases. Whipped cream communications.

If you are forced, against your will, to write a mission statement— write it with exciting, concrete words; action words that everyday people can understand. For example, instead of a mission state-ment like 'Our mission is to ameliorate global poverty by advancing economic opportunity with market-based, sustainable solutions for the base of the pyramid', you and I might be more turned on by: 'We create good jobs for poor people who have been royally screwed by the current economic system'.

Even if you and I eschew mission statements, we still need to tell the world about our organizations. If you want to gather people and pennies to your cause, you'll fail unless you can find words that are concrete and clear enough to get people on board. Veteran social entrepreneurs speak and write with specificity and modesty. Instead of 'my enterprise is pivoting' try 'my enterprise is switching from water issues to health issues'. Instead of 'my venture is looking for collaborating partners' try 'my venture needs a distribution partner to reach new clients' or even 'my venture needs to merge with a deep-pocketed partner to avoid filing for bankruptcy'. Instead of 'we're in the middle of a paradigm shift' try 'we're rethinking our effectiveness' (or 'after a lot of organizational soul-searching, we figured out that two paradigms equals only forty cents').

—∞—

To please the dictates of scholarship and accelerate the profession, social sector thought-leaders have used up a sizable number of words composing a pantheon of definitions for social entrepreneurship. I can't prove it, but I suspect that there may be as many definitions as there are social entrepreneurs.

Like a diner claiming that its pie is 'world famous', most social entrepreneurship definitions are overblown exaggerations. I can never tell if the author is a former writer of motivational posters, a fuzzy communicator by nature, or simply detached from reality.

Generally, social entrepreneurship definitions leave me feeling insignificant and slighted; dispirited and disheartened; unable to measure up. Please show me where the social sector demi-gods hide themselves. You know—the ones with penetrating moral vision, unparalleled organizational ability, unbridled determination, a system-disrupting social venture, inspirational oratory, knowledge of business and management, community connectivity, fast and flexible thinking, pitch-perfect leadership talent (ego enough to lead, but not overly egotistical), high emotional IQ, good listening skills, plus an endearing origin story of civic commitment. Oh, and did I mention physically attractive with a soft aura of sexual energy?

Maybe social entrepreneurship is hard to define because we haven't finished figuring out its full potential—or its limits. In fact, social entrepreneurship is more poetry than prose, more beta test than proven product. More about aspiration and belief structure than we sometimes care to admit.

Social entrepreneurs have no fixed theology. No catechism. No hymnals. No edicts, dogmas or boundaries. Social entrepreneurship – call it a vocation, a career or a profession – lacks a code of ethics. No widely-adopted best practices. No prescribed academic or vocational training. No universally-recognized professional degree. No guild or union. No dues. No secret handshake. Common sense, conscience and common decency guide us.

The phrase 'social entrepreneur' is not, comprehensively and unconditionally, a job description. Did you know that the US Bureau of Labor Statistics lists 'nonfarm animal caretaker' as a bona fide occupation, but not 'social entrepreneur'? The job duties of the former are to "feed, water, groom, bathe, exercise or otherwise care for pets and other nonfarm animals, such as dogs, cats, ornamental fish or birds, zoo animals and mice. Work in settings such as kennels, animal shelters, zoos, circuses and aquariums." A comparable delineation of duties does not exist for social entrepreneurs.

In our daily work, a social entrepreneur is like an overworked bartender in a bar with no closing time, mixing drinks from unlabeled bottles of booze. What you and I need to know is ambiguous, ever-changing, confusing and, uh, intoxicating. Consequently, for the sober among us, essential social entrepreneurial skills are nimbleness of mind, improvisation, flexibility, adaptation and leveraging unexpected opportunities. Of necessity, the definition of what we do remains in flux.

Unshackled from the dictionary, the actual practice of social entrepreneurship is rather straightforward: puzzle solving. It's the hardest crossword. The most complex chess game. The biggest Rubik's Cube. We thrill at the excitement of not knowing what's coming next. We soar on the updrafts of the unsolved.

With my fingers crossed, in hopeful anticipation, I tell myself that the various interpretations about who and what we are, what we do and what we should do, will be resolved in the *practice* of social entrepreneurship, not by our *definition* of it. To me, this seems a good thing. Let's have a big tent and trust that the chaos and disorder of our emerging field will bring in new designs, new directions and new dreams.

The ever-present danger, of course, is holding the line against the abuse of the term 'social entrepreneurship' for the purpose of white-washing, green-washing or poverty-washing (sorry, I don't know the color of poverty). "In an age of hype and sound bites, you must make sure you are not practicing *social manure-ship*," says Rebecca Hoffberger, Founder of the American Visionary Art Museum. For a good example, anthropologist Isabelle Clérié reports that "in Haiti, foreigners come here all the time and talk about factories being social businesses because they only hire women. Companies that are solar call themselves social businesses because they are environmentally-friendly. The truth is much less romantic: factories only hire women because they work harder and steal less; companies go solar because grid power is expensive and wildly unstable, so generators bleed cash. I really worry that the idea of social entrepreneurship is just a fluffy buzzword now."

What does it actually, really, truly mean when we proclaim "I am a social entrepreneur"? It must mean something more than merely a description about the way we go about our work. For example, if you call yourself a housing developer, I only know how you make your money. Nothing is implied about your values. You might build luxury mansions or low-income apartments. You might be a slumlord or a constructive (get it?) member of the community.

Indispensably, you and I insist on a social entrepreneurship definition that firmly reminds the world that our profession is about siding with the less powerful. No neutrality. And, yet an abundance of social entrepreneurship explanations skip over the whole point of social entrepreneurship—which is, definitionally, about justice, inclusiveness, fairness, saving lives, opportunity, hope and human development.

I launched MCE Social Capital in 2005, just as the phrase 'social entrepreneurship' was gaining currency. In those days, if the sector had enforced a defined set of even the most anemic professional standards, I wouldn't have made the cut. I still love calling myself a social entrepreneur, but I also know that I'm using the term because the 'social entrepreneur' label, with all its quirky vagary, has a certain cachet. Happily, it's still true that – without asking for permission or taking a vocabulary test; without jeopardizing your library card, your reputation or your sex life – you can start changing the world.

— ∞ —

Words are what I use to sanctify my most cherished commitments. Words are how I explain myself—first and foremost, to myself. Then, words are how I share myself with you. Words are how you and I understand the largeness of the work, and our small part in it.

Words are how we help others look at the world through our eyes. And, words are how we ask for help. Because social entrepreneurship stands on the shoulders of traditional community organizing, our most potent message framing puts the other person in the picture. Instead of 'support my organization to help us do great things', we say 'together, you and I will do great things'. This formulation is more than just a cheesy word manipulation. We use it sincerely because our work involves co-creation, collaboration and community-building. To change the status quo requires collective action, which is nothing more than lots of individuals – individuals like you and me – communicating and acting together.

A common trope is that social entrepreneurs are 'the voice of the voiceless'. To the contrary, our truth is that the poor, the marginalized, the disenfranchised, the discarded and the discouraged must have the power to speak up, speak out and speak for themselves. Until that day arrives, with the authenticity that comes from our lived experience as change agents, we bear the burden and the responsibility of communicating our despair and outrage about the overlooked places where social justice still sleeps.

When we use words in a hazy, confounding, complicated way, we violate our promise to be an inclusive social justice movement. It's really pretty simple: people can't participate in social change, social innovation or social movements that they don't understand.

You and I want to use our words, whether spoken or written, with the force and clarity our causes deserve. Our writing is especially important because, most often, when our words are read, we are not there to resolve the reader's questions or misunderstandings.

Write clearly. Proofreed karefuly.

Take Two: Words

Gerald Richards, 48, is the former CEO of 826 National, a network of tutoring centers to help students aged 6–18 improve their writing skills and learn to love writing. Hometown: Harlem, NYC. Favorite pastime: traveling. Guilty pleasure: binging on Chinese food with Jonathan.

"Words are power. Given the opportunity, words can start movements, topple governments, and change minds. I think what makes me bristle about this essay and its talk of business plans and mission statements is that it puts the words and their power to inspire (or not) in the hands of the social entrepreneur, rather than in the hands of those they serve and support. In many instances, the social entrepreneur in question is trying to communicate an experience, a change in a world they have only seen, and in some cases dropped into. They haven't lived it. The story is not theirs to tell, and so words fail.

"I work with young people of color from low-income communities helping them build their writing skills. You want a reality check? Read their stories in their own words. There is an honesty and purity to how they see the world and how they want the world to be. I would never presume to be able to convey our students' lived experience. My job, my honor, is to amplify those stories so the world knows what they think.

"As Jonathan talks about words and their use, or misuse, in business plans, I found myself thinking the problem is not in the inadequacy of the words, but in thinking the social entrepreneur is the one to convey the story of the work. Too many times have I, as a black man, sat in a room of white social entrepreneurs talking about the education work they are doing in an urban community and it's the entrepreneur telling the story and what is needed to create change. It's rarely the story of the students or the words of the community members served. It's great that your words talk about how you help a community, but what does the community think? In the end, it's the words of those we serve that the world needs to hear."

CONNECTIONS

The professional classes call the act of meeting people networking. I call it making friends.

In the first minute of the first hour of the first day of your new social venture, you are alone. When you begin a job search, a fundraising campaign or a new research project, you are alone.

'Aloneness' feels like teetering on the top rung of a ladder to the future. When I'm up there, I can envision more possibilities, but my perch is unbalanced, unstable and ultimately unsustainable. I can't be a social entrepreneur alone.

From the very moment that my moral imagination challenges the status quo or conceives a new social venture, my idea needs to marinate in the creative juices of colleagues and critics. We need force multipliers on Team Social Justice. That's why you and I network.

For change agents, networking is procreation; a way to multiply ourselves. For some professions, scarcity and exclusivity create value. The fewer plumbers or psychologists, the pricier their services. In social change work, our value comes from beehive abundance. The more changemakers, political activists, social entrepreneurs, crusading columnists, social venture executives and impact investors we can recruit, the better.

Above all, networkers talk about how we define community. When we are pitching and persuading, we are mobilizing potential allies on behalf of more than just a specific social venture, cause or campaign. We are 'selling' our vision for a *just society*.

Networking is a continuous process of creating a community of conviction. From social psychology, we know that peer pressure, social habits and unspoken societal norms are the hidden bedrock of our daily lives. When we are networked within a community, it changes us. One human inspires another. Fairness, kindness and decency coalesce at scale to become a system of justice. Without networking to find my tribe, the connective moral tissue of my social justice work atrophies. Justice is a collective, communal, connected, networked thing.

Regrettably, shared norms can also be anti-social. Graffiti begets more graffiti; demagoguery can feed on itself; mass movements can morph into mob rule. In a very real sense, we network to embed and secure our progressive social values both for ourselves (selfishly) and for others (with justice for all).

Networking is a continuous process of creating a community of conviction.

We also network because it's part of the indispensable human experience: the desire to be heard; the need to belong; the hope that our lives count for something. Networking (like social change) is about lasting relationships, alliances and collaboration. A network tombstones the truth that – through our friends and family, clients and communities, partners and protagonists – our good deeds (and fuckups) survive us.

Finally: change agents network because, for millennia, humans have connected with each other. When I find another human being who is alive with commitment, who shares my unrestrained excitement about social justice, a gentle euphoria (like a new crush) stays with me for weeks. Networking solidifies our interdependence. Networking confirms that we need each other. Networking is life.

—∞—

Occasionally, I don't network. I don't network when I'm asleep. I don't network when I'm showering or brushing my teeth. If I'm reading a particularly gripping espionage novel, I don't network.

Otherwise, any time and any place – conferences, receptions, parties, the local pub, bus rides, weddings, beauty salons, baby showers, pool halls, flea markets, the dentist's office – is a networking opportunity. Everyone you know (your best friend, younger brother, fellow students, teachers, librarians, teammates, *everybody*) is where to start networking for your cause, your next job, your social enterprise or your nonprofit NGO. Every human interaction is networking.

Since 90 per cent of communication is nonverbal cues (that is to say, your facial expression and body language count nine times more than your words), Carrie Rich, Co-Founder of The Global Good Fund, advises that "in a digital-crazy world, it's important to get back to our core, to remember that in-person networking is extraordinarily powerful... When it comes down to it, the best way to accelerate your success is to put aside your smartphone, make eye contact, engage in conversation and forge a lasting impression."

For the networking change agent, no individual is too unimportant, too untitled, too low in the ranks, to overlook. An anonymous dance partner at a costume party, a bored conference-goer, a total stranger in a restaurant, or a nameless shopper all share one characteristic in common: you and I don't yet have a clue about them, so it would foolhardy to assume that they're not interested in our social justice work. They could have expertise or contacts that could aid our social venture. They could be a prominent foundation executive. They could win the lottery tomorrow. They could be actively searching for their next civic engagement.

Networking for MCE Social Capital is a pretty decent demonstration for why talking to real people yields real results. In its pre-launch R&D phase in 2004, I worked on the financing concept for MCE in a comfortable isolation cell: my home office in the small town of Davis, California. I interviewed microfinance experts by phone, learned what I could from the internet, and studiously avoided time-distracting meetings.

One year later, I was convinced that the MCE social finance model was a really terrific idea. 'Really terrific' in the same way that jumping out of a plane without a parachute looks terrific when your feet are firmly planted on the ground. Still in its pre-business plan, pre-board of directors, pre-staff, pre-website, purely-theoretical stage of development, I figured the most realistic market test of the idea was whether or not anyone would actually commit to put their money on the line for an untested concept promoted by a volunteer with zero banking and zero microfinance experience. I decided to find out by networking at the Social Venture Network (SVN) conference.

In out the gymnasium-sized SVN exhibit hall, I collected literature and samples from fair trade food importers, ethical clothiers, organic bakeries, solar companies and a dizzying array of other progressive businesses. With a bulging tote bag, I stopped in front of a selection of handmade Afghan scarves in search of a gift for my mother-in-law. Next to me, another consumer was eyeing the same merchandise. In the way that total strangers sharing a taxi might do, we introduced ourselves and exchanged a bit of biographical information. My fellow scarf-shopper was a businessman from Alaska, and also a first-timer at SVN.

Trusting myself to his straightforward, unpretentious demeanor, I took a small conversational risk by inviting him to sit with me during lunch. Over salad, I asked him to critique the MCE revenue model. By sandwiches, he was reacting positively to the general concept. By dessert, he was volunteering a possible interest in signing up. By coffee, I had discovered a new friend and life confidant. Today, he and his wife are financial guarantors for microloans for thousands of impoverished women living in rural villages all over the world.

The next day, in the conference hotel lobby, a woman smiled at me, extended her hand and declared, "I'm cat woman." At the previous night's Halloween party, I had danced briefly with a woman in feline disguise, before introverting myself back to my hotel room. In the years ahead, as MCE took shape, my cat-costumed dance partner provided advice and early-stage donations to fund critical R&D projects.

A few years later, a benefactor and I were dining in a Washington, DC restaurant, a rare opportunity to get together. When friends of hers approached our table, I restrained my resentment at the intrusion. When the husband of the couple turned to me and asked the tried-and-true question, "What do you do?" I answered, "I work on economic development for poor women in the developing world." Unexpectedly, his eyes lit up. His high school-age son was reading a book by 'someone from Bangladesh' (FYI: *Banker for the Poor* by Muhammad Yunus). We exchanged business cards, talked two weeks later by phone, and today he is one of MCE's thought-leaders and a major financial backer.

Many years later, at a policy conference, I found myself standing at the back of a tiny, over-crowded, over-heated seminar room. Escaping for a rest, I slid along the back wall towards the door. In the hallway, I bumped into another escapee. Sheepishly, we bantered about our truancy. Before heading to my room to change my sweat-soaked shirt, I asked for his card and mumbled something about talking with him later. My new contact turned out to be the head of a foundation and a future impact investor in a number of my wacky social venture ideas.

Not once in any of these four examples did I pre-qualify people. I knew absolutely nothing about their values, economic situation, policy interests, political leanings, life histories, nothing at all. I simple started the conversation, listened to their interests, assumed a potential friendship and let the moment lead me on.

My takeaway? Networking is even more unpredictable than the butterflies in your tummy are telling you. At least, it is in the beginning. Continuous networking is continuous networking practice. It's the only way to get better at it. To schmooze like a pro, just talk with everyone.

— ∞ —

A crackerjack networker needs only two things: a mouth and a person you don't know yet. A good place to find everyone who you don't know is anywhere—but especially at social sector conferences, local social impact hubs, college symposia, local chapters of national organizations, centers for social innovation, lecture series with receptions and, well, you get the idea.

A crackerjack networker needs only two things: a mouth and a person you don't know yet.

Of course, most of us don't get to attend the 'brand name' conferences and events, so let's just agree here that 'conference' can really mean any and every gathering of peers that allows you to interact with colleagues or potential allies. Even a private party could become a *de facto* mini-conference if you choose to talk about your work, the challenges you face, the help you need and your dreams. That's not bringing your work with you. That's showing up ready to talk openly, humbly and vulnerably about what moves your heart.

Conference pheromones are a turn on. We are affirmed; our work appreciated. At well-organized, well-curated social sector conferences, we get a contact high—a feeling of belonging, a sense of communal place and purpose. For a few days, we are immersed in a mini-community of conscience, courage and commitment.

"Conferences can be so energizing. There's just something about all that collective vision in one place," notes Kyle Poplin, Editor of *NextBillion Health Care*. "If you get a bunch of like-minded people together... sharing success stories from the field, the feeling that it's possible to change the world returns once again, as if by magic."

I'm an avid conference-goer—and that includes receptions, fundraisers, parties and hot dog barbecues. I learn; I share; I network. I torture colleagues with bad puns. I collect new ideas; get feedback; extend my brand; sweet-talk funders and reconnect with my tribe.

Of course, not everyone has the 'conference-goer gene'. Unavoidably, we each bring our shyness, our insecurities and our mercurial self-esteem to every meeting. I'm no exception. It's normal to be normal.

Moreover, historically, the social sector conference scene has been dominated by white guys. If you are a younger changemaker, or a person of color, or a woman, there are power dynamics to manage. We both wish it were different, but it isn't. Not withstanding the sector's rhetorical commitment to inclusivity, we are still learning how to do it well.

Even at the best of conferences and most cheery receptions, I still can feel lost and alone—like I'm living inside my own personal Edward Hopper painting. Nonetheless, conferences are about getting something done. When I'm at a conference representing my current social venture or social justice cause and by extension, its constituents, clients or customers, it's on me to accomplish something of value.

Unabashedly, before I register for a conference or any meeting, my pre-screening criteria is crass and self-centered. When committing my time and my organization's money, I'm entitled to be self-regarding. You are too. Unfortunately, conferences aren't rated like movies: PG=Pointless Gabfest; R=Rude; X=Exceptional.

Absent a rating system—before registering I figure out three things. Firstly, and most importantly: Who else will be there?

Secondly: Does the culture of the event align with my temperament and personality, or will I feel like a dispossessed outsider? Lastly: Does the format fit my purpose? For example, if I am there to network—are there relaxed opportunities to mingle?

Conference and meeting impresarios usually pre-determine a theme, topic or theory of social change, so conferees self-select themselves by perspective, purpose and policy dogma. Infrequent is the Opportunity Collaboration delegate who has misgivings about collaboration. I register because the values-based problem-solving is pragmatic and reinforcing (also, as its Founder, I'm proud to be there). Infrequent is the Skoll World Forum registrant who questions social entrepreneurship. I register because it's my learning tribe.

As I sort out how best to leverage my budget and, even more importantly, my time, I want to know who will be in the audience with me. To my way of thinking, and I suspect to yours too, the registration fee purchases access to people who, in some way, might be useful to our respective missions (or job search). If the confirmed roster of attendees is not pre-published and readily accessible (on the conference website), beware.

My 'people criteria' is weighted heavily towards variety. I look for attendees with different life experiences from my own; from a different region of the world; with a skin hue different from mine; a different theory of social change; a different ethnic heritage; a different knowledge base. And – because social change on the ground depends on intellectual and financial resources – I look for registrants who are either rich in dollars or rich in ideas.

In-person networking is the hidden *why* of virtually every social sector gathering. For the same reason that graduate students fork over outrageous fees to attend 'the best' schools, or corporate executives pay exorbitant country club dues—at every gathering it's the person seated next to you, not the one on stage, who matters most.

—∞—

A cultural norm at many social change conferences, events and convenings is sugar-coated civility: a well-practiced form of collegial non-communication. With seemingly unbounded mutual admiration, we freely pass out compliments (and business cards), succumb to herd-think and sip from the punch bowl of convention. Rare are the voices that challenge the charlatans or call out my bullshit.

On this score, I'm as guilty as anyone. From conversational cowardice, I skirt past giving honest feedback. I tell lies to complete strangers. For example, if I'm opportunistically assaulted with an earnest (but prolonged) pitch—I proclaim 'awesome', when what I really mean is 'I'm late to a session' or 'I'm looking for the bathroom' or 'I'm more interested in talking about my social venture than hearing about yours'. I'm guilty of having a finite amount of mental bandwidth.

Cringe-worthy conference formats make it especially hard for you and me to pursue the all-important social connections and human capital development that underpin social entrepreneurship. Panels and plenaries coerce conference-goers into rows, facing forward like milk cartons on a supermarket shelf. The unmistakable design message: ignore the people around you. After a lifetime of honing my conference survival skills, I still find that part of the conference experience tiring and tedious. My mind drifts; I doze; I daydream. Admittedly, my lax concentration also evidences my substandard attention span—a problem my elementary school teachers addressed in the report card category labeled 'deportment'.

It doesn't have to be this way. The better event planners are increasingly making space for serious, extended dialogue. For example, the Opportunity Collaboration brings delegates together every morning in small groups for a facilitated, two-hour discussion about core social sector values. Moreover, the event insists on 'unscheduled agenda time' to encourage delegates to take private meetings with each other.

The unexpected, the spontaneous, the catalytic can happen anywhere—but rigid programming and a jam-packed agenda make it less likely. Meeting planners can't manufacture authentic, unselfish conversation, but they can sanctify the time and place for it. Most don't, so it's on us to create our own.

—∞—

Networking is doing what our mothers told us never to do: talk to strangers. The professional classes call the act of meeting people networking. I call it making friends. Being a stranger in a strange room simply means you're in a room full of friends you haven't made yet. Try these tips:

Smile. Smiling is the way that humans say 'I don't bite'. Smiling communicates confidence and cheerfulness. Smiling says trustworthy and safe.

Approach the loner. To find an ally in any room, look for the person who is visible, but invisible—especially if that individual stands out for reasons of their age, attire, skin color, disability or any other factor that suggests that they, too, might be feeling left out. Do I have to explain why this is a good idea?

Charm people. If you want people to think you're charming, take a genuine interest in their work and life. "One of our biggest mistakes... is attempting to make others like us. Counter-intuitively, it's not how others feel about you that matters most. Rather, it's how they feel about themselves when they are with you," says Kare Anderson in *Mutuality Matters: How You Can Create More Opportunity, Adventure & Friendship with Others.*

Use a snappy, understandable intro. Skip the elevator pitch. What's your short, instantaneous, rapid-fire, tweet-like reply when people say "what do you do?" If I'm representing MCE Social Capital, I say something super-fast such as: "I'm into economic opportunity for poor women in the developing world." Notice that I didn't mention the name of the organization, my title, my specific duties, my theory of social change or my favorite hot dog condiments. I also avoided jargon or political correctness in favor of simplicity: instead of impoverished or low-income, I said poor. My intro is a verbal trailer, not the whole movie—or the bragging end credits.

Be curious. Have real conversations. Every person's story leads to follow-up questions. "What do you do?" leads to "What do you like about your work/career?" "Are you finding the conference/meeting productive?" leads to "What have you learned?" "What challenges are you/your organization facing?" leads to "Can I be helpful in some way?" You get the gist.

Don't pitch. Don't talk at people. That's not networking. That's not even pleasant or personable. It's rude. "We spoil the magic by thinking that selling is a forced conversation, one that is heavily-scripted. I liken selling to having an authentic, purposeful conversation in which you are yourself, not some 'other' version that you save only for sales pitches," writes Michael Bungay Stanier in *End Malaria*.

Solicit real advice. Ask for help (or offer to help others). Bypass the small talk and go for a modicum of hard-edged problem-solving. Reveal a vulnerability by asking, 'My organization is struggling with (*insert your biggest headache here*). Do you have any advice?' Vulnerability automatically involves your listener in what you are saying. If you have all the answers, then you don't need me. Anyway, we are much more likely to appreciate honesty than be impressed by bluster and braggadocio.

Fully engage. Behave as if every nametag is a person, every business card a human being. Over time, you may find out that it's true. When the person in front of me turns out to be utterly disinterested in my cause-du-jour, I make a special effort to pretend I'm a decent person by not peeking over their shoulder to spot someone more important.

Manage your time. When you've concluded that the person in front of you is borderline psychotic, it's time to move on. *After* they finish monologuing (don't interrupt), then smile your best smile and say something like 'I need to make a call' or 'I think there's a fire in my garage'. Then, follow up with *everyone.* Even a self-centered buffoon might help you out in some unexpected way. If you promised to share information, do it.

— ∞ —

Back in the Sixties, a veteran community organizer passed along his conference survival advice to me. Over the decades, it's held up pretty well. "Learn one fact you can put to use on your first day back at work. Get one challenging idea to mull over in the months ahead. Make one new lifetime friend or ally. Then, go get drunk."

Networking is a personal and professional skill for changemakers. Networking simply means meeting lots of people and then triaging each one for follow-up. Classifications might range from volunteer to major donor, from incidental advisor to potential soul mate.

At the most basic level, networkers talk about their short-term need for information, a job, money, a place to stay, a new car, whatever. But in a fast-changing industry with practice boundaries constantly in flux, networking is also a way to stay current and connected to cutting-edge ideas and trends.

Learn one fact. Get one idea. Make one new friend. If you've watched me in public, I'm usually trying hard to take my own networking advice. You can be forgiven for assuming that I am an indefatigable and gregarious networker. Your data is skewed because you only see me in the public spaces of an event.

In truth, the real Jonathan gets rattled, intimidated and bummed out. Networking has its fair share of rejection, and I dislike rejection. Having someone look through me like I don't exist, even though we appear to be communicating, feels demeaning. Sitting alone, ignored and ignorable, hoping someone will say hello, feels like I'm back at the 'unpopular table' in the high school cafeteria. When I don't have any more energy for people, I'm sorely tempted to blow off the meetings and retreat to my room. These deflating moments can spoil an otherwise perfectly good conference.

When I have moments of intense shyness, I keep in mind that, in any given room, at any given time, other people feel as socially inept and as awkward as I do. Some days, I'm articulate and self-assured. Some days, I'm tongue-tied and timid. Some days, I even remember that approaching someone else may be an act of kindness because they may be feeling stuck and unwelcome, just like me.

If you see me on one of those shy days, remind me that networking isn't an end, but a means to an end. And, in the end, it's not even *about me*. I am a stand-in. By rights, the disenfranchised and the discarded should be in the room, networking for themselves. Since that isn't always possible – in the interim and in their absence – it's our job is to connect to the human capital, the intellectual capital and the financial capital necessary for moving our projects and plans forward towards social, environmental and economic justice for all.

Take Two: Connections

Pia Infante, 42, is Trustee and Co-Executive Director at The Whitman Institute, a private foundation promoting trust-based philanthropy. Hometown: Oakland, CA. Favorite pastime: paddle boarding. Guilty pleasure: Shondaland.

"In a *Wired* article entitled, 'It's Embarrassing How Few Black Female Founders Get Funded', we learn "of the thousands of venture deals minted from 2012 to 2014, so few black women founders raised money that, statistically speaking, the number might as well be zero."

"This is where I want to lovingly point out that the many, many great tips of the networking trade offered in this chapter will simply, inevitably, and structurally work better for some (white, male) than others. Here are few tips I'd add for relative 'outsiders':

"*Pick your conference battles.* Not all well-resourced (read: wealthy investors in attendance) conferences are worth your time. Find conferences that at least acknowledge the existence of inequity, have some inclusion intentions and practices, and where the design, location, and culture appeal to you.

"*Pick your conference buddy.* This is someone that can scoop you, debrief crazy shit with you, facilitate discernment, and celebrate when something magical happens.

"*You're not crazy.* You may notice that your proof-of-concept is interrogated more aggressively than those of your counterparts. You're not crazy. Racism and sexism are alive and well, even in the most (supposedly) sympathetic spaces. Use your intuition and your buddy to decide if an interrogation is worth your time.

"*It's okay to walk away.* You never have to respond if someone thinks you are the waitress or maid, and it is okay to abruptly end conversations that take demeaning turns (eg: 'How is someone so pretty so worried about climate change?')

"*Rejection is God's protection.* When something seemingly amazing falls through—more likely than not you're actually being protected from a dysfunctional relationship, months or years of trying to make something work when it doesn't. Feel the sting. Take a breath. Find your buddy. Keep it moving. Your genius is what the world needs."

MENTORED

*Mentors come in two basic categories: dead and not dead.
The dead ones eternally have your back. They might not
love you, but they'll never stiff you.*

The best time to solicit a mentor's advice is anytime. The second best time is before launching our social justice career or venture. The third best time is when we're in trouble. The worst time is never.

Every changemaker needs mentors, coaches, advisors, gurus, champions, counselors and wise voices. I myself could use a dozen of each. If your city ever wants to honor someone with a statue entitled 'Sorely Needed a Mentor'—I'm your guy.

In 2013, I was *definitely* that guy. For a few days each month, a red brick warehouse in San Francisco's trendy, multi-ethnic Mission District was the pop-up studio for Café Impact. We filmed interviews with consummate social entrepreneurs. Our goal was to reach hundreds of thousands of idealistic young people with the nitty-gritty 'mentoring' tips needed for a successful social change career.

The ironic backstory is how, without a mentor, I led Café Impact into bankruptcy. For the full story, see *Failure*. Whether or not a counsellor-in-arms would have called out my blind spots, challenged me, or made me brake before crashing is something I'll never know.

On a typical filming day, job before my alarm clock had a chance to do its job, anticipation jangled me awake. With my mind whirring like the spin cycle on a washing machine, I re-read my notes for the day's interviews. After re-adjusting my tie, re-inspecting my beard for rebellious hairs, and re-checking my pants zipper for the umpteenth time, I headed out the front door for the twenty-minute drive to the studio. It was the last twenty minutes of solitude that I would have until late that night when, still dressed and still sitting upright, I fell asleep on my sofa.

Entering the Café Impact studio was like going behind the scenes at the best-ever Disneyland ride, traveling in the cockpit of a jetliner, or hanging out in the kitchen at your favorite restaurant. While the crew positioned the lighting, checked the camera angles and tested the sound, I fidgeted in preparation for my fifteen minutes of on-air fame. Feigning composure, I chatted with guests or, to cope with nervous bowels, camped out in the bathroom.

After the last-minute instructions from the Executive Producer, we did the final makeup and sound check. *Lights. Camera. Action.*

Filming days brimmed with energy, excitement, exhilaration and exhaustion. They were intellectually demanding and emotionally intense. As the cameras rolled, my split-screen brain multi-tasked between listening to my guest and taking directional cues from the producer.

As Café Impact started to take shape, before a single dollar was spent, when it was still comparatively easy to reprioritize, I ignored three pieces of consequential advice. As I convincingly demonstrated, the thing about good advice is that I'm perfectly capable of ignoring it more than once:

1. John Anner, Founder of the Independent Press Association (now CEO of The Dream Corps), was the first to tell me that the easy part would be producing high-quality media content by high-quality social change agents. The hard part would be marketing and distribution. At the time, I had no idea what he was talking about.

2. Regina Starr Ridley, former Publishing Director of the *Stanford Social Innovation Review*, said: "The trick is marketing, advertising, getting viewers, but, if anyone can do it, you can." In a classic example of hearing what I wanted to hear, I was encouraged by the compliment when I should have been discouraged by her experienced assessment.

3. Victor d'Allant, former director of Skoll Foundation's
   Digital Communications (and the individual who first
   recruited me into the blogosphere), advised me to
   partner with a major, pre-existing media platform such
   as the *Huffington Post*. I didn't fully understand the
   implications of his counsel, but it sounded too difficult
   to pull off, so I closed my mind to the possibility.

Today, with time and distance, it's easy to see the repeating pattern that I missed. I wonder – oh, how I wonder – what Café Impact might have accomplished if I'd had a kickass mentor to whom I could have confided these cautionary conversations. Would she have guided me towards the obvious conclusion that I so foolishly missed?

Instead – faking it as the self-assured, self-confident leader – I kept horn-blowing about even the smallest thing, hoping (futilely, desperately) that each milestone might morph into a miracle. Operationally, I was changing course too often, erratically careening like a car without steering, from one revenue model to another, trying everything we could think of. Worse, I never stepped back or stopped long enough to ask if I was the best-positioned, best-equipped leader for Café Impact (I wasn't). At the time, it was more fun to do introspective interviews than to be introspective myself.

In the end, producing high-quality interviews with insightful social entrepreneurs was not enough to save Café Impact. Catastrophically, we failed to draw the viewership necessary to achieve our social mission. With the benefit of hindsight, I can see that I neglected to take to heart the advice that I'm sharing in this chapter.

— ∞ —

Most of us, especially in the early days of our social entrepreneurship, are ill-equipped to take our dreams to market, let alone grow our projects or our careers to transformative scale. Recalling the startup travails of Ashoka U, Co-Founder Marina Kim tells us in a *Forbes* magazine article: "Sometimes you just don't know what you don't know."

You and I need mentors, allies and guides because in social justice work there are no silver bullets. No instant cure-all. No easy answers.

In fact, the more I learn about social entrepreneurship, the more I realize how much I don't know.

A mentor can help pinpoint heretofore unseen problems or, even better, unseen possibilities. "You can't will something that is outside your capacity to imagine it," observes George Lakoff in *Whose Freedom?* "Free will... cannot operate on ideas you do not have." True in our personal lives. True in our social justice work.

Something I like about myself is that I rarely disagree with myself. Unfortunately, the advice that I already know is rarely the advice that I need. Tim Harford advises us that "we all need a critic, and for most of us the inner critic is not nearly frank enough" in *Adapt: Why Success Always Starts with Failure.* "We need someone who can help us hold two jostling thoughts at the same time: I am not a failure, but I have made a mistake."

If you only want positive feedback, you're not a social entrepreneur. Whether your social venture is spiraling downwards or hockey-sticking upwards (pursuant to the revenue forecast in your business plan), eventually you and I will bump into our own biases, presumptions, false narratives; our own conceit and hypocrisy. Not seeking the objective, probing, ventilating conversation of a mentor or advisor disrespects the importance of the causes that define our life's work.

Lastly, and perhaps most importantly, if your social justice career is kicking you in the ass, the conversational confidentiality of a mentor is like a balm—a safe retreat. A mentorship moment can be a big hug of protective caring, much like the extra squeeze a mom gives her kid on the first day of school. It's *that* good.

—∞—

Before I can benefit from mentoring, coaching or proffered wisdom, I need to find a mentor or two. No mentor, no mentorship.

Finding the ideal mentoring god or goddess can feel daunting, even intimidating. To quell the anxiety, let's surface three critical truths about your prospective coach:

1. Why do mentors mentor? Answer: mentorship is another way to effectuate social change. When you and I don't ask others for help or advice, we preemptively

disempower and disenfranchise them from contributing to our social justice mission. Bad move.

2. Your prospective mentor needs *you* as much as you need *them*. Over the course of our social justice careers, in our most private thoughts, we might think that we're unworthy of our mentor's time. That's complete bullshit. As any decent mentor will tell you: don't sabotage yourself. We're all members of Team Justice. Mentors need you to do the social change work they believe in, but can't do themselves.

3. Mentoring is also self-mentoring. When I'm advising a colleague, a secret gift that I get in return is the spur-of-the-moment satisfaction of collecting my uncensored thoughts and saying them out loud. Occasionally, I hear myself say something insightful, timely, or useful. When that happens, and before it slips my mind, I try to take my own advice right away.

To find a mentor, just ask for help. "It gets back to humility. You have to say *I need help on this*," states Jacob Harold, CEO of the nonprofit rating system Guidestar. Patrick Gleeson, former CEO of Meyer Family Enterprises confesses: "I absolutely feel insecure at times. I've tried to bluff my way, and it didn't work out so well. Just say you don't know. If you need help, raise your hand."

Like ships on the high seas responding to distress signals—a hallmark of the social sector is a sense of shared purpose, camaraderie and mutual aid. Every day, waves of generosity, collaboration and collegiality ripple through the sector. While some social entrepreneurs still cling to an outdated, competitive operational model, most of us are open-handed and open-hearted with feedback and counsel.

However, it's also true that no one likes backseat drivers, so typically the best mentors don't go around volunteering their advice. Obviously, I'm not referring to brainstorming meetings (where everyone contributes his or her viewpoint), parenting (unsolicited advice, aka 'nagging') or graduation speeches (homily-induced mass boredom). For myself, I try to avoid interjecting my opinion unless someone I love is about to do something seriously dangerous; in the case of my enemies, I keep my counsel.

Selecting a mentor is akin to a lifelong research project to ascertain your favorite Italian gelato flavor (currently, mine is licorice). Only extensive trial-and-error, sampling and re-sampling, works. Some flavors need to be tried twice, even three times. And sometimes, your tastes (aka your career needs) change, requiring that you start anew.

I myself prefer mentors who understand personal and political power, the byways and back channels of influence, the ways and means of money, the visible and invisible elements of leadership—what it looks like, how to get it, and how to use it. After all, if social entrepreneurship is about social justice (and it is), then it's also about the power struggle inherent in un-trenching the entrenched.

Unfortunately, not every person of accomplishment is going to make a good mentor. Among the titled and the untitled, the rich and famous, we've all encountered people without one observable iota of kindness or empathy. Particularly for mentoring purposes, avoid these brick-like people.

For mentors, I also shy away from experts (except on technical matters). They tend to be self-invested in their opinions; too cocksure of their recommendations; too attached to their solutions. Also, if their expertise interfaces closely with your mission, a psychological conflict-of-interest can develop between their desire to be respected with a paycheck and your desire to respect them with your gratitude.

We know that gated communities of the mind are dangerous. If all your advisers and mentors match your socio-economic profile, it's time to diversify your circle of confidantes. Resist the tendency of your team, friendship circle, fraternal order, political caucus or book club – or mentors – to homogenize a set of assumptions. To step beyond our dogmas, you and I need to engage with people unlike ourselves. People with different life experiences, different beliefs, and different dreams. One subject, for instance, about which we can never know enough is the lived experience and perspectives of people with racial, religious, ethnic, gender or generational identities different to our own.

I like mentors and advisors who are accomplished in their own right, who demonstrate a modicum of common sense, and who aggressively make me a priority. More than anything else, my non-negotiable gauge for a mentor is how I feel when I'm in their presence. I want to feel seen and heard. I want to feel with absolute certainty that they have my best interests at heart. And, most of all, in that special moment of mentorship, I want to feel like I am the most loved person my mentor's life.

—∞—

Typically, mentors come in two basic categories: dead and not dead. The dead ones eternally have your back. They might not love you, but they'll never stiff you.

For one example, I get leadership advice from a wood-framed lithograph that hangs in my office. The artist, Sixties political activist Sister Corita Kent (deceased), quotes American writer E.B. White (deceased) eulogizing President John F. Kennedy (deceased): "It can be said of him, as a few men in like position, that he did not fear the weather and did not trim his sails, but instead, challenged the wind itself to improve its direction and to cause it to blow more softly and more kindly over the world and its people."

Over the course of my social justice career, I can't say that I've actually been a 'mentee' in any formal sense. When people used that word, I'd always assumed that they were talking about a flavor of tea. Okay, that's a silly joke, but the point is that mentoring comes in many forms, only one of which is officially designated and structured like a classic mentor-mentee experience. For example, my first boss was an influential mentor and role model, but I'm sure that he never thought of it in that way. And, for my part, I was just a young kid trying, in the early days of my job, not to get fired. But from listening, watching, emulating and debriefing—I ended up being mentored by him.

Far and away, the most indispensable mentors are the victims of injustice. Wherever families fight for their futures, local knowledge, experience and wisdom are worth learning from. That's axiomatic for social entrepreneurs. Just by listening to local input, I am *de facto* accepting a form of mentorship.

Colleagues, friends, allies, partners, advisors, collaborators, cronies and total strangers have mentored me without even knowing it. Every single time someone asks you a *Why?* or a *Why Not?* question (or offers some similarly open-ended comment that intersects with your life)—if you pursue it, that's a mentoring moment. Take it. It's free.

Here are two 'mini-mentoring' case studies that influenced me (and, by extension, impacted you, my dear reader):

1. The year was 2013. It must have been winter because I recall the sun had fallen below the horizon early in the day. The place: a Peruvian restaurant along the waterfront in San Francisco. I am dining with friend and colleague Sally Osberg, CEO of the Skoll Foundation. In casual conversation, I'm sharing my increasing sense of ineffectiveness and personal ennui with large portions of my social sector work. Between the tuna ceviche and the entrée, she asks, "Why don't you take a break, a sabbatical, to write a book?" Startled by the suggestion, I responded playfully but dismissively, "Are you out of your mind?" I summarily rejected the idea, but the 'concept seed' was planted. Sally wasn't my mentor, but nonetheless I had been mentored. Mentors, after all, ask good questions.

2. Fast forward: two years later. By then, I was telling friends and close colleagues that I was taking a short break to write down a few private thoughts about my social justice career. In my mind, it was very low-key. No pressure. No deadlines. No disciplined commitment to an outcome. At the time, totally coincidentally, I found myself attending a lecture series that (in the privacy of my mind) I referred to as 'Talks by Authors I Have Not Yet Read'. During the Q&A, aspiring young writers usually asked the speaker about their 'writing process' and, over the course of the series, a composite image of the 'writer's lifestyle' planted itself in my head. One day, as I was crossing the street outside the lecture

hall, I suddenly realized that I was no longer a change agent on a temporary sabbatical to write. I was a writer. I was doing what writers do. To be sure, I was writing about social entrepreneurship careers, but the job title was 'writer'. In that instant, this book became a mental reality. I had been mentored. Mentors, after all, are everywhere.

Some mentors are more interventionist. "In my life, I have sometimes done things that I was absolutely certain I could not do only because friends told me I darn well should, and then made it possible by supporting me and taking away my excuses," reports Jan Piercy, former US Board Member of the World Bank. "Advice is not just counsel, but also sleeves-rolled-up-pitching-in to make possible the impossible. Mentors can help remove obstacles you are using to rationalize not taking the plunge."

In an amped-up world, a mentor is the calm, wise person at our side. A second pair of eyes and ears. A poster with a new perspective on an old problem. An editor to organize my sloppy thinking. A neutral thought-partner to help us think things through. A friend to ask the questions that you and I need to hear.

— ∞ —

Like any relationship between two people, the variations on how you and I will interact with our mentor are endless. Here are a few thoughts on how to get the most of that relationship:

Be fearlessly receptive. As Ann Patchett (one of the speakers in the aforementioned lecture series) cautions in *This Is the Story of a Happy Marriage*, "It's a wonderful thing to find a great teacher, but we also have to find him or her at a time in life when we're able to listen and trust and implement the lessons we are given." If you aren't set to 'listen-trust-implement' mode, maybe you should hold off meeting with your mentor.

Stand up for what you believe in. Believe in it enough to put aside your ego, show vulnerability and admit your ignorance. "We are taught from a very young age to have an opinion on almost everything. In school, you are asked to pick a side, for or against something, and build a case to support your argument. We are conditioned to think that our opinion on any given subject is important," suggests Sam Nemat Vaghar, Co-Founder of the Millennium Campus Network. "The problem with this system of education is sometimes the best answer is *I don't know, but I'd love to learn more.*"

Bring what you have to teach. Most conversations are better when we learn from each other. A cool mentoring moment is when our mentor arches an eyebrow and asks us: "What can I learn from you? How will you inspire me?"

Gracefully welcome negative feedback. Because I'm more thin-skinned than I like to admit, I can only handle so much 'constructive' feedback before I'm at the refrigerator, chasing calories and comfort food. A key component of the social entrepreneurship gig is handling chastisement or a stinging rebuke with grace. To minimize undermining your self-esteem or professional authority, ask proactive, take-charge, open-ended power questions: *What am I not seeing about this problem? How would you organize a venture like this? Are there other professional or personal skills I should acquire to get this job done?*

Expect tough love. While I am ostensibly seeking advice for my floundering organization or clogged career, it's *my* personal qualms and quivers, *my* lack of knowledge, *my* experience deficit, *my* errors, *my* limited vision, or *my* inadequate whatever that's under probing examination. When we engage with a mentor, you and I will hear things we'd never even thought of—even shocking things, revolutionary things, personally-rebuking things, and ultimately things to make us better.

Don't take yourself too seriously. The best mentoring relationships are filled with laughter, deflating self-mockery and comic perspective. Is there a word for laughing and learning simultaneously?

Speak up about the practical filters limiting your growth. You are the expert about your career and your organization's resources—and, critically, your bandwidth to effectuate change in your life and for your social enterprise. At Café Impact, we did not lack for suggestions. Switch to a reality show format; undertake traditional campus organizing; film before live audiences— the list goes on. What we lacked was the capacity to implement any of these wonderful ideas. Input without matching resources is a distracting time-waster. Convert the useless into the useful by asking *How?*

Be patient with your mentor. They may not be a trained coach. In my case, for example, more often than not, I fall into the bad habit of giving (what I think is) great advice in a patronizing and pedantic way. I also tell longish stories or invent convoluted analogies that fall perilously close to the fault-lines of political correctness. If you ever find yourself trapped in a room while I'm pontificating, just remember this quip from the movie *Inherit the Wind*: "I may be rancid butter, but I'm on your side of the bread."

Respect the moment. Appreciate that your mentor is sharing herself with you. Even the most fleeting conversation can feel close to the heart. "All advice is autobiographical," writes the film director Stephen Elliott. "When people give you advice, they're really just talking to themselves in the past."

— ∞ —

By the time it dawned on me that Café Impact was in serious trouble, I was already well under the influence of two irrational, well-documented behavioral compulsions. For the social entrepreneur, both are self-inflicted wounds. The *endowment effect* misleads us into over-valuing our social enterprises simply because we thought of them. The *escalating commitment effect* (aka senseless stubbornness) deceives us into defending a decision made today simply because we argued for it yesterday. Both mindsets forestall problem-solving, and smother creativity. Both are bad habits that a mentor can call out.

Whether your social enterprise is out of control or steadily advancing, it's better to ask questions than argue old answers. It's better to admit mistakes than fake solutions. Better to hear and heed advice than to blunder forward.

Compliments are cool because they make us feel good. Criticism makes us good enough to deserve them. Mentored advice makes us wise enough to keep both in perspective.

Take Two: Mentored

Lissa Piercy, 28, is Co-Founder and CEO of Strength of Doves. She is a spoken word poet turned social entrepreneur working to ensure social justice-focused artists can earn a living wage through their art. Hometown: Washington, DC. Favorite pastime: late-night poetry ciphers. Guilty pleasure: popcorn and podcasts.

"I exist in two communities: one of artists, the other of social entrepreneurs. The poet in me is eager for guidance and support. She finds mentors in friendship, in books and live performances, always assuming that she has something to learn from others. The businesswoman in me is headstrong and determined to prove herself, and when she doesn't know something, her first instinct is to fake it rather than admit that she needs help. I think this is something many young entrepreneurs face. This need to prove ourselves and show we are worthy of mentorship before actually finding it.

"As I read this essay, I realized that one of the reasons I don't reach out for mentorship is not knowing what questions to ask. When we are in the toughest moments of our business, it can feel like we are out at sea in a ship with five gaping holes—and who do you ask for help when you're trying not to sink? A good guide is the person who can take a step back, see the holes, and help keep the boat afloat while you find support for each individual one. A sort of umbrella mentor, if you will.

"In social entrepreneurship, though, young people especially can be so consumed by our own projects that we forget some of our best friends may have the answers we are looking for. I can't count the number of times the person I needed was sitting right next to me, but I didn't think to ask—or the times I had an answer for a friend who didn't ask me. Sometimes, too the first step towards mentorship isn't asking for help on your own project, but offering help to someone else, and then receiving something from them in return. In this way you can build the mutual mentor/mentee relationship that Jonathan describes."

FAILURE

Failure is not contagious. You don't get it from toilet seats. It's not transmitted by airborne pathogens. You don't catch it from talking about it.

From out of the passing crowd, moving at a brisk pace, a young woman with an effervescent grin closed in on me. I was standing curbside, waiting to cross busy George Street in Oxford, England. Not yet quite within range for conversation, she exclaimed, "You're Jonathan Lewis!" This didn't particularly impress me because (let's not mince words here) I already knew that.

As she neared, her words spilled out. "I've watched all of your Café Impact videos. They're the reason that I'm studying social entrepreneurship. I'm an MBA student here. I'm going back to Ghana soon." Presenting her hand to shake mine, she announced: "My name is Charlotte Ntim." As I would soon learn, she and I were both attending the Skoll World Forum—an annual convening of social venture leaders, progressive policy wonks, social impact investors, journalists, movie makers and scholars committed to social change through social entrepreneurship.

For a bittersweet, heart-twisting nanosecond, I felt famous and acknowledged. I was, after all, Café Impact's on-camera host and founding CEO. Correction: founding and failed CEO. After two long years, Café Impact collapsed, unable to sustainably finance itself.

The Café Impact story, as I've shared with my colleagues over many glasses of cabernet, begins in 2011, in the midst of an entirely different failure. At the time, I was a malfunctioning visiting lecturer at the University of California Berkeley's Blum Center for Developing Economies. I taught social entrepreneurship with gusto, but (like good social entrepreneurship) good professoring requires apprenticeship and practice. Back then I had neither, and, by my own standards, underperformed. (I went on to teach a similar course for the Reynolds Program for Social Entrepreneurship at New York University; my students reported that it was not the *worst* class they'd ever taken).

Through the eyes of my students, I discovered the scarcity of practical resource materials for aspiring social entrepreneurs. Following consultations with a broad sample of national student leaders, a plan emerged for a series of YouTube-style interviews with social entrepreneurs. Grandly, Café Impact's social mission was to democratize access to careers of conscience.

From the beginning, I insisted on superior production quality. Set the bar high and respect the viewer, I argued. My analysis of the competitive landscape concluded that the social sector had more than enough video material with a scripted, stiff, unpolished change agent peddling his or her program. I could not find a single colleague who actually watched these videos (unless, of course, they were featured). Somewhat pompously, I concluded that new entrants to the social sector deserved professionally-done (read: expensive) material.

In addition, we resolved to showcase only social entrepreneurs with replicable career paths. We considered interviewing celebrities, the rich and the powerful—but opted for realism over stardom. Our principled decision was right on the merits, but wrong on the money. In retrospect, if we had interviewed a few activist-celebrities, we might have attracted a higher viewership. There's a reason that Hollywood gossip columns get read. Ironically, the better approach was right in front me at the Skoll World Forum, which both honors frontline social entrepreneurs and showcases the sector-at-large by featuring Nobel Prize Laureates, noteworthy political leaders and marquee entertainers.

Into the filming studio we scurried, fully committed to producing videos with solid production values. We retained a well-regarded web design firm; selected a talented, female-owned film studio; hired a youth-led social media company and fundraised. Café Impact did not lack for startup capital, talent, vision, creativity or energy.

What we did lack was marketplace acceptance. Correctly, we identified the need for the videos. Incorrectly, we did not identify the market demand. I was asking the wrong questions. (As detailed in *Mentored*, this was all explained to me at the time.) The decision to focus on great content, instead of great marketing and great distribution, ultimately proved fatal. Unwatched videos are useless, not to mention financially-unsustainable.

Over the course of Café Impact's short life, we tried any number of revenue models. In fail-fast mode, we first went after individual paid memberships. Then, we sold advertising. Then, we explored university library subscriptions. Finally, we took to begging for donations. Of these, begging proved the most lucrative.

"We chose to move ahead with the project because we were getting positive feedback about the videos, rather than because we nailed the business model or the market opportunity," notes Executive Producer Chantal Sheehan in the postmortem. "Young social entrepreneurs often believe that if they build it, money and people will come. That, unpoetically, is crap thinking." In saying 'we'— Chantal is kindly sharing a responsibility that was mine alone. As it turns out, you don't have to be young to be full of shitty ideas.

Café Impact never achieved its dreamy social change mission of reaching millions of budding social entrepreneurs. Without thousands of eyeballs watching the videos, nothing we tried came remotely close to generating the revenue necessary to support a second or third season of filming—let alone generate a financial return on investment. Without even an obituary notice, Café Impact collapsed in bankruptcy. No money, no mission.

—∞—

In the middle of a social venture meltdown, social entrepreneurs can react (*gasp!*) exactly like regular human beings. As Café Impact struggled, I struggled too.

Goaded by the embarrassment of a looming failure, I obsessively threw myself at make-believe tasks, fabricated work for myself and kicked into overdrive. Spending time with student interns and fretting over website details sucked my time when I should have paid attention to the big and looming challenge of marketing the videos.

117

I was busy being busy, accomplishing little that was mission-critical. Hardworking trumped hard thinking.

Two years too late, my blinkered hubris was laid bare. Senior executives at *USA Today* and Participant Media (known for socially-relevant films like *An Inconvenient Truth* and *Food, Inc.*) unequivocally confirmed the difficulty of monetizing online video content. When I offered up my videos for free(!), they responded by saying, "You've got to be kidding. We haven't figured out how to make money on our own videos, let alone someone else's!"

I'm still proud of the work that we produced. The videos are pragmatic and inspirational; introspective and insightful. Viewer feedback gushed: "When you see the videos, you see the passion." "I ended up re-watching, like, 10 videos... They are really a huge comfort and extremely, extremely true." "I loved how the videos are both inspiring but also so authentic—the host and guest both admitting to being scared shitless on the first day of work... I can relate!"

I suppose some changemakers are untroubled by failure, but I've never met any. However, as often happens in the social sector, we had a chorus of admirers without a chorus of customers. Potential viewers who *needed* the video content didn't necessarily *know* they needed it. Viewers who valued the content didn't value it *enough* to pay for it. As the Roman poet Juvenal bitched, "All wish to know, but none want to pay the fee."

At the start of our changemaker careers, when you and I say yes to a social change opportunity; when we commit our time, talent and reputation; we're not thinking about falling or failing. "Nobody wants to fail. Ever. It hurts. It's embarrassing. It's lonely. Organizations, too, hate failure. They penalize it, rationalize it, ignore it, and some try to cover it up altogether," write John Danner and Mark Coopersmith in *The Other 'F' Word*. "Too often we shift instantly from describing a situation as a failure to describing the individuals involved as failures." And, that's exactly what I did.

As I signed off on the final legal documents to close Café Impact, I felt empty, unhappy, ugly and awful. I was angry with myself—and inconsolably embarrassed. My psyche ached with a deep woundedness. I suppose that some changemakers are untroubled by failure, that their souls are unmolested by the special responsibility of social justice work—but I've never met any.

—∞—

Failure is not contagious. You don't get it from toilet seats. It's not transmitted by airborne pathogens. You don't catch it from talking about it.

Nevertheless, in polite conversation among social entrepreneurs, failure – total, complete, abject failure – is taboo territory. It seems to go against human nature to readily acknowledge a mistake, let alone a failure. To twist a line from the poet Oscar Wilde, failure is the social entrepreneurship that dares not speak its name.

Even if we fall flat on our face and learn nothing whatsoever from the experience, just sharing our stories about failure normalizes open and frank dialogue. In my case, I feel I've earned the right to proudly repeat the badass words of management consultant Barry LePatner: "Good judgment comes from experience, and experience comes from bad judgment." Examining failure is cathartic, clarifying and cleansing.

Unexamined failure is a social sector scandal, a cover-up as unproductive as failure itself.

Unexamined failure is a social sector scandal, a cover-up as unproductive as failure itself. An un-scrutinized mistake leads to more of the same. Every airplane crash is automatically investigated by a team of taxpayer-financed independent experts. Industry-wide safety improvements ensue as a result, which is why, when I am in an airplane at 35,000 feet, it usually doesn't fall out of the sky. Professional sports teams debrief after every game. Military maneuvers are unpacked in war colleges. In Silicon Valley, failure is practically a badge of honor; without a few failures under your belt, no one thinks you're innovating enough.

In contrast, when a social enterprise crashes, we hardly hear about it. Without postmortems, quality improvement in the social sector remains elusive. Deprived of case studies about failure, we're left with the probability that our social ventures will be the next road kill, and the next, and the next.

We keep our failures hidden to puff up our personal brands and forestall becoming social sector pariahs. Failed organizations don't get marquee billing at social change conferences. Workshops about failure are ghettoized, not lionized. We know that success compounds (called the cumulative advantage effect); conversely, underdogs (by class, by race, by gender, by physical appearance and – yes – by past performance) suffer a cumulative disadvantage effect. Failure can prefigure our future prospects, right?

Contemplating failure can also undermine our confidence that our social enterprises are too well-designed, too clever, and too well-managed to ever drive into a ditch. Like drivers passing a highway accident, gawking for a morbid moment at the broken glass and mangled cars, we slow and stare and then (fueled by the delusion that we are better drivers than we are) we speed up. No change agent likes to see themselves reflected in the failure of others.

Change agents dislike discussing failure because it filets open our fears, cutting close to our insecurities.
Another reason to conceal our failures is that grantmakers, government decision-makers, board members, the media and everyone else prefer Hollywood endings to life's uncertain nuances. Good triumphs over evil. Boy gets girl. Social venture solves social problem. It's thorny to attract donors or impact investors with a story about mistakes, missed cues, fizzles and fiascos. Few funders fund R&D; fewer still will underwrite a flunking project for a second attempt.

Chiefly, change agents dislike discussing failure because it filets open our fears, cutting close to our insecurities. In comparison to everyone else's boastful press releases and proud Facebook postings, failure makes me feel small and unattractive. Worse, failure makes me feel unworthy of the causes I fight for.

— ∞ —

Even with the odds stacked against us, social entrepreneurs are undaunted. Indeed, according to most studies I've not read—social entrepreneurship is the leading cause of social venture failure.

In both the social and non-social business categories, I have architected several prime-time fiascos. Café Impact is just one of them. Another was failing to achieve commercial success as the Co-Founder of a high-end, hip, artisanal gift shop called Art Related Things; the popular pilot store never scaled. A third was a real estate development company revitalizing an urban neighborhood; impatiently, we gave up too soon. Late in my career, when I should have known better, I undertook the CEO-ship for a struggling social enterprise without properly vetting it; my role imploded. Still other failures I try to forget (but never do).

Moreover, in the nooks and crannies of my professional accomplishments, I've accomplished a thousand failures of character. At times, I failed to make a decision when one was needed. Other times, I acted impulsively, forgetting to pause long enough to consider all the factors indispensable to making a fully-informed judgment. I have failed in friendships and flagged in kindheartedness. Sometimes, I failed to live up to my own principles. Much to my surprise, I'm not perfect.

The Other 'F' Word catalogs a depressing array of failures up and down the ladder of life. "Between 50% and 70% of all new businesses in the United States fail within the first 18 months. Two out of five [new CEOs] fail to last 18 months. As many as 95% of new products introduced each year fail. Between 70% and 90% of mergers and acquisitions fail to add to shareholder value or meet their objectives. Most sales calls are failures, as are most advertising impressions on TV, the web or in print; internet ads, for example, get clicked about once for every thousand views. More than 99% of US-approved patents fail to earn a cent for their inventors; of 1.5 million patents in effect, only 3,000 of them are being used for something commercially-viable. Almost half of new marriages end in divorce. About 88% of New Year's resolutions end in failure."

After living most of their lives in near-poverty, these social innovators died penniless: Johann Sebastian Bach (composer: *The Brandenburg Concertos*); George Washington Carver (inventor: peanut butter); Vincent van Gogh (painter: 2,000 works of art, including *Starry Night*); Johannes Gutenberg (inventor: printing press); Herman Melville (author: *Moby Dick*); Socrates (philosopher: hemlock brand manager) and Nikola Tesla (inventor: alternating electric current). If our social ventures implode or our underpaid social sector careers flounder, at least we're in good company.

—∞—

If you get the choice, I recommend success over failure. Be that as it may, be prepared to make mistakes. Failure is how we live our lives. Things go wrong. It happens in life, in business, in government and, yes, in social justice work too. It behooves us to get good at the art of managing and mitigating failure:

Hug a colleague. Support each other. Send notes of appreciation. Even if you aren't failing, someone else is. When we acknowledge each other's contributions to a more decent world, we are nourishing and fortifying our collective resilience. For example, long after Café Impact closed, Chid Liberty, CEO of Liberty and Justice (a fair-trade apparel manufacturer promoting the Made in Africa label) emailed me to say:

> "So last year I got an email from a consultant at Bain, a Yale grad. She'd been following Liberty & Justice for a few years and wants to know if she can come work for us for a little while as a Bain extern. They pay; I get a super-talented young mind. I said, 'Where do I sign?' Fast forward a year. We've won an award for the project I assigned her. She's now left Bain to come work for us full time as a Senior Vice President. The other night, she casually mentioned that she actually first heard about us on a Café Impact video and started following our progress from there. If you knew how much of a gem she is, you'd know how grateful I am to you."

Avoid self-delusion. As a balm for bruised pride, I'm often tempted to revise history, redefining my screw-ups as stepping stones to eventual success. This kind of happy-talk is common in bragging memoirs ('I-failed, I-never-gave-up, I-learned, I-improved, look-at-me-now'), but sometimes a flop is just a flop. Rewriting our mission statements *ex-post facto* is toxic and dishonest. After Café Impact collapsed, a colleague tried to console me: "You accomplished a lot. Look at how much you learned." That's true, but our mission statement called for a self-financing educational program. It didn't mention one single thing about professional development for me or the senior management. Social entrepreneurs measure success not by how much they self-improved themselves, but by how much they improved the world.

Mess up early and often. The most-timely feedback occurs during pre-launch practice sessions or in apprenticeship. Before game time, sports teams scrimmage. Theater companies schedule previews before live audiences. Minimum-viable products and pilot projects are self-justifying prep tools used to increase the chance that your failures will be small ones. Get advice early enough to use it.

Share your failure. "Every year around Thanksgiving, I write a personal letter to our community," reports Carrie Rich, CEO of The Global Good Fund. "In the letter, I highlight my failures from that year... I make my failures widely known, I own them, I take responsibility and I share what I learned. Then, I thank our community for sticking with me. The practice keeps me authentic and real. It also gives permission to others to be imperfect." Following Carrie's advice, I wrote this essay.

Maintain perspective. Before you decide that you are tragically-fated to suffer catastrophe after catastrophe; before you order a barrel of embalming fluid—talk to colleagues. When we are feeling down, the best tonic is a big gulp of remembering that we're not playing the failure game alone.

Hang in there. If the social entrepreneur's path presumes a few wrong turns, cul-de-sacs and dead-ends, it also presumes perseverance. "Survive long enough to get lucky," advise Kevin Lynch and Julius Walls in *Mission, Inc.* For example, until you succeed, you have a 100 per cent failure rate at finding a new apartment. Learning to play a musical instrument begins with utter failure followed by zigzags towards competency. Searching for a life mate is pretty much a case of short-term, repetitive disappointment followed by joyful discovery. As a breed, social entrepreneurs channel Thomas Edison who (having testing thousands of filaments before the light bulb came on) said, "I have not failed. I have successfully found 10,000 ways that will not work."

A failure is not a permanent verdict on either of us. Temporarily, but only temporarily, failure shrivels my self-esteem and my brand. An F grade is merely an assessment of my particular ability to implement a particular idea at that particular moment in time. That's it. Nothing more.

—∞—

Failing sucks. When a project fails, if we care enough (and of course we do), then it's heartbreaking. As if replaying, over and over again, a failed friendship in my mind, I never quite get over a social venture crash and burn. The wincing memories and recycled self-doubt remind me that I'm human and vulnerable. They also remind me to treasure the heart-filling, awe-inspiring psychic rewards of social justice work.

Accepting the prospect of failure means that I can shed paralysis-by-analysis. Our social venture failures can have unintended good consequences. Even if I fail my own social mission, I might – inadvertently, serendipitously and happily – help yours. Even if you and I fail to reach our large and laudable objectives, the very act of making the attempt role models commitment. Social entrepreneurship-in-action publicizes what we are made of, and what we stand for.

When I am rejected (by the marketplace, by funders, by whomever, by whatever), my thoughts whirl with questions: *What did I do wrong? What could I have done differently? Will I be stigmatized as incompetent? Am I worthy of social entrepreneurship? Am I worthy, period?*

Whether we're a CEO-Founder, or one of the vital middle managers, consultants or volunteers working for an NGO or social venture, we each have our own ingredients to add to the collective stew of failure. With all the headlines and hype about social entrepreneurs and scaling innovations, it's easy to lose sight of the fact that winning (or losing) at social change is a team sport. We can all succeed at failure.

The anatomy of social change, and the core of our social entrepreneurship, depend on taking risk after risk for our convictions. Daring to fail is part of the job description.

Social entrepreneurship is gambling for people with a conscience. Realizing with absolute certitude that I'm going to lose (probably more than once) is liberating. Accepting the prospect of failure means that I can get started right away, shed paralysis-by-analysis, and confront stagnation. ('Stagnation', if anyone asks you, is not a country densely populated by adult male deer. Nope. Stagnation is the granite face of the status quo—the social entrepreneur's eternal enemy.)

After burying my social enterprise; after the funeral wreaths wilt; after I've exhumed whatever lessons I can, it's time to heal and try again. "A heart still works even when it's broken," Charles Blow tells us in *Fire Shut Up in My Bones*. The human need, and the pressing social injustice, that first called my heart to action remain as urgent as ever.

A dead social venture leaves survivors that demand our redoubled efforts. "When a tech startup fails, it's inevitably a harsh time for the founder, the employees, the investors and the customers. But when a social enterprise shuts down, its failure also affects those populations or ecosystems that the business was supposed to serve," blogs Leticia Gasca, Co-Founder of the Mexico City-based Failure Institute and FuckUp Nights. If the latest e-gadget or app fails to turn a profit, no one contracts malaria, wastes away in a refugee camp or goes hungry as a result. In the marketplace of the poor— the stakes are high.

Every time we launch a social venture or accept a social sector job, you and I can't know if it's our destiny to succeed or fail. If I'm a social entrepreneur, I only know that it's my destiny to try.

Take Two: Failure

Chid Liberty, 37, is CEO of UNIFORM and Liberty & Justice. He is a pioneer in ethical fashion and manufacturing in Africa. Hometown: Monrovia, Liberia. Favorite pastime: playing guitar. Guilty pleasure: The Bachelor.

"Do social entrepreneurs fear failure too much, or too little? After all, even some terrible ideas still bag funders, customers, great press, and highly-coveted awards. Some would argue that my idea to build Africa's first fair trade-certified apparel factory in post-conflict Liberia was a terrible idea. Filled with hubris, I shamed those who brought to light any reason that starting such a factory might be too risky. After all, who could say *no* to providing jobs for women in Liberia?

"Four years later, the Ebola outbreak shut down our factory for nine months and nearly put us out of business. Of course we couldn't have predicted that Liberia would experience an Ebola outbreak. Nor was it our fault that it was the worst outbreak in history. But, we'd spent so much time silencing those who disagreed with us, that maybe we underestimated the red flags they raised, such as Liberia's unusually high country risk—calculated by investors to assess the comparative risk of doing business in any given country. Liberia's score could not have specifically predicted an Ebola outbreak, but was a clear indicator of why manufacturing in Liberia is so much riskier than using factories in San Francisco, a fact I often failed to accept as gospel truth.

"Failure and success can be deceptive. No matter what, there will be hacks whose failures appear to resemble amazing entrepreneurs whose plans just never really panned out. There will also be hacks who somehow find success beyond their wildest dreams and put themselves in the same category as our most-lauded heroes.

"I hope that our obsession with success and failure never overrides our ability to recognize those who make it their duty to humbly serve others. And that whenever we are unsure of the risk of failure (or promise of success), we have the wisdom to balance our inner truth with the wisdom of the tribe."

ABANDONMENT

A commitment to community empowerment means being there when you're needed—and stepping aside when you're not.

By the time I'd turned 18, my dad had saved up enough money to pay for the bare basics at my taxpayer-subsidized college. In keeping with his frugal Depression-era values and his lower-middle-class earnings, 'bare basics' translated as tuition, books and dorm housing. In keeping with my teenage values, I wanted money for clothes, beer and other college 'essentials'. So, in the long, slow summer months before leaving for the University of California at Davis, I worked in a neighborhood retail store: stocking shelves; unpacking boxes; pricing and dusting merchandise; changing light bulbs.

On Saturdays, free to do whatever I wanted, I transformed myself into a combatant in the War on Poverty. Summoned by President Lyndon Johnson to enlist, I became a foot soldier in the national campaign against economic inequality and racial injustice. Under the aegis of the revered Booker T. Washington Community Center, I volunteered as a remedial reading tutor for a preteen African-American boy living in San Francisco's Fillmore District.

Following the 1906 earthquake, the Fillmore was home to successive waves of Jewish-American and Japanese-American communities. By the Sixties, it had become the city's primary African-American neighborhood, and where (with equal parts prejudice and protectiveness) my parents warned me not to go after dark. (Not that I listened to them. On Saturday nights I danced at the Fillmore Auditorium among dope-smoking hippies and psychedelic light shows. To the music of Jefferson Airplane, the Grateful Dead, the Doors and Santana, I tested the resilience of my eardrums.) Today, the Fillmore is a historic jazz district, a Japanese cultural hub, and a vibrant African-American community. Back then, however, the bus ride from my house to my pupil's, along the length of Fillmore Street, took me from the grand mansions of Pacific Heights to the peeling paint, broken windows and boarded-up doors of the Lower Fillmore. From antique shops to pawn shops. From my privileged life to a life of housing segregation, discriminatory banking and economic decay.

—∞—

All summer, every Saturday, my young companion and I traversed the city—riding buses and trolleys, making the rounds of the zoo, the natural science museum or any other public institution with free admission for students. I made a few half-hearted efforts to encourage him to read the advertisements plastered above the tattered bus seats. One ad touted Volkswagen Beetles (nicknamed 'The Bug'). Another promoted a school for radio announcers. Mostly, we just sat across from each other, lost in our own thoughts.

Prior to our day trips, as I later found out, my 13-year-old protégé (a grand word for my silent sidekick) had never once traveled beyond his four-block neighborhood. In turn, until that summer, I had my own invisible boundaries, marked by the routines of class and race. We were – to state the obvious – totally ignorant of each other.

Returning to his house at the end of each Saturday's outing – my feet tired, my mind worn out – his mother invited me to stay for refreshments. She was warm, enthusiastic, encouraging. The house was modest and clean. One wall of the living room prominently displayed a black velvet painting of President John F. Kennedy. I felt welcomed—but awkwardly, in the way of youth fumbling through unfamiliar social situations, I begged off.

As autumn arrived, so too did information from the University of California. I devoured every word of every document: dormitory housing forms; orientation week directions; my first college course catalog. On a mental teeter-totter, as my excitement about college went up, my interest in tutoring went down. As my loyalty slowly shifted from our fragile, two-person community to my future collegiate community, I didn't notice my transformation—but my watchful ward did.

One day, without fanfare or observable feeling, he said, "You're leaving." Caught off guard, I muttered something banal and stupid. I think I promised to stay in touch. We both knew I was lying. A week later, in an act of emotional cowardice, I telephoned him to cancel our final day together. It was an inexcusably shitty thing to do.

Abandoning or leaving a relationship, community or social enterprise doesn't make you a bad social entrepreneur or a bad person. Abandoning or exiting in an unthoughtful, precipitous way does.

Leaving a relationship doesn't make you a bad person. Leaving it in an unthoughtful or precipitous way does.

Fifty years later, I still regret my youthful insensitivity. I regret my poverty of kindness, the paucity of awareness. I regret not being able to hear the unspoken words he meant to say. I regret not being a better friend to a young boy whose name I wish I remembered—the young boy whom I carelessly abandoned.

—∞—

As social entrepreneurs, we community organize, community empower, community create, community fund, community invest, community embrace, community extol, but, in the end, we community abandon. When our social business plans fail, when funding runs dry, when career paths veer in a new direction, when college classes resume, when our love life calls us home: we leave. When we grow bored with one social change paradigm, we leave to chase after the next hot, new theory of social change or economic development.

We are the legion of experts, do-gooders, students, volunteers, foundation executives, healthcare workers, academic researchers, impact investors, government professionals, religious missionaries and anyone else who, sooner or later, goes home to their 'real' community. As individuals, planned abandonment is a structural element of the work we do—it's professionally normal and perfectly understandable behavior.

Importantly, let's distinguish between the various kinds of exit, or (if you prefer) abandonment. The words sound similar, but the ethical ramifications and social change issues play out differently.

For example, as individuals, "one of the principal virtues of free-market choice is that it gives people the opportunity to express their displeasure by exit. Social relations are different," writes Barry Schwartz in *The Paradox of Choice*. "We don't dismiss lovers, friends, or communities the way we dismiss restaurants, cereals, or vacation spots. Treating people in this way is unseemly at best and reprehensible at worst... Exit, or abandonment, is the response of last resort." For the social entrepreneur, an unthoughtful, uncaring exit is unacceptable, albeit sometimes unavoidable.

A new employment opportunity, for example, triggers my exit. It's not a betrayal of my core values to accept a new job with a better salary, more responsibility or more impact. Indeed, loyalty to a particular program, strategy or community may be, in your case or mine, secondary to our larger social justice mission. Nonetheless, no matter how justifiable, no matter how forthright and collaborative the process of planning for our respective exits, it is an abandonment of our existing community engagement. It just is.

Still, change is the natural lifecycle of a career in social entrepreneurship. Indeed, as a life insurance salesperson might dispassionately tell us, every social entrepreneur's career comes equipped with its own built-in obsolescence and final exit. Social entrepreneurs, funders and volunteers make abandonment decisions all the time. Consider these four voices:

1. A dual-citizenship changemaker colleague, working on the very toughest economic development challenges in his poverty-plagued country, confided to me, "I feel like leaving my country is a betrayal because, when I returned after the civil war, it felt like an act of courage. But, the woman I love lives in America. I want to have kids. Plus, opera and modern art rejuvenate me."

2. Wrinkling her nose in self-critique, Karen Keating Ansara (of the Ansara Fund) says, "We're constantly creating abandonment. If we don't exit, we don't have

the flexibility to respond to new opportunities. It's more exciting to fund what's new than what's tried and true. The new lover is better than the well-known partner. Staying committed to partners in philanthropy is hard. I can't say I've always done it well."

3. "I feel like I've abandoned things in my social justice career and that's hard to come to terms with. There are huge amounts of frustration and guilt because we've all left projects and communities we care about... We all sway between feeling really crappy about it and then making ourselves feel better by reminding ourselves that we had good reasons. It's not a clear-cut thing," muses Natasha Goldstein, former CFO of MCE Social Capital.

4. Volunteers know this too. "I received countless hugs, an unreal amount of admiration and tears as we said our goodbyes... However, after leaving, I realized how much I despised myself for the adoration I had received from the children," reflects Charlotte Robertson, Ithaca student and author of 'Voluntourism: Why Helping Abroad Isn't Always Helping'. "Though I still have ambitions to be an active part of creating change, I have new ideas on how to do it, and it doesn't involve me using my Western privilege to so easily enter and exit the lives of others."

Of course, these voices are only half the chorus. The *really* important singers are the clients, nonprofits, collaborators, business enterprises, local organizers and community leaders with whom we partner. Until we ask them, we are left guessing whether our swan song is off-key. Until we ask, we can't know if our social entrepreneurship has been enriching or depleting. As the playwright, Oscar Wilde taunted, "Some cause happiness wherever they go. Others, whenever they go."

To mitigate the downside of our eventual exit, we need to plan for it with the same care and energy that we marshal in planning our entry. The human work of social entrepreneurship is always personal and always unpredictable. That's why Ellen Pasquale, an international affairs student at American University, once schooled me at the Opportunity Collaboration: "We can never fully prepare for [the full ramifications of an] exit because attachment to other humans is what humans do." Consequently, an attitude of humility, coupled with a commitment to partnership, is the better way of doing things.

— ∞ —

We need to plan for exit with the same care and energy we marshal in planning our entry.

At the organizational level, the permutations for engagement are nearly endless: humanitarian relief agencies, economic development partners, technical assistance providers, grant funders, business investors and government agencies. As social entrepreneurs, the core of our work is building long-term, durable organizations that will be steadfast, reliable partners. If there is an exit, it is a mutually planned-for and agreed-upon exit—not a one-sided abandonment.

Take for example my work with MCE Social Capital. For any number of valid reasons, MCE may wrap up a funding relationship with a local microfinance partner. Reasons (on both sides of the partnership) might include: shifts in local financial conditions; lack of MCE capital to loan; the local partner outgrowing MCE; depleted staffing resources; and so on. Every reason has its rationale, so ground rules are talked over and ironed out at the beginning of the partnership, not imposed unilaterally or unexpectedly by one party later on. Moreover, there is no artificial exit strategy. Indeed, if the working partnership is accomplishing good things and both sides are realizing their respective social missions, why in the world would we even consider exiting?

MCE Social Capital doesn't enter into a partnership planning to blow it up at the first sign of difficulty. That's not what allies do. Ted London and Stuart Hart write about the same idea in *The Next Generation Business Strategies for the Base of the Pyramid*, "Base of the economic pyramid (BoP) venture leaders must ground their dialogue in mutual respect... [with] three guiding perspectives as they develop relationships in BoP communities: be patient, stay longer and come back."

In the best-case scenario, you and I simply work ourselves out of a job. Nick Tilsen (CEO of Thunder Valley, an economic development enterprise serving his Native-American community) sets the bar at the right level when he says that "experts, volunteers and aid workers from outside always leave. We insist that outsiders train their replacement. Our non-negotiable goal is local capacity for, and by, Native Americans." Could either of us have said it better?

Let's craft exit strategies that *strengthen* our partners, colleagues and communities. A water group, in partnership with a local village, digs a well or installs a sanitation system, develops a self-financing mechanism, trains local leaders to run it—and then leaves behind a viable water system. An educational NGO builds a school, designs a sustainable fee structure, trains and hires teachers—and then leaves behind a functioning school. A technical assistance provider undertakes a capacity-building knowledge and skills transfer. 'Sustainability exits' mitigate dependency on outsiders, leaving behind local leaders with co-created, self-sustaining solutions.

The invigorating challenge is to get enough done to justify our predictable, and forgivable, abandonment. To assure that when we do exit, local allies are stronger for our presence, and emboldened by our absence. The inescapable truth is that a commitment to community empowerment means being there when you're needed—and stepping aside when you're not.

A respectful partnership starts with transparency between the social entrepreneur who can never shed the freedom to leave, and the local leader who can never shed the responsibility to stay. Honest consultation with local partners is the only sensible and commonsense way to jointly decide when it's appropriate (or necessary) to leave.

It's a truism that how we *react* to change largely depends on how it's *implemented*. For example, discovering someone to whom you and I have formed an attachment (a close friend, a coach, a community partner, or summer tutor) has left the relationship before us feels demeaning, deflating and disempowering. No wonder that the word 'dumped' has a damaged, debilitating ring to it.

133

Authenticity is the preferred antidote for averting the abandonment blues. From day one, we can't pretend to be what we aren't, or make promises (implied or otherwise) that we simply can't keep. Serious friendships and productive social change don't start that way. If we strive to bring our whole selves to the work of social justice, that means one hundred per cent of our beautiful, ugly identities—including our probable exit.

"It turns out that there is no surefire way to 'do good' in the 21st century. There are no pat or pure answers," cautions Courtney Martin in *Do It Anyway: The New Generation of Activists.* "There are no true heroes—and those who cast themselves in this light probably haven't thought hard enough about the complexities of their work or explored the terrain of their own souls with enough honesty."

With the exception of home-grown social entrepreneurs, most change agents undertake social action work in communities where we start out as strangers. And even in our home community, we are always learners. *How* we do our work matters as much, maybe even more, than the work itself. In every community, even our own, we are not there to solve everyone's problems, but rather to problem-solve collaboratively.

In my home community, I live a *togetherness* with my fellow citizens. I don't treat them as clients, or categorize them as recipients. In short, solidarity with my 'real' community does not stop at the edge of a single program, or when I 'leave' a particular role. My civic participation is unbounded by an arbitrary exit date. I don't need to cauterize myself or my neighbors against the haunting, unhappy knowledge that someday I will be leaving.

In the social sector, fulfillment for us comes when clients and causes succeed. Wonderfully, sometimes an exit celebrates the handover of operations so that a community can control more of its own destiny. Joining a community with the best of intentions and then leaving a community stronger are two ends of the same hot dog.

—∞—

The altruistic instinct to do something about human suffering, about social and economic injustice, is inarguably a good thing. Acts of kindness, empathy, caring and solidarity are intrinsically uplifting. So too is the instinct to get out there and learn about the world as it is, warts and wonders aplenty.

As individual social entrepreneurs, we place ourselves in the world in reference to a marginalized population, a constituency, a cause, a community, a group of people whom we care about. For us, the latitude and longitude of our connection to the community are mapped with feelings of mutual obligation, duty and allegiance.

As much as witnessing injustice activates and enlarges our compassion, it reminds us to handle our leave-taking with grace and respect for those we leave behind. Since exit is a built-in feature of social entrepreneurship, let's say so with greater clarity from the start. Let's not over-promise. Let's not succumb to everlasting savior complex. Let's not wear a martyrdom badge.

Fundamentally and irrevocably, exit confirms privilege. We can leave. We can board an airplane; we can escape to better health care, better schools, better roads, better water systems, better *everything*. And, yes, to the comfort of our loved ones.

As we go about the daily business of social entrepreneuring, you and I learn, and re-learn, that Social Change 101 is the art of continuous, two-way communication. If we stay in sync with our colleagues and allies, if our own humanity is part of our work, our local partners will (with any luck) want what is best for us, just as we want what is best for them.

To state the obvious, my summer of tutoring was the quintessential real-life learning experience. In some haphazard, indefinable way, it must have contributed to my future civil rights activism, to my collegiate interest in African-American studies, and to my general opinion that reparations for slavery are not a wholly-unthinkable proposal. Small comfort, though, to the boy who I left behind.

I remember my mistake, not with guilt and not with any false promise that I won't accidentally repeat it, but with sadness. I'm certain you understand why. If you've ever stumbled like I did, you might be sad too.

A universal cliché of career optimism is the notion that, when one door closes, another opens. As social entrepreneurs, when we can't sleep because we remember a stupidly-executed abandonment— our conscience might be telling us that the door that we closed was slammed in someone's face.

Take Two: Abandonment

Tabitha Mpamira-Kaguri, 32, is Founder and Executive Director of Edja Foundation. Being a mother of two boys and twin girls energizes her to fight sexual violence in Sub-Saharan Africa. Hometowns: Kigali, Rwanda; Kampala, Uganda; Okemos, Michigan. Favorite pastime: watching thriller movies. Guilty pleasure: sleep.

"I am a Rwandan who grew up as a refugee in Uganda due to political instability that later turned into genocide. As a Rwandan in the work of social justice, I am particularly sensitive to abandonment. As a country, the world looked away as my ethnicity was slaughtered. We watched the UN extract their workers when it deemed it too risky to fulfill their obligation. Therefore, I find some parts of this chapter too simplistic and filled with assumptions that come from a place of privilege, especially the phrase 'abandonment blues'.

"My family moved to the US when I was 14, and I had to leave yet another home. Fast forward to adulthood, I returned to Rwanda to work with women and children who had been raped during the genocide. Soon after, my mother died in a car accident in Michigan, so I had to pack up and return to the US, leaving behind a group that had trusted me with their struggle. Abandonment is an inevitable part of life, especially for those of us who grow up in marginalized situations.

"Future social entrepreneurs: you have to start by being honest with yourselves, especially about the fact that 'abandonment blues' are the privilege of those who have something to go back to. Most people you will serve know abandonment well. Take heart in knowing that you will not be the first, nor the last, to abandon them, but remember to walk into any situation prepared to listen to those who will be staying when you go. Recipients usually do not fool themselves into thinking you came to stay. Instead, they enjoy your presence and service, and then move on, because they still have to figure out how to actually survive."

BRUISED

Social entrepreneurs are midwives—birthing new opportunities for greater economic, environmental and social justice. At the same time, we are hospice workers—helping old paradigms to die. In the clinic of social change, our bedside manner can lose its mojo.

Social entrepreneurship is not always awesome. Not every day is a good day. Some days are bruising. Some days, feeling isolated and broken, devastated or angry—I just want to cry.

As social entrepreneurs, you and I have chosen causes and careers that, day in and day out, place us in the crevice between humankind's most noble aspirations and its most ignoble behaviors. We watch horrible, hideous, staggering, unspeakable and entirely preventable sorrows unfold. The human instinct is to look away.

Bearing witness to meanness, misery and malice burns the human heart. It leaves scar tissue. Ernest Hemingway observed, "The best people possess a feeling for beauty, the courage to take risks, the discipline to tell the truth, the capacity for sacrifice. Ironically, their virtues make them vulnerable; they are often wounded, sometimes destroyed." You could be one of those best people. You probably are.

Social entrepreneurs are also bruised by working interminable hours, sapping stress and recurring disappointment. We are worn thin by the pressure to sell solutions and pitch programs. To be the hot new idea—or at least pretend to be. To be super-human.

Because managing a social enterprise means handling competing crises with a chronic shortage of resources, it's hard to achieve a sense of stability. For sub-par pay, we pursue picture-perfect mission statements. It's true for the well-funded. Even more true for the under-funded.

In some fundamental ways, social entrepreneurs are just regular entrepreneurs running in the rat race. Whether we are leading a start-up or mid-level-managing an established social venture, whenever and wherever we fully commit ourselves, changemakers can become Type-A workaholics in drag—cross-dressing as humanitarian agents for justice.

Living a fast-paced, change-the-world 'suitcase career' feels no different than any other pressure-cooker job. Working long hours, we have less time for savoring life's pleasures: tending relationships; pursuing hobbies; extracurricular reading; rambling walks; relaxed meals; lingering kisses. Eventually and inevitably, personal relationships fray.

The secret insecurity of every social entrepreneur is that we might fall short, prove unworthy of our loftiest ideals.

Sometimes, social sector jobs are further complicated by the twin burdens of internalized oppression and societal expectation. When she stepped away from an exalted job title, a large operating budget and great pay in the private sector to run the *Stanford Social Innovation Review*, Regina Starr Ridley questioned her decision, recalling, "Sometimes I felt like I'd let other women down." The weight of class, gender and racial 'tribal representation' is heavy.

The secret insecurity of every social entrepreneur is that we might fall short, prove unworthy of our loftiest ideals, or let down the causes and people that we care about. No surprise then, that social sector performance anxiety sets in.

If you believe that injustice disfigures our planet; if you believe that the responsibility for fixing it belongs to each one of us; then the cliché 'don't take it personally' is pure gaslighting. Even while my head is rationalizing phrases like 'it's just business' or 'we received many worthy proposals', my heart only hears shattering rejection. The result is a sense of increased vulnerability and exaggerated fragility.

Bruises are just part of the job. That's because every change agent worth a damn is in the business of undermining the status quo. Our social change workday is defined by asking uncomfortable questions, exposing hypocrisies, forcing institutional change, and pushing back against the powerful. People don't instinctively invite disruption into their lives, and so negativity and hostility are inescapable. As social entrepreneurs—we know that we are pains in the ass; agent provocateurs; pariahs at the party. We also know that enervating isolation is part of the social entrepreneurial lifestyle.

—∞—

Social entrepreneurs are midwives—birthing new opportunities for greater economic, environmental, racial, gender and social justice. At the same time, we are hospice workers—helping old paradigms to die. In the clinic of social change, our bedside manner can lose its mojo.

As gratifying as fighting the good fight is (and it is, it is!), I can't count all the times my wonderful, glorious, uplifting, satisfying, spectacular social change career has felt wobbly and worrying. I'm not alone. Listen to five reports from the field:

1. "I [left school] vibrating with grand notions of what it meant to live an ethical, examined life... Just five years later, I felt extinguished. The real world was not a place of perfect forms and pat answers. It was messy, bureaucratic, painful." –Courtney Martin in *Do It Anyway: The New Generation of Activists*

2. "A sense of isolation would envelop me, and there were nights that ended in tears of tiredness and sadness for a world that didn't seem to want to see the possibilities right there in front of it." –Jacqueline Novogratz in *The Blue Sweater*

3. "I'm... freaking the fuck out about how I'm going to meet my budget shortfall, how tired I am, how much I crave making a difference. I'm wrestling with hope and despair." –Nonprofit Executive Director (in a private email to me)

4. "There is a point in an entrepreneurial venture when the adrenaline starts to run out. Burnout is incredibly common [for] social entrepreneurs... [from] the constant feeling that much of the world's problems are bearing down on their shoulders." –Marina Kim (Co-Founder, Ashoka U) in 'The Burnout Phenomenon'

5. "Lately, I've been feeling a lot like checking out. The stress of my job is really getting to me. I'm not sure if I am just putting pressure on myself or if I just want so bad for this venture to succeed... or if I am frustrated seeing colleagues the same age as myself making three times my income... I feel like I lack the courage to swim upstream these days." –Marketing Director of a social enterprise (in a private email to me)

They're not the only ones. When I was a young activist, naïvely convinced of my invincibility, I thought I could 'win' by working harder, and then harder still. In the 1970s, when I accepted responsibility for leading a public interest organization called the California Tax Reform Association (CTRA), I learned differently.

CTRA had the audacious mission of campaigning for tax justice and, in particular, closing corporate tax loopholes. Then and now, anti-government forces abused tax reduction rhetoric to advance a tax code that redistributed wealth and income *upwards*. Regardless of how small or how large you might like your government, to my way of thinking, it seems right and reasonable that we should all pay our fair share for it. No loopholes. No free riders. No exploiting the underclasses.

Fighting against an unfair tax system – zealously guarded by fat cat beneficiaries and corporate welfare recipients – battered me. Confronted with plenty of legislative and political setbacks, my mind was constantly churning, often late into the night. Almost every afternoon, to stave off stress headaches, I was swallowing aspirin. After work, too exhausted to eat dinner, I passed out on my sofa. While traveling, often staying in a cheap hotel to save a few bucks, I'd wake up in the middle of the night and rush to the bathroom to vomit away the tension. I started grinding my teeth. My driving got faster and more reckless. One night at 2am, driving northbound along the California coast, the highway patrol clocked me at close to 100mph.

When I took over leadership of CTRA, it had 70 citizen-members and a total asset base consisting of one roll of postage stamps. Three years later, we had 4,000 dues-paying members. Elected officials, labor unions, senior citizen organizations, local governments, social service agencies and the media routinely turned to us for trusted commentary about fair and equitable tax policy. A decent accomplishment, and I'm proud of it, but it came at a bruising personal price.

CTRA became my identity. When it lost a fight, I felt it personally. And we lost spectacularly, and often. With the wisdom of time, I've learned that workplace martyrs make lousy social entrepreneurs. Today, the tax code is still a golden playground for the richly undeserving. It still pisses me off, but I've stopped taking it out on myself.

—∞—

Once you get to know a few social entrepreneurs, you start to discover we are defective and flawed in all the standard ways. We can be heedless, feckless, insensitive, insecure, self-centered—the usual range of human infirmities. Some of us spend unproductive hours watching junk TV, over-eating and not exercising. Some of us obsess about 'fixing' our life partners. Some of us even forget to put down the toilet seat.

The idea that we need to be super-human, super-clever or super-innovative is not only wrong, it's super-unhelpful.

The notion that any social entrepreneur needs to be super-human, super-smart, super-clever or super-innovative is not only wrong, but also super-unhelpful. By fantasizing ourselves into superhero cult status, we inadvertently discourage what the world needs most: every ordinary non-hero doing heroic things.

Social entrepreneurs talk with enthusiasm about financial and institutional sustainability, but less often (and less loudly), do we talk about *personal* sustainability. In 'Decelerate to Accelerate' Michel Bachmann and Roshan Paul of the Amani Institute (a global social entrepreneurship training program) observe, "It's ironic that the people who seek to create a more sustainable world often live the most unsustainable lives of all, sacrificing their finances, their relationships, and sometimes even their health to pursue a broader social mission."

A life well-lived has its own markings. There's a time to learn. A time to take risks for our convictions. A time to become a social entrepreneur. A time to rest and replenish the soul. A time to nest with our families. When you and I embrace personal accountability for economic justice and for human rights, for earth stewardship and for global peace, our work is never done. We need to pace ourselves.

Personal development underpins both having the social justice career you want, and becoming the mindful change agent the world needs. When fissures and flaws in our social entrepreneurial lives appear—take a break; stand down; take responsibility for a bit of self-care. When you're feeling in top form again, the world's troubles will still be here, waiting for you.

—∞—

Social change takes time. Winning hearts, minds and imaginations takes time. Overcoming entrenched political and economic interests takes time. On the other hand, no one should ever be asked, or forced, to wait for political or economic justice. In the words of the potent legal truism, *justice delayed is justice denied.* Holding these two truths in my brain simultaneously gives me a headache.

The worst feeling for any social entrepreneur is the sinking sense that history is not on your side. Nothing sucks our energy more than the depressing feeling that we are losing, that justice is lurching backwards.

It's perfectly reasonable for social entrepreneurs to think that our time – if not the worst of times – is far from the best of times. Consider America's sidewalks—where stray bullets, gang bullets, and police bullets terrorize our families. Consider the one in five people in the world who can't affordably drink clean water. Consider the one in three women – very likely, a woman in your immediate social circle – who has experienced physical or sexual violence. Consider the many irreplaceable species moving towards extinction, even as the human species is moving to kill itself.

When badness outweighs goodness, when pessimism engulfs optimism—I console myself by comparing the present day with 1948, my birth year. It was a time of hopeful progress and menacing new threats. Of change, and resistance to change. Of things to laud, and things to lament.

Countries acted with high-mindedness, malice, or both. 1948 was the first year of racial apartheid in South Africa. 1948 was also the first year of universal health care in Great Britain.

Across the world, the forces of self-determination and colonialism, freedom and fascism, war and peace, competed for the future. The Berlin airlift answered the Soviet Union's Berlin blockade. Korea split into two and, soon after, went to war with itself. A massive American taxpayer-financed act of compassion, the Marshall Plan, began to rehabilitate war-ravaged Europe. The term 'cold war' was used for the first time. In elementary school, I practiced ducking under my flimsy wooden desk in case of a nuclear attack.

American society took a few more small steps towards being more inclusive. President Truman issued an executive order ending racial segregation in the military. The California Supreme Court declared interracial marriage a protected constitutional right. The first African-American played in the US Tennis Open. The first woman was promoted to permanent military rank. The Supreme Court declared that public-school religious instruction was unconstitutional.

A sense of global citizenship took root. The Organization of American States, the World Council of Churches and the World Health Organization were each established. The International Court of Justice began hearing cases. The United Nations adopted the Universal Declaration of Human Rights.

Alexandra McGee, a community organizer at MCE (a clean energy program in California) and a member of the millennial generation, observes that "the underlying question is the issue of time. Of impatience with things not changing fast enough, versus seeing things in historical perspective. Of the short-sightedness of humans in the angst of living in the present tense, especially for millennials who have a smaller scope of living history."

In the end, we can only do what we can do. "When I consider how long I sometimes take to learn a new lesson, I have greater compassion for humans writ large," reflects Akaya Windwood, President of the Rockwood Leadership Institute. "No one of us is in charge of the pace of change. We are only in charge of our piece of it."

"Although the problems are urgent and so important, I need to have more patience," concludes Jessamyn Shams-Lau, CEO of the Peery Foundation. "I'm not going to solve problems on my own. You're not going to solve them. I'm an apprentice in life. I'm an apprentice in [social justice] problem-solving."

For my part, I'm reassured, even encouraged, when I remember we have more social justice today than we did 100 years ago, 50 years ago—even 25 years ago. We are entitled to celebrate without becoming complacent. And, as changemakers, you and I can fortify ourselves with the certain knowledge that, whether it's 1948 or 2017, every time is the perfect time to fight for what we believe in.

—∞—

When I'm emotionally black and blue, in addition to shoving my face into a pint of ice cream or escaping into an espionage novel, I pick from the following mix-and-match options:

Create high-five moments. Windwood, in her article 'Celebration', rejoices: "We celebrate because it satisfies our souls and increases the overall happiness in the world. This is not about denying our pressing difficulties or putting our collective heads in the sand... Humans need the solace and comfort of remembering and honoring the magnificent things of which we are capable."

Accept being you. Human contradictions characterize most change agents. "I accept being mediocre. I am not perfect. Even if I focused on just one or two things, I still would not be perfect at them," claims Wanjiru Kamau-Rutenberg, Director of Kenya-based African Women in Agricultural Research and Development. With a giant grin, she adds, "I spend all day running an organization empowering women, and relax at night by reading romance novels about women who get carted off into the sunset by burly men."

Stay focused. "There are a million causes I support. I fully recognize the inter-relatedness of racism, sexism, environmentalism, classism, capitalism, ageism, etc... As activists, we have a really hard time figuring out where to begin and how to best expend our energies," writes Natasha Thomas-Jackson in '6 Things I Need Activists to Stop Doing Now'. "Global change is achieved by hitting one mark at a time. Scattering energies and shifting agendas only create confusion and disillusionment."

Trust individual-level change. When I was growing up, in my all-boys high school, homophobia was an unchecked social norm. Shamefully, I used hurtful language, told immature jokes and behaved with callous prejudice. Today, that kind of crap is unacceptable to me. If I can learn and grow, others can too. If others can, so can society as a whole.

Find a hammock. Or, Saul Alinsky writes in *Rules for Radicals*, go to jail. "The revolutionary... must, now and then, have an opportunity to reflect and synthesize his thoughts. To gain that privacy... the most convenient and accessible solution is jail. It is here that he is emancipated from the slavery of action." Personally, I'm going with the hammock option.

Validate a colleague. I'm strengthened by the people who lead by courageous example, who loan themselves to social justice work and, therefore, loan themselves to me. When I tell my colleagues, peers and role models that I'm grateful for their acts of decency, kindness, and compassion—it cheers me up.

Find your tribe. "Finding a tribe of people who are making similar life choices is critical for sustaining your energy... There is tremendous value in being with people who understand where you are coming from, and rejoice in seeing you grow," write Bachmann and Paul.

Don't multiply the bad moments. One lousy experience or rejection is not predictive. In psychological terms, don't let your mind anchor your negative experience. In military terms, don't fight the last war. In human terms, don't prejudge your next potential ally.

When I'm feeling beaten up; when I feel like stepping off the endless treadmill of tragedies; when I'm septic with issue fatigue— acknowledging my bruises helps. That's why connecting with a colleague, confiding a weakness, admitting insecurity or sharing a dumb joke are non-negotiable parts of my social change work. In those moments, perhaps the bravest sentence we can use (quoted by Courtney Martin in *Do It Anyway*) comes from a female change agent struggling to reclaim her self-worth and personal power. She simply says: "I think I need to talk."

—∞—

Change agents, like everyone else, have interior lives and hidden histories. The ranks of social entrepreneurs are populated with trauma survivors, people with unseen physical and mental health challenges, and changemakers in the process of burning out. We're not robots.

At the extreme end of depression and despair, suicide is a human instinct so desolate that you might think that life-affirming social entrepreneurs are immune from it. Think again. It's entirely possible for a social entrepreneur with good friends, a supportive family, a measure of financial security and a brilliant social enterprise to also harbor private thoughts of suicide.

My first experience with a friend committing suicide involved an older white male (the highest suicide rate demographic). He was rich, civically-active, gregarious, popular and fun-loving. In his swank condo overlooking Chicago's Lake Michigan, he ended his life with a shotgun in his mouth.

My second experience was triggered after a charity banquet of mediocre food and elongated speeches. As a social sector colleague and I searched in the parking lot for our respective cars, we multi-tasked by trash-talking the event and sharing updates from our lives. As the sky dulled into dusk, as the moody darkness enveloped us, my friend – a single mom – blurted out, "I'd be worth more to my kids dead than alive." Without another word, she stepped into her car and drove off.

Unnerved, I hurried home to study suicide prevention websites, all of which urged me to take any talk of suicide seriously. Intent on communicating my concern, I unleashed a hailstorm of emails and phone messages. A few weeks later, my colleague nonchalantly mentioned that she was, in anticipation of wearing a bathing suit poolside at the Opportunity Collaboration, exercising more. Realizing that she wasn't really considering suicide, I felt more than a little sheepish about my panicked response. Nevertheless, why take a chance with anyone's life—especially the life of a fellow social entrepreneur whom you like and respect?

No social entrepreneur walks alone. If you're sinking, or know someone who is, call the US National Suicide Prevention Lifeline at 800-273-8255 (or your national equivalent).

— ∞ —

Even as our hearts are enlarged by the humanity of our social justice work, the crushing enormity of social injustice can make us feel small and insignificant. It's a lousy trade-off.

You and I don't run away because, no matter how stressed, frustrated, ineffective or trivial we might temporarily feel, fighting for justice and a healthy planet is beyond awesome. We don't run because our social change work defines us, and we can't run away from who we are.

A changemaker career blurs the traditional line between work and the rest of our lives. Describing the holistic social entrepreneurial personality, David Bornstein, author of *How to Change the World* and Founder of Solutions Journalism, observes that "although it is probably impossible to fully explain why people become social entrepreneurs, it is certainly possible to identify them. Every decision – whom to marry, where to live, what books to read – passes through the prism of their ideas."

While it's undeniably true that social entrepreneurship comes with its share of heartaches, it's equally true that watching small bits of progress happen in front of us, maybe even with our help, mends our fractured hearts. Even more, when we're fully engaged in our social justice careers: cynicism, fatalism and despair are replaced with aspiration, purpose and connection. I'm affirmed. I'm happy.

On the days when I feel like screaming at the world, a powerful cathartic is the work itself. To be sure, it's a counterintuitive paradox. You and I can – and must – attack injustice like the furies and then, when needed and necessary, we should take sanctuary to replenish, re-energize and restore ourselves.

Being a social entrepreneur doesn't make me a better person. Being a better person makes me a better social entrepreneur.

Take Two: Bruised

Amy Paulson, 40, is Co-Founder of the Global Gratitude Alliance.
She works at the intersection of healing and social justice, transforming
cycles of intergenerational trauma into legacies of healing and
resilience. Hometown: San Francisco. Favorite pastime: eating spicy
food. Guilty pleasure: dancing to 80s music.

"In the world of social justice, our incessant drive is led by the myth of the martyr activist. If we sacrifice our lives for the cause, we are praised as heroes. If we only work ten hours a day, we aren't committed enough. Others struggle every day. So must we.

"Living from that place of scarcity during the first 30-odd years of life led me to depression, anxiety, repeated burnouts, and a prediction that I'd die before I turned 40. When my physician muttered that it would be from suicide, I was deeply offended. Then it hit me. Not caring for myself was akin to a slow suicide.

"These days, there are tools and apps targeted at (recovering) overachievers like me, helping us 'hack' self-care. But, the truth is, we already know what to do: sleep, exercise, eat well, spend time in nature, and cultivate joy, gratitude, and connection to community. These simple things build the resiliency needed for a lifetime of activism. So, how do we overcome the guilt that prevents us from prioritizing our own well-being?

"I've learned that the secret isn't about bubble baths or massages (though I recommend both). It's about remembering to put on our own oxygen masks first. It's about breaking cycles of harm, including those against ourselves. And, it's about building a new paradigm for activism, rooted in radical love, for others and ourselves.

"So, when I'm grumpy about going to morning yoga, or stressed about squeezing in an evening with friends, I remind myself that these are 'oxygen mask moments'. They are bold actions of self-love.

"I'm happy to say that I made it to 40. And, by nourishing my mind, body, and heart, I may just double my lifespan. Because no doubt, the world of social justice will still be calling."

MISGIVINGS

So much of what we do is a matter of judgment and nuance, of balancing competing priorities and concerns. Doing one thing in one place, and doing something else in another.

Like every other occupation, social entrepreneurship has its share of conventions, assumptions and operating norms. How we think about our social sector careers; what we think is worth doing with our professional lives; and the expectations we set for ourselves are all framed and influenced by an assorted mix of contradictions and conundrums, paradoxes and parables, myths and muddles.

When it comes to certain brands of conventional wisdom: I have misgivings. I'm not so much in direct disagreement with them as I'm cautiously waiting to learn more, to better understand their full implications and unintended consequences. To extend the 'are-we-on-the-wrong-bus?' metaphor of Nobel Prize Laureate Wangari Maathai, I feel like I'm sitting in a bus terminal waiting to see where each departing bus is headed, even as I know (from history) that some buses will have accidents, run out gas, confront detours or get hijacked. I also know that most buses arrive at their destination, safe and sound. No changemaker journey is well-mapped. Cognitive dissonance sets in when we sense we've boarded the wrong bus and might be moving away from our social mission.

Let's talk about three topical areas of keen interest to social entre-preneurs: selling goods and services in the developing world, scaling our programmatic impact, and the buy-one-give-one model.

—∞—

For some pioneering social entrepreneurs, consumer demand in the developing world is a potential 'fortune at the bottom of the pyramid', as coined by management professor C.K. Prahalad in 2006. Since that time, the handy acronym 'BoP' has come to describe those millions of low-income consumers around the world who buy goods and services, frequently in small amounts. Some are these are basic necessities (such as soap or medicine); some are productivity improvements (think: water carriers or agricultural tools); some are lifestyle-enhancing (for instance, beauty products or soft drinks).

From field experience, we now know that product re-engineering and repackaging (plus marketing and distribution innovations) are required to access the BoP marketplace. In 2014, Erik Simanis (Managing Director of Market Creation Strategies) reported in 'The Rise and Fall of BoP Ventures' that "while many initial BoP pilot projects offered compelling... evidence of positive community impact, rarely could they show a realistic path to profitability— particularly within the investment time-frames expected by corporations. Consequently, a number of corporations are turning away from BoP investments. And those that do move forward typically do so as corporate social responsibility or philanthropic projects, without the expectation of competitive returns." That's disappointing, but plausible because all businesses (especially multinational corporations) have many competing uses for capital. In other words, a BoP product might be profitable, but not profitable enough to compete with other divisions within a company.

Nevertheless, the dream that large multinationals might unlock the BoP market (and become a force for good within the world) remains seductive to social entrepreneurs. We cling to this hope for two reasons. First, whether our social enterprise is organized as a for-profit or a nonprofit, the social entrepreneurial *modus operandi* resonates with leveraging marketplace forces as a listening platform for staying in close communication with clients, customers and communities. Second, many of our social ventures are starved for expansion capital and senior managerial talent. Thus, Paul Polak and Mal Warwick in *Business Solutions to Poverty* proselytize that "a virtually untapped market numbering 2.7 billion potential customers is simply too big to overlook. The emerging economies of the Global South, not even counting China and Russia, collectively generated $12 trillion, or nearly 1/5 (18 per cent), of the world's total economic output... In developing countries, more than 50 per cent of the purchasing power resides in the bottom of the pyramid segment."

For the social entrepreneur, a handy distinction splits economic development based on consumption from economic development based on financing in-country businesses. Setting aside that distinction for now, let's take a peek at three BoP products and services: soft drinks, consumer catalogs, and small business loans.

For an example of a multinational selling to the BoP: Coca-Cola employs 68,000 people in Africa and, through its distributors, bottlers and retailers, creates work for ten times that number. It is the largest private employer on the African continent. By 2020, the company will complete a $17 billion investment in Africa—equal to the entire GDP of Botswana.

For a social venture example: consider for-profit Copia Global, the Amazon-like consumer catalog that I co-founded. In 2017, while still in its start-up R&D phase, Copia has already increased the incomes of female shopkeepers in Nairobi, Kenya by 34 per cent; lowered prices for 50,000 mostly-female BoP consumers by 4–5 per cent; and sold reliable, top-quality merchandise (such as school supplies, bulk animal feed, motorbikes, sewing machines, healthcare items and solar lights), that shoppers can't readily find close to their homes or farms. Copia itself employs 100 Kenyan nationals. For more about Copia's pro-consumer, pro-women policies, see *Hegemony*.

For a third example: MCE Social Capital (which I founded) issues $50 million of debt capital annually to locally-run, locally-controlled nonprofit microfinance partners in 33 countries. Our ultimate business partners, and the reason we exist, are rural women at the absolute bottom of the BoP. Wherever we can, we actively promote and finance microfinance programs that are coupled with social services such as health education, women's business training, financial literacy and gender empowerment. We also lend money to small and growing businesses. MCE is a nonprofit, but has operated in the black without any external subsidies for over ten years.

Every year in the developing world, approximately 125 million people – about 80 per cent of whom are women, and most of whom live in rural areas – voluntarily borrow, and then repay, roughly $100 billion in uncollateralized microloans. For the most part, they use this money to start or expand a micro-business: making and selling empanadas; raising and slaughtering pigs or chickens; buying yarn to knit sweaters; stocking dry goods in a neighborhood store; getting a home-based beauty salon started by purchasing nail polish or hair brushes. Average loan amounts range from $200 in South Asia to nearly $3,000 in Eastern Europe.

Women in emerging markets typically reinvest an impressive 90 per cent of every dollar earned in education, health and nutrition for their children. Some borrowers don't see a net increase in spendable household income, but instead put aside a little money for a rainy day, or reduce their work hours to devote more time to their children.

Of course, each of these three enterprises has its critics. Perhaps you don't think poor people should drink sugary beverages. Perhaps you don't want poor people to have access to the same consumer goods that you and I routinely buy from Target, Costco, Home Depot, CVS Pharmacy or Amazon. Maybe you dislike the fact that some poor women occasionally over-borrow, or redirect their loan money to non-business purposes such as medicine for a sick uncle, or a cell phone so that a father in a faraway country (sending remittances to his family) can talk with his children.

If those are your concerns, why?

Shouldn't a poor person have agency to decide what's best for her family and herself? If a microloan powered her choice: good. If she wants to buy a small luxury item for her home: good. If she wants to treat her children to a Coca-Cola: good. Within the limits of her finances, why the fuck should a poor woman be denied the same consumer choices that you and I enjoy?

Here's the deal: unlike other worthy interventions to alleviate poverty and create economic opportunity, all three of these BoP examples don't depend on donations, grants or government funding. In other words: economic justice and job creation can occur without the need for charitable fundraising appeals, fights in Congress over foreign aid budgets or foundation grant applications. If you've ever worked for a nonprofit, then you know what a big advantage this is.

That said, for all the blessings that business brings into our lives (employment, technology, entertainment, telecommunications, life-saving medicine and, of course, hot dogs) profit as a prime motivator for social good is suspect. Before we succumb to the allure of building BoP companies, you and I have to decide what we think about some ethical and operational issues.

1. Advocates of profit-spangled opportunities at the BoP typically glide past the fact that a global market doesn't actually exist. As Vijay Mahajan and Kamini Banga point out in *The 86 Percent Solution*, "there is no Chinese market. There is a market in Shanghai, or in a neighborhood in Shanghai. There is no Indian market. There is a market in Mumbai or Chennai, or in their local neighborhoods. Developing countries are a collection of fragmented local markets in a country that is gathered loosely under a single flag." The mind-set matters because, as we explore later in this essay, you and I want to grow our social enterprises without sacrificing community-facing, client-focused social impact and high-quality customer service.

2. Contrary to what economic fabulists claim, even the most robust capital markets are not a panacea for allocating society's resources efficiently, rationally or wisely. In theory, investment capital flows to its highest and best use, but 'best' is always defined without regard to social or environmental impact. As Confucius noted, "The superior man understands what is right; the inferior man understands what will sell." For convincing proof, look to the very profitable slave trade, or Big Oil, or Big Banking. Or, what about the killer profits of Big Tobacco or the gun industry? What about AIG, Goldman Sachs or Enron? The Great Recession? As noted by the political economist John Maynard Keynes: "Capitalism is the extraordinary belief that the nastiest of men for the nastiest of motives will somehow work for the benefit of all." For social entrepreneurs at the BoP, ethical and social impact self-policing becomes a critical responsibility.

3. It's almost quaint that some American social entrepreneurs are spreading the gospel of consumer capitalism
to the BoP. Mass consumerism (complete with national
holidays devoted to buying, giving and returning merchandise) has yet to create either unbounded economic
opportunity or economic justice in the United States.
In 2015, there were 43.1 million Americans in poverty
(or 13.5 per cent of the country—roughly on par with
Hungary, Indonesia, Romania, Slovakia and Thailand).
Are we somewhat carelessly, if not hypocritically,
pushing a shabby economic growth model?

4. In developed markets, competition and creative
destruction deliver improvements in product
design and pricing. Survival of the economic fittest is
a necessary consequence of progress: some businesses
succeed, others fail. If my new app to manage your
photos goes bankrupt, no one gets hurt besides my
investors and me. But, where the poor live, mistakes in
the marketplace are paid for by the most vulnerable—
mostly women and children. If my social enterprise
fails, babies may end up drinking filthy water, get sick
and maybe die. Or, crops may not get to market. Or,
medicine will be unaffordable. Or, girls will not get an
education. Does neatly tagging the marginalized as 'the
BoP' risk depersonalizing millions of human beings
into a financial idiom that shields us from the full
implications of our developing world investments (and
failures)?

5. In ideal markets, prices are set by willing buyers and
willing sellers. Competition lowers prices and improves
products. Consumer protection and financial transparency are enforced by governmental policy and in a
court of law. In contrast, where the poor live, scarcity
and monopoly live side-by-side, inflicting shoddy
products and predatory pricing on captive consumers.
Financially-impoverished usually means legally-

impoverished; by and large, the disenfranchised have neither lawyers, nor the law, on their side. Look no further than the US court system where, despite a constitutional right to due process, money buys unequal justice. Hopefully, high-minded business-es marketing to the BoP can be counted on to never exploit their monopoly power, but – on the off chance they do, as history suggests they might – who, or what, will stop them?

As economic justice advocates, we respect the fact that businesses create jobs, but we also know that in the real-life marketplace where the poor live and shop, a miracle-making invisible hand is not writing storybook endings of economic efficiency and opportunity for all. If there *is* an invisible hand, it's a hard slap to the face. The poor are burdened with a myriad of terrorizing market imperfections. Even in devel-oped economies, we appreciate that, like E.B. White (author of *Charlotte's Web* for children, and *Elements of Style* for college students), points out: "The trouble with the profit system has always been that it was highly unprofitable to most people."

People living on the unpleasant edge of economic life have the same requirements for food, clothing and shelter, and the same human wants and weaknesses, as you and I do. The obvious difference is the poor live in a complex, high-consequences world of competing and unmet basic needs, few choices and many hardships. As Michael Holman reports in *Last Orders at Harrods: An African Tale*, a life lived in poverty is "fragile, cheap, dangerous and unpredictable."

The urgent question for us is this: what are you and I going to do about it? Every platform for change has its merits and demer-its. Our common sense tells us that no single program, by itself, solves poverty—let alone creates economic justice. If one option is undesirable (or unworkable), what are the realistic, actionable alternatives? If someone suggests that one of our BoP social ventures is harmful or inadequate, we might want to ask: *compared to what?*

—∞—

Unless you're a fish or a snake, what's so great about achieving scale? For social entrepreneurs, the task of scaling our social enterprises (or not scaling them) induces heartburn.

Social entrepreneurship calls us in the direction of big, brash, system-disrupting, system-stopping, system-innovating solutions. Without growing our social ventures, without moving our careers up the ladder of professional success, without achieving economies of scale, without becoming big enough to be seen by funders and journalists, without a 'scalable model', are we doing enough? Are we reaching our full potential as changemakers? If our programs are small in size and stature, do you and I matter?

To give the notion of scale its due: we are in an urgent fury to achieve system-wide, broadly-reaching social justice. We take it personally that a billion people can't drink clean water. We take it personally that 29,000 children die every day from poverty. We take it personally that our globe is getting hotter. We take it personally that women are abused or sexually-trafficked. That 2.5 billion people don't have basic sanitation. That wars are the macho solution for government officials who don't fight or die in them. That, around the world, on this very day, 27 million people are enslaved. The internal moral pressure to do more, get bigger, reach greater numbers and forestall total environmental disaster weighs heavily on our hearts—and in our organizational planning.

Thinking big is a time-honored tradition. In business: economies of scale mean greater efficiency, lower prices and higher profits. In government: scale means inclusiveness, protecting the rights of every citizen and participatory decision-making. In ecological terms: water and air ignore man-made borders, so comprehensive, scaled environmental action is the only way to save the planet.

At the other end of the scale (so to speak), Tiffany Persons articulates the anti-scale rationale. Tiffany is the Founder of Shine On Sierra Leone, an educational and economic development program. After growing her program, enlarging its programmatic reach and achieving international recognition, Tiffany hit the brakes. As she tells it, "I asked myself how I was feeling about how big and how fast we were growing. It hurt my heart to realize the people that I was working with didn't feel part of the change. What are we really changing if the people we are working with don't feel connected?

I was sold on the idea of scale, but now I am the anti-scale. I've decided to focus all of my energy and all of my love into one community."

Amy Paulson, Co-Founder of the Global Gratitude Alliance, adds: "In community development, small is good. Scale forces us to look at people as issues to solve, not as individual humans with complex and unique needs. Scale brings up many other difficult questions, like what metrics really make sense, not for our donors, but for the communities we serve? How willing are we to forgo quick wins for long-term, messy and complex sustainable change that can often take decades or generations? Does our desire to define scale as volume, rather than impact, represent another form of colonialism?"

For social entrepreneurs, the important thing is progress towards social justice—not organizational size, geographic coverage or budget. "Can you really help everyone?" asks Dylan Hrycyshen, Community Development Coordinator at a Canadian small business incubator. "Tell me what your product or service actually does, and skip all the fluffy language about being the most socially-conscious provider. Stop scaling before your idea becomes a [reality]. It's about the real way your service improves lives within your community. Impact is about connection, and that doesn't happen when scaling is the objective."

Different social entrepreneurs think about growth differently. If our social venture is a product solution, like solar lights or treadle pumps, then growth might mean wider distribution to realize economies of scale. If our thing is social services, like health care or education, the more people served, the better—provided that our touch is deep, tender and life-affirming. If we stand in opposition to political corruption and the denial of civil liberties, then turning the gears of government more humanely is our way of thinking about scale. Some organizations grow organically, and some do not; for example, some partner, collaborate or replicate. Some grow inwardly, scaling deeper into the communities to which they have committed their careers. The permutations are uncountable.

Obsessing about size and scale is fraught with growing pains, most often experienced as sharp pains in the ass:

+ As our social ventures get larger, they require new lead-ership skills, new internal systems and new budgets. "Anyone who has worked in an organization with more than a dozen employees recognizes institutional costs. Anytime you are faced with too many meetings, too much paperwork or too many layers of approval, you are dealing with those costs," notes Clay Shirky in *Here Comes Everybody: The Power of Organizing Without Organizations.*

• For some organizations and some leaders, scale becomes psychologically addictive, a gateway drug leading to mission drift. "The more he conquered, the more he had to conquer," is a warning from the life of Genghis Khan, as reported by Jack Weatherford in *Genghis Khan and the Making of the Modern World.*

• Not all programs are scalable. Not all projects can produce a profit. Not everything worth doing earns recognition, wins a competition, attracts fat cat donors or garners a foundation grant. For many worthy social justice organizations, chasing scale is unrealistic.

Bigger is not always better. There is no 'best' organizational size. As change agents, we are caught in the crossfire between the change that we know matters, and the change that others think matters. Bigger is not always better. There is no *best* organizational size. An admonition from the co-author of *The Communist Manifesto*, Frederick Engels, comes to mind: "Quantity changes quality." Getting and maintaining the balance is, well, a balancing act.

Trust-based change doesn't miraculously materialize out of thin air, summoned into existence by our brilliant insights, penetrating analysis or compelling oration. It takes time, and small actions. And then, small actions beget larger actions. "Great work is often built on the mundane. Great cathedrals start with bricks, great paintings begin with paint and great novels start with words," notes Michael Bungay Stanier in *End Malaria*. We celebrate our small victories— not just to nourish ourselves, but because small victories really do matter. They are victories.

To my way of thinking, social entrepreneurship honors itself when it honors change agents at all levels of impact and in all spheres of human endeavor. Parenting, to pick one important example, is so commonplace that we tend not to consider it to be heroic social change work. But raising a child is investing in a better tomorrow just like any social impact investor or charitable nonprofit. Parents expend patient financial capital in the form of real money, real time and real mission commitment. Think of the social change gifted to us by the parents of Emily Greene Balch, Mahatma Gandhi, Dag Hammarskjold, Dr. Martin Luther King, Jr. or Nelson Mandela. Single moms and dads—take note.

Because social progress is human progress, it's really thorny to isolate what drives, or impedes, social change. People lead varied and complicated lives. Within the borders of our lifetimes, people laugh, dance, drink water, fall in love, fall out of love, sweat, work, fuck, raise kids, cook food, make music and make mistakes. We have dreams; we have nightmares. Deep inside the ecology of a community, so much of what happens is intangible, without clear causation. So much of what binds a community of people or creates economic opportunity is invisible, and hard to capture with measurable certainty.

"Few of us can do great things, but all of us can do small things with great love," avows Nobel Prize Laureate Mother Teresa. If we can't do it small, can we ever hope to do it large?

— ∞ —

TOMS Shoes pioneered and popularized the buy-one-give-one corporate cause marketing model. For every pair of shoes that you and I buy, the company donates a pair of shoes to a shoeless child in the developing world. Copycat social enterprises are metastasizing: eyewear, toothbrushes, baby clothes, bicycles, soccer balls, fruit snacks, jewelry, purses, coffee, blankets, lamps, hammocks, and children's rain boots. Clearly, the buy-one-give-one model is here to stay.

TOMS Shoes has left a sizable, albeit muddied, footprint on the American psyche. "When asked, almost one in three Americans can't name a single socially-responsible organization. But, the people who can [name one] cite TOMS Shoes, Whole Foods, and Microsoft most often—even ahead of nonprofits like the American Red Cross and The Salvation Army," reports Ariel

Schwartz in 'Americans Think TOMS and Whole Foods are the Most Socially Responsible Companies, Sort Of'.

"On college campuses," blogs Johnathan Favini, a student at Lafayette College, "just about every twenty-something knows the name. You can spot TOMS Shoes on college campuses across the country, often sported by young, socially-minded students. The buy-one-give-one promise captures the hearts of the young idealistic demographic quite well, satisfying its two greatest cravings simultaneously: one, the desire to feel a part of change... and two, the desire to look cool."

To get to the foot of the matter, are buy-one-give-one models the real deal or junk social entrepreneurship? After all, even a company claiming a 'soleful' purpose might be shoe-washing. If I'm wearing a pair of TOMS Shoes, am I walking the talk? It's complicated, because there are three aspects to the buy-one-give-one model for us to unpack:

First, is it a sustainable and ethical revenue model for social entrepreneurs to emulate? *Yes*, is my cautious answer.

By all accounts, TOMS Shoes is a cause marketing success. According to the company, it has distributed 10 million pairs of free shoes. To manufacture a pair of canvas shoes costs approximately $5 or less (according to experts), so that means that this one social venture, if you choose to call it that, has generated $50 million of shoe-charity for the developing world. On its face, that's a good amount of money.

As a matter of policy, however, you and I might question the wisdom of spending our way to social justice. The implicit appealing (and appalling) message of the buy-one-give-one model is that economic development can be bought on the cheap. Still, as an ardent shopper, I find the prospect rather enticing. If shoes, why not shovels, shirts, shorts, shampoo, soap, spoons, saws or scissors? In that respect, buy-one-give-one doesn't fundamentally differ from any other corporate social responsibility program or consumer-facing business charity. It's *shop 'til you drop* meets *be the change*. TOMS' message is not all that distinct from a charity that tells potential donors that it can save the world, or at least a child's life, for a few pennies a day. A world with great misery offers opportunities for great hype.

Second, as conscious consumers, is the buy-one-give-one model a prudent way for us to support social change? Not really.

As social entrepreneurs concerned about the cost-effective use of our money, the buy-one-give-one approach ranks pretty low on the dollars-reaching-recipients efficiency-meter. Let's compare a buy-one-give-one model with a run-of-the-mill, nonprofit (hypothetical) charity. We'll take TOMS Shoes versus Tanya Teachers. I spend $50 with each organization—in one case, making a donation; in the other, buying a pair of canvas shoes (the 'classic' retails in that price range).

Let's assume that both organizations have overhead costs totaling a whopping 30 per cent of total revenues, thus, leaving $35 after my donation or shoe purchase for other expenditures.

Let's also say that Tanya Teachers sends me a crummy $5 coffee mug as a thank-you gift. That leaves $30 for training and paying teachers, plus hot dogs for the staff party.

By comparison, TOMS spends $5 manufacturing one pair of shoes for me, and another $5 to make a pair of shoes to send a poor kid. That leaves $25 for profits.

Obviously, these numbers are pure guesswork, but the conclusion is pretty clear: a direct donation to a cause I care about is the more cost effective way to go. In our little example: For the same $50 out of pocket, Tanya Teachers generates $30 for teaching, versus $5 of shoe charity from TOMS. Parenthetically, if I happen to buy a more expensive pair of TOMS shoes, the charitable benefit is still only one pair of shoes donated, whereas increasing my donation to Tanya Teachers has a commensurate 'do good' benefit.

Finally, my donation to Tanya Teachers is tax-deductible. Shoe purchases are not.

Of course, if either of us was planning to buy a pair of canvas shoes anyway, a pair of TOMS shoes might do a bit of good in the world. We simply need to be honest with ourselves: shoe-shopping is what it is, and it isn't smart philanthropy.

Third, is the buy-one-give-one model, at least as executed by TOMS Shoes, a sensible, impactful economic development model to copy? Not even close.

As reported on the company website, "In 2006, TOMS Founder Blake Mycoskie befriended children in a village in Argentina and saw that they didn't have adequate shoes to protect their feet. Wanting to help, he created TOMS Shoes, a company that would match every pair of shoes purchased with a pair of new shoes for a child in need."

Imagine, if you will, showing up one day in an economically-depressed village. Subsistence farming is the town's principal employment. We note the absence of electrical lines. Women, still fully dressed for modesty, are bathing in a nearby stream. Young girls use flat stones as washboards. Unemployed men huddle in small groups. An old church doubles as the health clinic. At the end of town, feral pigs feed in an open garbage dump. A small school, staffed by one teacher, lacks sufficient books. We hear songs and laughter. Boys and girls flirt. Babies cry. Meals are cooked. Life has meaning. Taking this all in, you or I decide the most pressing priority is free shoes for barefoot children. Really?

In economic development terms, TOMS Shoes is product dumping with a heart.
If TOMS' CEO, at the time of his shoe epiphany, had looked into what poor children require to realize promising lives, he might have come up with a buy-one-give-one business plan for TOMS Health Care, TOMS Jobs, TOMS School Books or TOMS Who-Knows-What. Of course, you and I don't know what he might have learned. More to the point, neither does he.

As social entrepreneurs, you and I reject the wheezing argument that 'anything is better than nothing'. We also dismiss the cringe-worthy implication that the shoeless poor are helpless and, therefore, whatever we in the West dole out is 'at least better than nothing'. No one wants the economic development bar set so low that, one day in the future, we might be shopping for the best in TOMS Shoelaces.

TOMS Shoes is the oldest form of altruism known to humankind: alms for the poor. In economic development terms, TOMS Shoes is product dumping with a heart. Dumping is the predatory practice of exporting a product or commodity into another country at a price below its cost of production. Even cutthroat corporations consider this an unsavory business practice, and seek government protection against it. When TOMS walks into a village, local leaders focused on economic opportunity are wise to worry about their local shoemakers and cobblers. 'Free' is a difficult price point to undersell.

"Charitable gifts from abroad can distort developing markets and undermine local businesses by creating an entirely unsustainable aid-based economy," writes Cheryl Davenport in 'The Broken 'Buy-One, Give-One' Model: 3 Ways To Save TOMS Shoes'. "By undercutting local prices, Western donations often hurt the farmers, workers, traders, and sellers whose success is critical to lifting entire communities out of poverty. That means every free shoe donated actually works against the long-term development goals of the communities we are trying to help. TOMS isn't designed to build the economies of developing countries. It's designed to make western consumers feel good."

Contemplate this hypothetical: according to the National Center for Children in Poverty, "more than 16 million children in the United States (22 per cent of all children) live in families with incomes below the federal poverty level—$23,550 a year for a family of four." Undoubtedly, some of those children need new shoes. If a Chinese shoe company implemented a buy-one-give-one program, Chinese volunteers would soon be landing at American airports, then fanning out into inner cities and poor rural communities to give away free shoes to American kids. American shoe manufacturers, retailers and repair shops would explode in jingoistic protest.

Our rejection of the TOMS Shoes giveaway program is compounded by the way the program presents itself to the general public. Characteristically, the TOMS Shoes CEO is pictured on bent knee fitting new shoes on the feet of grinning brown, black or yellow children, imagery reminiscent of the Pope washing feet on Holy Thursday. TOMS' optics are reminiscent of the white, Western savior. It's a paternalistic narrative that informed social entrepreneurs religiously avoid.

Worse, when interviewed for the Australian magazine *Dumbo Feather*, the company CEO revealed an insulting ignorance about the nonprofit sector. In 'Blake Mycoskie is the Chief Shoegiver' he says, "when people look at charities sometimes they see huge percentages going towards overheads and the CEO's high salary, and it's off-putting... We're a business and hopefully we're going to be a really big business and make lots of money but in the process we're going to help lots of people." Is it churlish to note that TOMS Shoes (privately-owned before its sale to Bain Capital for $625 million) doesn't publish its 'overheads and the CEO's high salary'? In stark contrast to nonprofits which are legally-obligated to be transparent, you and I were not given a shred of information about the company's operational efficiency.

We only know that TOMS' profits are symbiotically laced together with welfare shoes for poor kids: no free shoes, no motivated customers. When life's essential products and services (like health care, education, decent roads, clean water) depend on vagaries of American consumer purchasing patterns, it seems like the opposite of committed social change.

Perhaps the buy-one-give-one model makes sense for products that are unimportant, or at least less important. Perhaps the TOMS buy-one-give-one model seems reasonable to us because, in the final analysis, shoelessness is a comparatively trivial part of the poverty puzzle—a symptom of economic injustice, not its root cause. Anyone who says otherwise probably owns stock in a shoe company.

— ∞ —

I love doing the work of social entrepreneurship precisely because it is more art than science, more about morality than about markets. Because it's grounded in people and principles. So much of what you and I do in social justice work is a matter of judgment and nuance, of balancing competing priorities and concerns. Doing one thing in one place, and doing something else in another. If you've chosen the life of the change agent, and if you're expecting sharply delineated, well-trod, well-lit pathways, you have my condolences. There are no firm, fixed answers—only the continuing responsibility to fight, side-by-side, with people who have been less lucky in the lottery of life.

Take Two: Misgivings

Natalie Conneely, 32, is Director of Resource Development for Dalai Lama Fellows; and Executive Director of Changing Stories, where she amplifies the stories and voices that have traditionally been muted. Hometown: Santa Cruz, Bolivia. Favorite pastime: dancing. Guilty pleasure: frozen yogurt with all the fixings on a hot summer's day.

"In my experience, when we are chasing the concept of 'big' we often forget the word 'enough', a word that defines what is *actually* needed in a society where 'big' means 'more'. In the world of good intentions, the first step to creating change is often missed. In order to find our own 'big', we must first understand ourselves and our reasons for doing the work in the first place. Before reaching for the stars, it's important for us to ask ourselves if we need to 'till the soil' of our own intentions for the work and energy we want to put into the world, to ensure that it is aligned and alive enough within us.

"At Dalai Lama Fellows, we balance the demand for scale (by funders and individual donors), with the knowledge that our program is best delivered to small groups, in order to accomplish transformation at the individual level. Every year we pick a few more Fellows than the previous year, in our effort to reach more individuals. However, we make our decisions following our core value of 'humbition', a made-up word which brings about the necessary balance between humility and ambition. We strive for our own version of 'big', based on the knowledge that in order to have transformative change in a group setting, we can only work with a handful of individuals at a time. Recognizing that the challenges are big in our increasingly connected and ironically isolated world, we know that unless we build towards a world that works for all of us, it won't work for any of us."

PLURALISM

I'm an economic bi-sexual. I favor capitalism, and I favor socialism. My policy instincts are socialist. My tools are capitalist.

Government solutions versus private-sector solutions. For-profit versus nonprofit social enterprises. Social service programs versus political action campaigns. Entrepreneurship versus intrapreneur-ship. Secular institutions versus faith-based institutions. Impact investing versus philanthropy. In these debates, I take both sides. I call myself a pragmatic pluralist.

A drowning person doesn't ask, or care, who paid for the lifeguard.

A drowning person doesn't ask, or care, whether a taxpayer, a shareholder or a nonprofit paid for the lifeguard. Doesn't ask, or care, who owns the life preserver, or how it was financed. Doesn't ask, or care, if it was governmental policy or the marketplace that failed to value free universal swim classes.

I'm an economic bi-sexual. I favor capitalism, and I favor socialism. My policy instincts are socialist. My tools are capitalist. As practicing change agents, you and I have seen the truth of the Polish proverb: "Under capitalism, man exploits man; under socialism, the reverse is true."

Ideological rigidity is a luxury of the privileged, and a sanctuary for the stupid. A social entrepreneur's mind is dogma-free. Flexibility of approach is our secret sauce. As Osberg and Martin, in *Getting Beyond Better*, note: "challenges demand new models; they call on us to contest existing assumptions, and they encourage us to create new paths rather than follow the existing routes. This fluid and adaptive approach distinguishes social entrepreneurs, no matter the specific legal structure or tax status of the organization in which they work or the domain of their pursuit."

The moral core of social entrepreneurship is defined by what we *actually do*. We pursue practical solutions for achieving the deepest impact for the greatest number of people. We don't search for answers in ideological theory, partisan agenda or abstract economic policy. Instead, we draw on pragmatic pluralism.

"It's time to move past the simplistic caricature that running a business for profit will make a person a greedy automaton who cares only about getting rich and not making the world a better place, who may not sleep at night but at least will have enough money to buy all the Prozac needed to numb the pain of having sold out," demands Kyle Westaway in *Profit and Purpose*. "It's also time to move past the view that if you're on a mission to do social good, you've got to take a vow of poverty, which is okay because at least you're compensated by the reward of making the world a better place."

To reach our goals, social entrepreneurs experiment with every possible solution and every possible platform until we find the one that unlocks social justice. When I eat a hot dog, I don't eat it with a pro-marketplace or anti-marketplace, pro-government or anti-government, ideological mindset. Usually, I eat it with mustard. But, as a social entrepreneur, I'm also constantly taste-testing, or if you prefer, iterating and innovating, other hot dog toppings to determine which one I relish the most.

—∞—

To help us imagine what pragmatic pluralism in action looks like, let's consider the following three scenarios:

Traffic safety: At a particularly dangerous street intersection, schoolchildren are dying with unacceptable regularity. What should we do about it?

As a social entrepreneur, to address the problem I might first start a for-profit social venture charging parents a fee to escort their kids safely to and from school. Some deaths are avoided, but only the children with affluent parents are protected.

Next, we might try a nonprofit solution. Winning a grant from a community foundation and raising donations from local businesses, my nonprofit hires hard-to-employ individuals as safety guards in reflective vests who, during peak traffic times, keep the human bodies and the car bodies separated. More lives are saved, but it's too expensive to provide 24/7 coverage. Plus, this option requires fundraising into eternity.

Finally, we organize a citizens' political advocacy group, mobilize community opinion, turn out voters, elect a safety-conscious city council and get stop signs installed at the intersection. The day after the signage is installed, every car stops at the intersection, accidents abate, and every kid stays alive (no matter how wealthy or conscientious their parents are).

Weeks later, some moron writes a letter to the editor to complain that the signs are an example of government overreach, because they force all cars to stop even when there are no pedestrians in sight. The letter also snipes about 'socialized street safety' and 'the erosion of individual responsibility'. In reply, you or I write a blog pointing out that governmental action is the only practical at-scale solution. Only government has the power and resources to effectuate universal compliance. Only government can make us stop at a stop sign. We are all safer for it.

Community knowledge: In San Francisco, the main branch of the public library anchors one side of an expansive public plaza. Nearby, the majestic City Hall building, the imposing Federal Courthouse and the Asian Art Museum bespeak civic pride and civic ownership. Just across the street from the library is a small shop selling various items, including an excellent selection of newspapers. Inside the library, the same publications are available for free. A few blocks from the library, a bookstore does a brisk business selling novels, non-fiction, art books, poetry, business books, magazines, children's books and cookbooks—all of which are also free at the library. To my knowledge, no one has ever accused the public library of undercutting the free market, nor railed against the retailers for profiteering off a necessary public good (knowledge and information).

Street litter: If we are good socialists, we believe in public street sweepers. After all, street cleaning is a public responsibility;

litter should be removed by decently-paid government workers. If we are good capitalists, we think that private sector merchants, incentivized to attract more customers, should sweep in front of their shops. Either way, thanks to behavioral economists, we know that neighborhood social norms, rather than economic theory, determine whether or not perambulating social entrepreneurs walk on clean or dirty sidewalks.

John Kenneth Galbraith, economist and author of *American Capitalism*, famously destroyed the ambiguous public-versus-private-sector divide. He noted that our quality of life depends equally on vacuum cleaners and street cleaners. The worker who manufactures a vacuum cleaner to clean inside a store, and the worker who cleans the sidewalk in front of that store, both produce needed goods and services, both pay taxes, both raise families, both are engines of national prosperity. Both are necessary for clean living.

In all three examples, the lines are blurry. Moreover, as the world turns, new formulations are emerging every day: B Corps, hybrid models, public-private partnerships, social impact bonds, etc. For us, the only takeaway is a rigid commitment to not be rigid, as we problem-solve society's messes. Let's not quibble or quarrel over which legal entity or institutional framework is the superior purveyor of goods and services. Even the synthetic debate about which comes first – economic development or political and human rights – can feel distracting. Justice is *one* thing.

As social entrepreneurs, our urgent assignment is to make each institution as compassionate and effective as possible.

As social entrepreneurs, you and I seek out the cleanest, neatest, most sustainable solution. Our urgent assignment is to make each institution as compassionate and as effective as possible. To make government, banks, businesses, churches and NGOs function well. In this era of rending social fabric and frayed social trust, it's a radical idea.

— ∞ —

The social entrepreneur's conceit is that we can innovate a better solution than anyone else; that our creativity, visionary thinking and advanced management skills will pioneer the next social justice breakthrough. Martin Luther King, shake hands with Steve Jobs. Frances Perkins, meet Henry Ford.

For a role model in pragmatic pluralism, you and I can't do any better than Benjamin Franklin. Excluding his personal blinders and prejudices, his early ownership of slaves versus his eventual opposition to slavery—his overarching life story is one of social entrepreneurship implemented across the topography of societal institutions.

Walter Isaacson (in *Benjamin Franklin: An American Life*) describes this iconic social entrepreneur applying his innovations to civil society, the private sector, science, government and impact investing: "A fundamental aspect of Franklin's life, and of the American society he helped to create, was that individualism and communitarianism, so seemingly contradictory, were interwoven. The frontier attracted barn-raising pioneers who were ruggedly individualistic as well as fiercely supportive of their community. Franklin was the epitome of this admixture of self-reliance and civic involvement, and what he exemplified became part of the American character."

Terry Breverton (in *Immortal Words*) records that "Benjamin Franklin [was] a scientist, inventor, printer, musician, economist and philosopher. [Among] his inventions were bifocal glasses, a flexible urinary catheter, the Franklin stove for heating homes more safely, an odometer and the lightning conductor. He started *The Pennsylvania Gazette* and pioneered lending libraries in the United States. In the War of Independence, Franklin was ambassador to Europe for the colonies, negotiating French help for America. When he signed the Constitution of the United States of America in 1787, he was the only Founding Father to have signed all five documents that established American independence." We also fondly remember Franklin's proposal for a progressive tax to fund police departments. It probably never even occurred to him to think in silos, because silos are not the way that social entrepreneurs think.

Of course, not everyone is a polymath like Franklin. Most of us pick a single area of career concentration. No matter what we do, and where we do it—we carry the responsibility to put our heads and hearts to work for the public interest. No theory of government and no marketplace (whether failing or functioning) can change the reality that we are blessed and burdened with a moral compass. It's liberating. Energizing. Exhilarating.

—∞—

If there's a thing called social entrepreneurship, then there ought to be a thing called community entrepreneurship. Or, public entrepreneurship. Or, civic entrepreneurship. Which one sounds better?

Whatever we call it, a return to the idea of civic entrepreneurship deserves more of our time and attention. As agents of change, we cannot reach our goals for environmental, economic, racial, gender and social justice if we ignore the public sector.

For social entrepreneurs, and for the causes you and I care about, government is not some vague, take-it-for-granted abstraction. My government's helping hands are everywhere. My government provides libraries, public parks and street lighting. My government investigates the safety of products, drugs and airplanes. My government pays for the National Weather Service, the Peace Corps and the National Park Service (no, it's not a valet service). My government is the rule of law. My government funds universities, collects the garbage, conducts medical research, provides worker disability insurance, teaches kids to read and requires my mattress to be nonflammable. My government guards my freedom to gather and protest.

Every time I get in my privately-owned automobile to decide for myself where I want to drive, a collectivist, command-and-control government requires all the other drivers to obey speed limits, drive soberly and stay on their side of the road. The same authoritarian government makes automobile manufacturers include seatbelts and airbags in my car. If I run out of fuel on a publicly-financed highway, a public servant in a police uniform stops to make sure I'm okay. In a snow storm, a socialist snowplow clears the socialist roadways for my capitalist car.

"An inventor can develop a breakthrough in solar technology, but if our governments continue to deny or downplay the role green-house gases play in climate change, we are doomed. A researcher can discover a vaccine that will prevent an intractable disease, but if our governments can't find the political will to make its dissemination a priority, [can't] build the social structure and outreach necessary to ensure its use, then the innovation will lie dormant," observes Sam Daley-Harris, Founder of the Center for Citizen Empowerment and Transformation, in *Reclaiming Our Democracy.*

A poem chiseled into a cement wall at the Yerba Buena Gardens in downtown San Francisco asks, "Dare We Dream in Concrete?" Yes, we do. Over the years, the American government, thanks to its citizen-taxpayers, has built 45,000 miles of concrete freeways, at a cost of $185 billion. Today, the interstate highway system remains the largest public works project in human history, generating approximately $800 billion of private economic gain.

Some of the best parts of government are invisible, which might account for why some social entrepreneurs can't see themselves in satisfying public sector careers. Unless a bridge collapses, bridge maintenance goes unnoticed. Public park landscape maintenance is mostly hidden from public view. Building inspectors only get their due after a horrific fire.

In the same way that we pay for health insurance, but don't want to get sick—some parts of government are a grudge purchase. I pay the government to keep the fire department on alert, but I'm not planning to set my house on fire. I pay into social security, but I would really prefer not to think about growing any older. I pay my fair share of taxes for a strong military, but generally oppose using it.

A significant part of civic entrepreneurship is fighting to assure that civilization's highest and most sacred ideals are available to everyone without regard to race, color, religion, sex, or national origin. The belief structure that we proselytize is venerated, immutable, enshrined and old-fashioned: free speech, participatory democracy, community empowerment, human rights, earth stewardship, sanctity of life (defined as you choose), individual dignity, economic opportunity, family, privacy and peace.

In addition to all that, the social entrepreneur's relationship to the government goes much deeper than a cluster of itemized services. It's more personal. More intimate. More soulful. The government is our collective moral voice.

In our name, government hugs little children fleeing danger, or sends them back to the mean streets of Central America. In our name, the government keeps watch at the bedside of our 9/11 first responders, or looks away as they die from toxic exposure to asbestos. In our name, government welcomes refugees, or abandons them to the terrors of war and genocide. In our name, the government stands up for Native American tribes protecting their sacred lands, or bows to the oil and gas titans who despoil our air and water. In our name, the government is outraged at injustice—or not. More than anything else we can name, that's why civic entrepreneurship is worthy of us.

—∞—

Because the zeitgeist of our times dislikes big institutions, government service has fallen out of favor. Instead, from coffee cooperatives to artisan workshops, from organic farming to neighborhood retailing, from microfinance to mobile money—the social entrepreneurial mind turns towards non-governmental market solutions. "Social entrepreneurship is a rigorous approach to solving a social problem, using business skills—whether it's marketing, finance or negotiation skills," summarizes the Founder of Weal Life, Keely Stevenson.

Taken to its extreme, 'poverty capitalism' privatizes essential governmental services, creating private water companies, corporatizing prisons, making sick people pay for life-saving health care, financing social bonds and so on. The pragmatic social entrepreneur raises a quizzical, and agnostic, eyebrow. Yet free-market idolatry only takes us so far. "A wise man should have money in his head, not in his heart," advised the poet Jonathan Swift.

"The trend towards the privatization of the public sphere in the latter half of the 20th century has gradually transformed the idea of the citizen from that of an active political participant to that of a consumer. The political consumer makes individual, market-like judgments about the delivery of government services, but decreasingly sees his or her role as joining with others to shape or change government policy," reports Bruce Sievers in *Civil Society, Philanthropy and the Fate of the Commons*.

In rebuttal to this cheapening of our civic lives, Benjamin Franklin reminds us, "The good [that] men may do separately is small compared with what they may do collectively."

The American heart, we are told, is a generous one. However, individual generosity is not the same as community solidarity. Look no further than America's healthcare system. Americans donate to healthcare clinics, hospitals, migrant care, senior citizen centers, medical research, programs for people with disabilities, and so on. Profitable hospitals, health insurers, medical groups and pharmaceutical companies deliver excellent health care, if you can afford it. Nonetheless, without a governmental guarantee of health care access for all, America bleeds health injustice.

Without question, seasoned social entrepreneurs concede the limitations of their social ventures. A chain of charter schools is not national education reform. An enterprise providing affordable bottled water to slum dwellers is not a city-wide system with safe, clean water pouring from every tap. A sustainable microfinance program is not a well-regulated banking system prohibited, by law, from discriminating against women or redlining minority neighborhoods. A community program to improve race relations is not a local ordinance banning police profiling.

—∞—

Trash-talking government is easy. It's a lot tougher to do something about it. It's easy to win the argument that government has failed you. It's a lot tougher to admit that *you* have failed *it*.

Despite occasional, exasperating and heartbreaking reversals, democratizing democracy is worthy work for a social entrepreneur. "Setbacks in trying to realize the ideal do not prove that the ideal is at fault," observed former UN Secretary-General Dag Hammarskjold.

As an American social entrepreneur, I'm an American patriot. I love my country in the same way I hope that my best friends love me: accepting my faults, but expecting better of me. I believe in an exceptional America without believing in American exceptionalism. I want our country to be exceptional *without* wanting it to be treated exceptionally.

In America, the public rhetoric is fiercely individualistic, but our physical and emotional needs are communal. In case you're wondering, that old 'less government equals more freedom' polemic is total bullshit. Neither of us is freer or happier when life is random. Chaos and uncertainty are not liberating. There is little freedom, less opportunity and insecure human rights without a strong, well-functioning government.

Even the common assumption that social innovation happens more rapidly, more readily and more rationally in the private sector is untrue. We tend to forget that the formation of the US government, with its constitutional system of checks and balances, was *the* social innovation of its time. So too was the invention of free public schools, putting a human into space, England's universal health-care system, ridding the world of smallpox, planting public parks, installing sewers, patent protection, public fire departments, and so much else that we call a 'public good' (and take for granted). Social innovation is not unique to one institutional arrangement over another, one kind of legal structure over another.

Moreover, innovation, in itself, is amoral; an instrument for good *or* evil. Gadgets, mobile devices, inventions, lab creations and software don't come with a conscience. The first suicide vest was a disruptive technology. The internet, a platform for online learning, exposes millions of young kids to bullying and lewd content. Sub-prime mortgages and redlining were once innovations in the financial services industry. Innovation is not what drives social entrepreneur-ship. Social justice is.

Shortly after the election of the Trump/Republican Wasteland, I was interviewed by a popular social entrepreneurship podcast. The interviewer noted that some social entrepreneurs hoped that lower taxes and deregulation of business might benefit social enterprises. I exploded: "The author of that statement is not a social entrepre-neur. The key word in social entrepreneur is social, not entrepreneur." We are not in the business of profiting off public policies that hurt the very people we are pledged to fight for. Head-in-the-sand rationalizations for government-by-greed are unworthy of us.

H.L. Mencken once said: "Every decent person is ashamed of the government he lives under." Our question: are we ashamed enough to move public service up higher on our list of changemaker career choices?

—∞—

As things stand, 'social entrepreneur' is a more prestigious job title than 'government worker'. Public service doesn't sound as glamorous as running a startup social venture, working at a social impact investment fund, or inventing a new app to address an unmet community need. Very few of us start our changemaker careers imagining ourselves as a small cog in a big bureaucratic machine; one of 22 million American civil servants. Of course, we're entitled to wonder whether or not either of us has the fortitude, vision, wisdom, talent, character or heart for public service. What's not open for debate is whether the fight for 'people, planet and profits' is complete without politics. It's not.

In the early years of our social entrepreneurial careers, you and I can probably accomplish more in a government role than most anywhere else. At the risk of oversimplifying, take one example: A mid-level budget analyst with an MBA, five years out of school, working for a social impact investment fund might influence decisions affecting *millions* of dollars. The same individual working for a state government budget office might influence decisions affecting *billions* of dollars.

"Public entrepreneurs around the world are improving our lives, inventing entirely new ways to serve the public," reports Mitchell Weiss in 'Government Entrepreneur is Not an Oxymoron'. "They are using sensors to detect potholes; word pedometers to help students learn; harnessing behavioral economics to encourage organ donation; crowdsourcing patent review and transforming Medellin, Colombia with cable cars."

For a biting example, each day that we *don't* see a malaria-carrying mosquito is a victory for public health departments staffed by government-paid doctors and bossy bureaucrats spending our taxpayer dollars. In 1951, malaria in the US was eradicated after a government program sprayed five million households across the Southeastern states.

In Papua New Guinea, the Heineken beer company (to its credit) infuses its beer boxes with a natural, eucalyptus-based mosquito repellent, because the company learned that its customers drink beer around a bonfire, burning discarded beer boxes for fuel. As the boxes burn, the mosquito repellent is released, affording the beer drinkers some measure of protection against malaria-carrying mosquitoes.

It's a worthy, but ultimately unsatisfactory, substitute for a concerted, well-designed government mosquito-abatement program to protect the entire population, from babies to beer drinkers.

In Africa, malaria kills 500,000 people annually. The Global Fund to Fight AIDS, Tuberculosis and Malaria has financed 450 million insecticide-treated mosquito nets that are distributed free to at-risk villagers. Unfortunately, the nets are sometimes misused as fishing nets because starvation is the more immediate threat (even in families that have already lost a loved one to malaria). Just think about that for a moment. For lack of a strong, well-funded, community-wide, government mosquito abatement program—a parent is forced to choose between feeding a child and protecting it from malaria. *WTF!?*

If health justice is our goal, what's worth doing? Working for an NGO handing out free mosquito bed nets? Political work strengthening African governments? Working at a corporation to redesign products for better health outcomes? Working for a public health department? Manufacturing mosquito nets? All of the above, of course.

When my heart droops with disappointment, or I'm blood-red angry about an injustice, the realistic, relevant and morally-ripe question is: *Where can my talents make the biggest difference?* As social entrepreneurs working across the spectrum of social change—we want to build and upgrade institutions that are big and bold enough to answer the challenges crushing our collective humanity. Social entrepreneurship is about systemic change. It's about power—who has it, who doesn't, and whose side we fight on.

Social entrepreneurship is not just a career. It's also a way of showing up, a way of thinking about social change. Everywhere you and I go, in every room – whether a government building, a corporate office or a nonprofit shared workspace – courage, conviction and innovation happen because we are there to make sure it does. It's not about ideology. It's about who we are. I'm not being cute or cliché about this. It's as true about us as anything in the world.

Take Two: Pluralism

Ezra Limiri Mbogori, 60, is Executive Director of Akiba Uhaki Foundation, a homegrown human rights and social justice organization. Hometown: Nairobi, Kenya. Favorite pastime: being a fly on a wall. Guilty pleasure: driving aimlessly.

"In the early Sixties, the British Prime Minister made a famous speech to the then 'whites only' Parliament in South Africa. He observed that "a wind of change was sweeping across the African Continent."

"Kenya attained self-rule three years later. I recall adults questioning the distinct differences between communism and capitalism. Those who preferred communism talked about its closeness to African traditions—the spirit of care for one another and minding the welfare of the all. But they also spoke about who was influencing their thinking in respect of these ideologies—the west or the east. The dangers of capitalism were equated to its 'man-eat-man' nature. Similarly, those who were more attracted to capitalism warned that communism implied that everything (including your children) belonged to the State.

"Soon 'African socialism' became the happy medium embraced by African leaders struggling to locate themselves. This was the preferred African ideology. Pluralism at the time was a luxury that detracted from the twin challenge of nation building and development. "We must relentlessly wage a united attack on poverty, disease and ignorance," our politicians said. Unfortunately, the generation in leadership at the time failed to transfer appropriate 'ownership' of these challenges to those who *should* have taken over from them in pursuit of social justice. In many cases, those 'future leaders' are still waiting to take leadership.

"Could it be that the attempt to pass the ownership baton is failing even today? Are we communicating with millennials as we should? Young people must call us out if we appear condescending—because we could still lose the battle for social justice, despite our best intentions."

BYSTANDER

The lesser of two evils is less evil. Voting for the lesser of two evils is a shitload better than giving power to the more evil of the two evil options. I'm in favor of less evil.

In my college years, every student rally included a fiery speech protesting South Africa's racist apartheid regime. In 1990, I cheered when, after 27 years in prison, Nelson Mandela walked free. In 1994, following the end of apartheid, I tearfully celebrated when black South Africans, in their country's first fair and inclusive election, voted in the African National Congress. Behind my office desk, in a simple red frame, hangs a paper ballot from that election.

Twenty-two years later, in 2016, in an act of democratic infamy, the United States elevated to the presidency a xenophobic, racist, sexist, bigoted, willfully ignorant, dishonest leader. As the election results were announced, my body convulsed with the very same feeling I had when my dog, the best dog in the entire world, died from cancer.

It's as if the United States voted for a politics of apartheid. Even if it's not apartheid in the legalistic sense, it's still an ugly hate, a heartless cruelty, that's been installed in the White House.

Every election year, in a rather moralizing tone, we are informed that the act of voting has been reduced to an unsavory choice between the lesser of two evils. We are told that our vote only serves to validate a corrupt, centrist, corporatized two-party system.

Newsflash: the lesser of two evils is less evil. Voting for the lesser of two evils is a shitload better than giving power to the more evil of the two evil options. I'm in favor of less evil.

As citizens and as social entrepreneurs, sometimes we don't get to choose our battlefields. We do, however, get to choose whose side we are on in the long struggle for environmental, economic, racial, gender and social justice.

As change agents, we are obligated to pursue every opportunity, every avenue, every available forum, to advance progress. From soapbox to ballot box, politics is a changemaker power. Use it or lose it. The term 'apolitical social entrepreneur' is an oxymoron.

"Change requires more than righteous anger... To bring about structural change, lasting change, awareness is not enough. Passion is vital, but you've got to have a strategy. And your plan better include voting—not just some of the time, but all the time," advised President Obama in his 2016 commencement address at Howard University. "People try to make this political thing really complicated. You know what, just vote. It's math. If you have more votes than the other guy, you get to do what you want. It's not that complicated. When we don't vote, we give away our power, disenfranchise ourselves..."

If you're not a committed voter, you're not a committed social entrepreneur.

Not voting is the same as averting your eyes; looking the other way; censoring yourself; not taking responsibility; succumbing to cynicism. Nobel Peace Prize Laureate Elie Wiesel recalls, "In the place that I come from [Auschwitz and Buchenwald concentration camps], society was composed of three simple categories: the killers, the victims and the bystanders." In a democracy—not voting is bystanding.

—∞—

Just between you and me—if you're not a regular voter, then we have a problem. Actually, I can't believe I need to say this, but apparently I do. I really didn't want to tell you. It's a sour note on which to start an essay. I almost deleted it. Reluctantly, here goes:

If you're not a committed voter, you're not a committed social entrepreneur. You might be a perfectly good person and you might be exceptionally proficient in your social sector work, but if you are a spectator in the democratic process, then you lack the applied courage of your convictions.

In the same way that I am stunned into temporary silence when I hear someone who I thought I respected say something blatantly bigoted, I'm dumbfounded when a social sector colleague, student leader or community activist tells me that they don't vote. If you aren't a resolute, purposeful voter, it will be a long time before I forget, or forgive, your transgression against the world we both say that we want.

In the Sixties, we boycotted; we burned draft cards; we conscientiously objected; we picketed; we leafleted. We taught teach-ins. We signed petitions. We wore peace buttons. And we voted.

Over a lifetime, I've organized, marched and protested. I've worked for political campaigns. I've donated. I've impact invested. I've social entrepreneured. And I've voted.

For the causes we believe in, we do everything.

—∞—

Regrettably, some non-voters are blocked from the pleasure of fulfilling their civic duty by extenuating circumstances, such as voter suppression laws, inadequate childcare, illness, working multiple jobs, etc. Those who duck their civic duty without a legitimate excuse are selfish parasites, free riders on the body politic. Selfish in the same way that shirking your share of household duties is selfish. Selfish in the same way a filthy restroom confirms that the people who used it before us were selfish. Selfish in the way that the Trump/Republican Wasteland is self-centered about tax cuts for the wealthy and well-to-do, and insensitive jerks about the struggles of nearly everyone else.

In contrast, you and I aren't the selfish types. And, we aren't cynical. In a fucked-up world, when cynicism seems entirely justified, social entrepreneurs refuse to be cynical. In our line of work, the terms 'cynic' and 'apathetic' are used in the pejorative sense.

If you're not a regular voter, how do you reconcile your political alienation with a career committed to community empowerment? By what leap of logic did you conclude that every single person on the face of the earth should have agency to manage their personal affairs, advance their financial future and participate in the body politic—everyone but you?

'I voted' is so much more than a statement of personal accomplishment. It's a profound expression of our commitment to each other. People who vote share a bond of common kinship. In the same way that saying 'I love you' defines my relationship to another human, 'I voted' defines my relationship to the people in my community. Our votes affirm that we care about each other's welfare.

'I voted' also implies the reciprocal question, 'Have you voted?' That is to say, 'Do you love me too?' When I vote, I'm confessing my interdependency, my vulnerability and my need for you to vote with me. I'm asking for solidarity and your support.

Our votes build and strengthen our community's emotional resilience. Voting adds our voices to the crescendo of conscience that defines the world we want. As social entrepreneurs, we dream of communities where individuals have economic power, personal power and political power. We don't dream of communities of indifference and disengagement.

—∞—

From soapbox to ballot box, politics is changemaker power. A not-uncommon experience is chatting with people who share our progressive views, but who still don't vote. In the 2016 US presidential election, 90 million eligible voters did not vote, so there are plenty of opportunities for you and I to test drive these discussion points:

Voting is one way, the official way, to let others hear my broken heart. To shout back at dangerous stupidities. To deny barbarism in the public square. Voting is the über-poll, our opportunity to be publicly counted (even if our candidate or cause loses). No one can vote for me but me. I can't outsource my indignation.

When you don't vote, you double the vote of someone else. Long before PowerPoint, Plato articulated the powerful point of voting: "One of the penalties for refusing to participate in politics is that you end up being governed by your inferiors." Either you vote by casting a ballot, or you vote by not casting a ballot.

A cliché non-voter excuse is the perfectly preposterous falsehood that a single vote doesn't matter. Does it matter that I recycle? After all, it's just a bit of newspaper. Does it matter that I tutor a child? After all, it's only one kid. Does it matter that I make a donation to a charity? After all, a few dollars doesn't balance a nonprofit's budget. Yes, our vote matters because you and I matter. Voting is a question of self-respect, of refusing to sideline or sabotage ourselves.

Political elites and the ruling classes count on us to voluntarily surrender our franchise. Numerous business models work the same way. For example, health insurers lose money if you and I actually use the healthcare system. Not voting is akin to not getting that free annual health checkup you paid for. Power, privilege and the influence of money profit from passivity at the ballot box.

With so much power arrayed against social justice, we can't afford to waste any of ours. As activist-author Danusha Goska explains: "The problem is not that we have so little power. The problem is that we don't use the power that we have." If you and I don't trouble ourselves to register as voters, come election day, we're shit out of luck. We're powerless to vote our self-interest, let alone the public interest.

Our vote is a bulwark against government propaganda. The 'big lie', a phrase admired by Adolf Hitler in Mein Kampf, is how the Nazis sold the German people on anti-Semitism. It's how the Trump/Republican Wasteland is selling racism, bigotry and xenophobia. As summed up by Barry Schwartz in the *Paradox of Choice:* "When you hear the same story everywhere, you assume it must be true. And the more people believe it's true, the more likely they are to repeat it, and thus the more likely you are to hear it. This is how inaccurate information can create a bandwagon effect, leading quickly to a broad, but mistaken, consensus."

Voting mitigates our feelings of political melancholy. When society seems to lack a moral compass, steered by bad people doing bad things, if I cast a vote for progress, and if you do, and then someone else, and then another person—eventually the critical mass of humanity turns towards justice. For me, voting feels more hopeful than sniveling about how terrible things are.

When our worldview is in the minority (in my case, frequently), that's when it's most important to be counted. Every election is another opportunity to demonstrate what we believe; another day to resist plutocracy and oligarchy; another day to stand up for justice.

Voting is what holding people accountable looks like. Because we are part of a democratic, participatory national community, we own it. Just like shareholders 'share' responsibility for how a multinational corporation makes its profits, we are morally liable for our collective deeds and disgraces.

Voting puts us on the right side of history. "Apartheid was legal. The Holocaust was legal. Slavery was legal. Colonialism was legal. Legality is a matter of power, not justice," teaches comedian and social critic Chris Rock. For all posterity, the marks on my ballot connect my private conscience with the public use of power.

Compared to demonstrating in the street, voting is quite easy. You don't need to dodge tear gas at a protest march, spend a disagreeable night in jail after a civil disobedience, or sweat in the hot sun during a political rally. The secret ballot avoids all those unpleasantries. Not only that, but many polling stations come equipped with a thermostat-controlled climate system that we get to use free-of-charge.

Abdicating our electoral duty manifests privilege and entitlement as much as anything else we are likely to do in our daily lives. It's odious proof of a narcissistic disregard for our community.

—∞—

Elections have consequences for the causes and communities that you and I care about. Consider two life and death examples. First: killing moms and babies. Second: war and peace.

Right now, somewhere in an under-developed, under-served part of the world, a woman who we don't know is in labor. Let's assume that she lives in an isolated rural village. Nine months ago, she probably didn't have access to family planning information, let alone contraceptives. As her contractions intensify, complications ensue. She is without medical care. No doctors, no primary health clinic. By the time you finish reading this essay, she'll be dead.

"Every minute, at least one woman dies from complications related to pregnancy or childbirth—that means 529,000 women a year. In addition, for every woman who dies in childbirth, around 20 more suffer injury, infection or disease—approximately 10 million women each year," reports the World Health Organization. In the developing world, 220 million women lack access to basic family planning and contraceptive health care.

Non-existent reproductive health care steals a woman's chance to make, in the trenchant phrasing of the UN Population Fund, "crucial choices about their own bodies and futures." Reproductive services (information about safe sex, family planning counseling, contraceptives, child-birthing care and affordable access to safe abortions) are life-saving.

If you didn't know any of these facts—my mistake. I had assumed that you were an informed global citizen.

Adhering lockstep to Republican doctrine and practice, four days into his administration, the new president re-imposed the so-called gag rule, banning any nonprofit organization funded by US foreign aid from even talking about abortion. Marie Stopes International predicts that, as a result, by the next inauguration there will be 6.5 million unintended pregnancies, 2.1 million unsafe abortions and 21,700 maternal deaths. The horror compounds when babies die at birth.

If health justice for moms and babies matters to you, you don't have to be a gynecologist or public health worker to do something about it. You don't need to start an innovative social venture delivering healthcare services. You don't have to make a donation to a women's health clinic. You don't even have to hold open a door for a pregnant woman. You do need to vote for political candidates who support women's health and reproductive rights. I vote against any political party that, driven by either principled conviction or political kowtowing to its fundamentalist, religious base, opposes family planning services in US foreign aid programs.

The woman about to die in labor, and the other women in her village, can't vote in the next American election. But we can.

—∞—

Let me take you back to the year 2003. The United States is on the verge of invading Iraq. On February 15th, in the frosty early morning hours, protesters gathered near the California State Capitol. The skies were clear, but our hearts and minds were clouded at the prospect of war.

Spandex-clad parents pushed strollers decked out with peace symbols; scruffy students carried hand-printed signs dripping in blood-red ink; aging peaceniks with gray hair looked sadly fatalistic as they marched. The diverse complexion of California joined together in common cause, and joined 36 million people worldwide in public demonstrations against another ill-advised American war. Humans on the move, united in a movement, have rhythmic power, and I felt it that day. Voices combined; a chorus of conviction. Power to the people.

But peace never had a chance. Without even so much as a flickering pause to acknowledge our collective concern, the war hawks and the chicken hawks started bombing. The Bush-Cheney Administration, aided and abetted by a cowed Congress and a stampeded media, took the nation to war. A lone Congresswoman voted *No*. The night sky over Baghdad flamed open with terror and death. Without electoral power, the peace movement watched: impotent; powerless; paralyzed.

If, three years earlier, the Bush-Cheney presidential ticket had been defeated, these war crimes might have been avoided. We'll never know for sure. We do, however, know the Florida vote margin that brought about the George W. Bush presidency: 537 ballots.

—∞—

Some social sector analysts and academics parse social entrepreneurship, partitioning it off from public service, political activism and committed citizenship. The distinction is sophistry. Voting with your impact investment dollars, voting with your volunteerism, voting with your donation, voting with your career choice, and voting with your ballot are all on the same continuum of change-making social entrepreneurship.

Understanding how change happens, and doesn't happen, is central to our social action work. For one example, women's *economic* empowerment would hardly exist if women's *political* empowerment hadn't emerged from the Dark Ages. "Those who came before us risked all of their property, their reputations, their freedom and their lives to push the boundaries of democracy," writes political activist Jim Hightower in 'Rebellion Is What Built America'. "Elizabeth Cady Stanton, Lucretia Mott, Lucy Stone, Susan B. Anthony, Sojourner Truth, Sarah and Angelina Grimke and others organized a movement in the 1840s to obtain voting rights for women. They were ridiculed, harassed and defeated again and again. None of the founders lived to cast a single vote." The 19th Amendment to the US Constitution followed, and today women (and men) have the power to vote for (or against) economic sexism.

Elections force us to get outside the echo chamber, to stop editing out people with whom we disagree. Most days, social entrepreneurs are on autopilot, a feedback loop of unexamined political correctness and policy orthodoxies. For example, I assume that neither of us are wingnuts in denial about environmental science. Likewise, I assume that we acknowledge ingrained institutional racism and shun hateful, racist reactionaries. Good for us, but lasting social change depends on dialogue with our adversaries. Elections are an opportunity to do just that.

Elections reveal and reinforce my civic values and character. Walking a precinct, talking to a neighbor or posting a sign in my window are the public ways that I authenticate my progressive hopes for the future.

What would we think of an environmental scientist who researched in the morning, but littered in the afternoon? What would we think of a foundation that, in the morning, made grants to peace groups, but in the afternoon invested in gun merchants? What would you think of me if I wrote this essay, but failed to vote my conscience on election day? You might well decide that I am a hypocrite, morally suspect and intellectually dishonest.

Before we qualify as changemakers, there is the small the matter of the soul beneath our social entrepreneurship. I vote for the same reason that my heart beats and my head thinks. I'm politically-active because I'm a social entrepreneur.

—∞—

If you follow the daily news, it's pathetically simple to find an excuse for not voting. Maybe you've decided that not voting is political purity—a form of protest. Maybe you're in a chippy mood because politics is corrupted by big money, controlled by special interests and corroded by polarized political debate. Every social entrepreneur, including me, shares your dismay. However, abstention is not, in and of itself, social change.

Trash-talking politics is as mundane as fantasizing about what I would do if I were the boss of everything. Unless I'm voting for myself, no candidate will ever be quite good enough.

For my entire my adult life, no major or minor political party has had the wisdom to endorse 100 per cent of my policy positions. Likewise, no individual candidate has passed all of my policy and political litmus tests. Persistently and reliably, my government has disappointed me. Always, it moves too slowly. Often, it moves sideways or backwards. Frequently, it doesn't move at all.

Trash-talking politics is as mundane as fantasizing about being the boss of everything. Unless I'm voting for myself, no candidate will be good enough.

As change agents, sorrowed by the world's difficulties, our tolerance for political bullshit is zero. We want candidates who are informed, empathetic and genuine. We want candidates with coherent, comprehensive policy plans and, dammit, we want those plans summarized succinctly and with conviction.

Election time, on the other hand, seems like a cascade of cracked mirrors and crackpot theories, of political mumbo-jumbo, inauthenticity, empty promises, prepackaged candidates, anodyne policy views, hypocrisy and sanctimonious lecturing. It's all a turnoff.

For all that, elections are about governing priorities, not purity. As concerned citizens, we care about a nearly-infinite array of issues—from jobs and trade to education and public health; from racism and sexism to clean energy and rebuilding bridges. Not all issues, like not all law-breaking, are equally important. Illegal parking is not as grave as grand theft auto. Littering is a misdemeanor, but denying climate science is a clear case of global assisted suicide. Over-funding the military is more threatening than under-funding the arts. If every issue and every grievance are equally urgent, then none are.

Not voting, or voting for an obscure candidate, is the practical equivalent of abandoning any realistic chance that our justice agenda will come to fruition. As pragmatic social entrepreneurs, that's not a legit option. We show up to make the hard choices. Of the candidates who have some reasonable shot at winning, I vote for the most progressive. However you define the word 'better', a better candidate who loses, loses.

When I pick a candidate to support, I recall Reverend Jesse Jackson's speech to the 1988 Democratic convention: "This is not a perfect party. We are not a perfect people. Yet, we are called to a perfect mission. Our mission: to feed the hungry; to clothe the naked; to house the homeless; to teach the illiterate; to provide jobs for the jobless; and to choose the human race over the nuclear race. My constituency is the desperate, the damned, the disinherited, the disrespected and the despised."

As activists, social entrepreneurs and citizens—we engage. In the era of the Trump/Republican Wasteland, there are five platforms for resistance: investigative journalism, public interest lawsuits, public demonstrations, acts of personal resistance, and the next election. All options reject the temptation to normalize political meanness and cruelty. Each one stiffens our spines; reminds us that we are not alone; recognizes that the Trump/Republican Wasteland lost the popular vote; and reassures us that America has not lurched to the political right. When we protest, we send a message of solidarity to oppressed groups suffering the latest political atrocity. Let's face it, there's something uplifting, inspiring, simply gorgeous about people marching for justice.

That said, when we march, when we clamor at town hall meetings, when we stay informed, and when we file lawsuits: we're playing defense. When we win elections: we're playing offense. The only *proactive*, politically-sustainable option is to beat the Trump/Republican Wasteland in the upcoming 2018 mid-term congressional elections. This is so obvious that I blush even to mention it.

If justice and social progress are on your life agenda, it's a rookie mistake not to vote early and often. Even if you don't have any political views, register to vote anyway. You might stumble across your citizenship on the way to the polls. If not, you can always borrow mine.

Take Two: Bystander

Rosalinda Sanquiche, 49, is Sustainability Consultant and Board Member of the International Society of Sustainability Professionals. Hometown: St. Augustine, Florida/San Juan, Puerto Rico. Favorite pastime: biking, reading. Guilty pleasure: movies with fast cars.

"Jonathan and I once indulged in a rant against non-voters in which he articulated the cogent and emotionally-appealing arguments he puts forth in this essay. I would add that if you don't vote, how can you complain? Complaints motivate social entrepreneurs—against pollution corridors; racist international aid; mine worker conditions. Complaining helps me identify the bad, and act. In a tirade against the actual people mandated to do good on our behalf, I can point out their stupidity, greed and conceit.

"Can we rant if we did nothing to prevent their election? Can we non-hypocritically march against a malicious law if we didn't vote in favor of a human rights ordinance protecting the LGBT community?

"If you don't vote, you can't bitch. Jonathan will call you on this. I will deny you a complaining technique better than #DreamAct. I have on fax speed-dial my elected officials down to the district legislature representative. Faxes show you care enough to write your grievance, find the number and take the minute to fax. One fax counts as 1,000 to 10,000 constituents. These work—I've gotten personal calls from local reps. How cool is that? I'm happy to share this list along with names and addresses to cc: everyone (including the President of the United States). I'll even template the letter for you.

"'Dear_____, I'm concerned about_____. I am an active and vocal constituent in [city/state] and I vote'. If you can't complete this sentence, you don't get my speed dial. I don't trust you to be informed, to take action. Emailing you my letter is a 90-second waste, time better spent with people who have proven they give a damn.

"Jonathan will call you out. I won't listen to your whining. We both will lose respect for you. The good news, you can get back in our good graces by voting next time! If you do, and you live in Florida, call me. I have a nifty way to reach your representatives."

POWER

The first power of social entrepreneurship is the power to raise hell.

Powerless. It's the feeling that you get just after your mouth says the one thing that your brain really did not want you to say—and it's too late to apologize. It's the feeling in college when a lecture turns boring—and you're stuck in the front row. It's the feeling when your best friend falls in love with the wrong person—and you can't do a damn thing about it.

Powerless is a woman encircled by social norms that make her feel vulnerable and alone. Powerless is an African-American male in a police spotlight during a routine stop. Powerless is a refugee family. Powerless is a prisoner of poverty.

Powerless is invisibility. It's being dissed as unpatriotic for criticizing the government. It's hearing 'Black Lives Matter' echo back as 'All Lives Matter' (as if to say 'Cure Breast Cancer' automatically implies 'Don't Cure Heart Disease'). Powerless is not having a voice or a vote.

Early in our careers, change agents discover that power is dynamic, relative, interactive, evolving, elusive and personal. A thousand faults of history have fated us to live in a refracted world of one-sided, multi-faceted power relationships.

Some days, I am power. Some days, I am not.

— ∞ —

If you are in a social group that is marginalized, you already know that not having power is nothing to be pleased about. From birth to death—our social conditioning, cultural norms, people's predetermined expectations about us, what we look like, and a zillion other factors define the outer edges, the limits, of our power. If you aren't clear-headed on what I mean, ask someone with a hijab, dark skin, foreign accent, physical disability or some other visible sign of *Otherness*.

In *The New Jim Crow*, Michelle Alexander reminds us that without power, "public discussions about racial caste in America are relatively rare." She also notes that "more African-American adults are under correctional control today (in prison or jail, on probation or parole) than were enslaved in 1850, a decade before the Civil War began." A myriad of deplorable reasons drive this national disgrace (read her book), but one clear reason is that, without sustained political power, communities of color struggle to keep their issues prioritized with other pressing public policy matters.

For an international example, consider the maldistribution of food. One out of seven people in the world is without the minimum daily calories needed to survive (300 million are children). They are slowly starving to death in a global concentration camp of hunger and deprivation. It's a genocide against the poor. A war crime without a war. "There's more than enough food on earth today to feed the world one and a half times over. The reason that people go hungry is because of the way we distribute food... as private property, and the people who starve are simply too poor to be able to afford it," concludes Raj Patel in *The Value of Nothing*. Social entrepreneurs are not suggesting that food, a basic life necessity, be socialized like roads, libraries or the military. We are suggesting that disruptive, radical, revolutionary alternatives should be on the public agenda. Instead, without power, the hungry are left to beg or die.

Power is ubiquitous in the life of the social entrepreneur. It's archaic nonsense to claim otherwise. In fact, to ignore or shun power is to sabotage the social justice work we care about, and is itself an act of power and privilege. That's why you and I need to talk about it.

—∞—

Power is like a gray San Francisco fog: a swirling miasma of leadership and followership, of haves and have-nots. Some days, we welcome its familiar embrace. Other days, it chills us.

On one hand, we admire the strong social sector CEO-founder-innovator-pioneer-visionary; the undaunted superhero surmounting insurmountable odds to produce meaningful change. At the same time—we adore collaboration, consensus, partnering, power-sharing, crowdsourcing, co-creation and singing kumbaya.

We want individuals and communities to have both personal and collective power. We want our human interactions (in particular between races, ethnicities, religions, genders) to occur with the least possible power differential. We want the powerfully rich to use their 'good cents' with good sense.

As American social entrepreneurs, we are comparatively fortunate. We enjoy status, money, freedoms, mobility, opportunity and privilege that we did not earn. Even if you and I don't feel privileged within the dominant American society, we are privileged in relation to the rest of the world. Consequently, for you and me, and for every other agent of change, one kind of power is the power to impose (or at least promote) our ideas, to social engineer the kind of world we dream of.

If wielding power is a social entrepreneurial sin, then I'm a first-class sinner and unrepentant recidivist. I prefer having authority, leadership, power to delegate, power to decide—the power to use power. My default setting is Founder/CEO Type-A 'hero-preneur'.

The Opportunity Collaboration is one example. As it stands today, this annual 'unconference' of 450 economic justice leaders from around the globe is essentially self-governing. Every minute of the four-day agenda is comprised of delegate-led group discussions. There are no plenary speakers, no expert panels, no PowerPoint presentations to get in the way of delegate-to-delegate dialogue. The recruitment and selection of new delegates are done by the delegate community. But, in its formative first years, before all this community collaboration and shared governance could materialize, the Opportunity Collaboration (which I founded) was an exercise in tyrannical, one-person rule. Sure, I listened and listened (and listened) to suggestions and ideas from lots of people and organizations, but as a practical matter, decisions had to be made on very tight timelines (hotel booked, staff hired, people invited, agenda printed, website started, financial risk taken, etc.). I was a committee of one.

As changemakers, empowerment and agency can't possibly mean never using our power. That would be like going out to dinner and not eating. Or witnessing injustice and not acting. Social entrepreneurs avoid the trap of empowering everyone but themselves. We may be scared of power for its own sake, but we trust ourselves to use it wisely. Change agents tilt their power towards peacemaking, social progress and inclusive economic opportunity. We marshal the power at our fingertips to create the world we want. Power is a tool, a means, a commodity, waiting to be applied to the problems that piss us off.

—∞—

The first power of social entrepreneurship is the power to raise hell. Every changemaker is a one-person bully pulpit. One of our coolest superpowers is the power to be first in our community to raise our voice. There is, of course, power in numbers and in collaboration, but that power arises from the amalgamation of individuals like you and me, each with their singular perspective. Every Opportunity Collaboration starts with a single delegate. Every petition starts with a single signature. Every picket line starts with a single picket. Every call-to-arms begins with a single shout.

In most places and in many circumstances, the mere act of asking a question upsets the entrenched and annoys the complacent. Indeed, the heart of social entrepreneurship is the oft-quoted George Bernard Shaw line from *Back to Methuselah*: "You see things; and you say *Why?* But, I dream things that never were; and I say *Why not?*"

Social activists use the question marks in our heads to challenge the status quo. "When you are tempted to make a statement, ask a question," taught renowned Sixties community organizer Fred Ross. Over time, gadfly questions insinuate themselves into the mainstream. Unanswered questions hover like pesky bumble bees. Our progressive point of view may not sting (yet), but we should always refuse to buzz off.

Questions beget follow-on questions, often snowballing into an avalanche of fresh thinking. For social entrepreneurs, questions catalyze controversy—a politics of new perspectives. It's the powerful core of the powerful social entrepreneur.

You and I can't do our social justice work without debunking, exposing, challenging, decrying the institutional rigidities that impede social progress. A posed question signifies that longstanding traditions and staid social norms are open to challenge—itself a heretical, disruptive and powerful social entrepreneurial idea.

Taking on the monumental stupidities – the false narratives, myths, canards, confusions, fictions, hypocrisies, folklore and urban legends – that enshrine the status quo is the fun part of social entrepreneurship. "There is something personally satisfying about being disagreeable by advancing the truth," rejoices John Kenneth Galbraith, former presidential advisor and Harvard economics professor (and a superhero of mine).

Even if we don't get called upon in a meeting (or, if we're talked over), we can ask questions during intermissions, in hallways, in letters to the editor, on talk radio, on social media—everywhere. As it happens, the majority of people you meet aren't mind readers, so it's on us to speak our truth or ask a probing question. Before you know it, without even breaking a sweat, we're questioning authority. It's a form of street democracy. Anyone can do it.

Wherever the councils of government are closed; wherever elites hide in guarded country clubs; wherever class, race, status and financial wherewithal influence the courts; wherever economic opportunity is sparse; wherever justice is a distant dream: a lacerating question is like a searchlight shined on a cockroach.

Crucially, hell-raising is also a survival tool. Even if no one is listening, it reminds all of us that *you* are *you*. Peter Dreier, in *The 100 Greatest Americans of the 20th Century*, recounts the story of the pacifist minister A.J. Muste. Night after long night in the Sixties, Muste kept a single candle burning in front of the White House as a vigil of conscience to protest the Vietnam War. One evening, a journalist challenged Muste, asking if he realized that his one-person demonstration was ineffective and unlikely to change government policy. Muste replied, "Oh, you don't understand. I'm not holding a vigil to change the government. I'm holding a vigil to make sure the government doesn't change me." When I ask a question, I re-ignite my flickering conscience. I light a candle.

—∞—

Another social entrepreneurial power is when you and I act in concert with others. Collaboration is power. Community organizing is power.

In our social sector careers, networks are a functional tool for finding a job, fundraising, starting a political action, and so on. But, as we talk about in *Connections*, there's more to it than that: community empowerment and social justice put down deep roots when we build networks of trust and collaboration. In some respects, the totality of social entrepreneurship depends on social capital 'wealth creation'.

Think of all the ways in which social trust facilitates life. Asking someone to 'watch my stuff' at a coffee shop or airport lounge while I use the restroom is a simple case of social trust. The sharing economy (think: Lyft and Airbnb) means trusting the total stranger we let into our personal space. The base-of-the-pyramid consumer catalog company that I co-founded (Copia) depends on customer-merchant trust: customers pay in advance for their merchandise and then wait two days for delivery. Microfinance programs throughout the Global South depend on village-level social trust among groups of borrowers. In the pre-incorporation phase of my newest social venture, soliciting informal feedback about my business plan requires social trust—the common, and usually unspoken, expectation that my idea will not be 'stolen' or plagiarized.

As meeting conveners, you and I decide the agenda and – of equal importance – we also decide who receives an invitation. If we are thinking clearly, we use our invitational power to unmarginalize the marginalized (defined however you like). In the cracks between justice and injustice, we raucously clamor for more inclusive decision-making, more engaged communities, for bigger boardrooms. We are continually asking: *Who deserves to be part of this decision? Who has privilege and power excluded? Who is not in the room?*

—∞—

Whatever our brand of social change, our justice missions and our social ventures need us to show up with a clear-eyed understanding of our capacity (a power word) to leverage political and financial resources (a power phrase) to make things happen. We are each powerful, in our own way and in our own time.

As our adult lives and professional careers begin, it's under-standable to feel as though everyone has power but us. Everyone else (parents, professors, police, politicians, even parking lot attendants) seems to have an ordained measure of authority. No matter who we are and what we have accomplished, for our entire lives there's always somebody more powerful, more grandly-titled, more financially well-off.

The only antidote is to find your own power. Whining about the authority or influence that we *don't* have may be cathartic, and an accurate observation, but social progress is not served by wallowing in our victimhood. Likewise, to call ourselves virtuous because we are powerless is moronic—like boasting that we are frugal because we are poor.

To increase your power, use the power you have. I've assembled a few notes about claiming power, each one actionable; ready to go; locked and loaded. The missing element in each? You.

Outrage is power. Offended indignation is power. Enraged sorrow is power. Righteous anger is asymmetric power; typically, the comfortable and the complacent don't use it.

Truth is power. Even if you have to softly whisper it, speak the truth when no one else will. Kwame Anthony Appiah, in *Experiments in Ethics*, recounts this story: "The historian Martin Gilbert tells of a Polish peasant woman, during the Second World War, who happened to hear a group of villagers planning to throw a little Jewish girl in a deep well. The woman said, 'She's not a dog after all', and the girl's life was saved. The peasant offered no indication of grand theory, the inherent dignity of man, the inequity of Nazism, the injustice of religious discrimination, the workings of natural law, the sacredness of life, or the primacy of rights. Just a simple comment."

Tenacity is power. Our social justice careers start slowly, then momentum takes over, moving us forward faster and faster. Patience and perseverance, sustained and unrelenting pressure, builds our power. "It takes a certain kind of person to step forward when hope is hard to find. Changemakers have a relentless persistence," observes Kennedy Odede, the Founder of Kenya-based Shining Hope for Communities.

Audacity is power. The unexpected is power. The unconvention-al is power. As one anonymous social critic teaches, "When tempted

197

to fight fire with fire, remember the fire department usually uses water." This is also the thesis of Malcolm Gladwell's book *David and Goliath* with its tantalizing subtitle: *Underdogs, Misfits and The Art of Battling Giants.* In military terms, remember the winning guerrilla tactics of both the American Revolution, and the Vietnam War. And, remember the American civil rights movement's use of non-violence to stop the violence of Jim Crow.

Naming is power. When the characterization fits, name the destroyers and the haters. Anything else is sanitized bullshit. "There is an expectation that we can talk about sins, but no one must be identified as a sinner; newspapers love to describe words or deeds as 'racially charged' even in those cases when it would be more honest to say 'racist'; we agree that there is rampant misogyny, but misogynists are nowhere to be found; homophobia is a problem, but no one is homophobic," writes Teju Cole in 'The White-Savior Industrial Complex'.

Simplicity is power. Complexity favors the status quo. "You have to turn the invisible into something other people can see," says Austen Kleon in *Show Your Work.* Of course, you and I both realize that issues and problems require serious, nuanced, sophisticated, holistic solutions, but part of our job description as change agents is to simplify what we have to say, so that everyone is empowered to understand us.

Knowledge is power. Change happens when people armed with knowledge use it. Learn from the wisdom (and mistakes) of others. We are not the first to try to change the world. There's a decent chance that other good people have things to teach us, experiences to share, and good jokes to tell.

Money is turbocharged power. Every dollar spent, every dollar invested, every dollar donated is a vote for or against something. My views are hardwired inside every budgeting decision I make. Money talks, bullshit walks.

Citizenship is power. As we discuss in *Bystander,* your opinion is important, but mouthing off within your circle of friends or on social media is weak tea compared to casting your vote and, even more powerfully, electioneering. Luckily, you can pursue any career you want and still vote your informed conscience. If you tutor a child, you might be tutoring the next President of the United States of America;

when you vote, you're creating a community of conviction worthy of that child.

Chutzpah is power. Assume your power to be seen and be heard. We all know people who seem to have a personal authority, a kind of command charisma. Neither of us can change our personalities, but you and I can practice owning the room by owning our right to be there. Simple tricks: 1) Speaking succinctly is more powerful than prattling on; 2) Prefacing remarks with a self-deprecating apology undercuts the message; 3) Eye contact is powerful.

Listening, just listening, is power. Listening is also a form of power-sharing. "When we listen, we must also consider the lens through which the person is speaking. Peoples who were colonized, exploited, abused and whose voices have never really been heard often do not have the language or confidence to speak their truth. Therefore, we must be mindful of the power dynamic that may inherently play a role in our conversation. We must learn how to ask more open, generative questions to hear what is actually being said," counsels Amy Paulson, Founder of the Global Gratitude Alliance.

Forgiveness is power. Forgiveness reinforces empathetic behavioral norms and caring values. I try to follow the unforgettable advice of psychiatrist Thomas Szasz in *The Myth of Mental Illness*: "The stupid neither forgive nor forget; the naïve forgive and forget; the wise forgive, but do not forget."

We are power: You and I don't need an exalted title, a prestigious office or the traditional trappings of power to move our social justice agenda forward. As Jim Hightower, former Editor of *The Texas Observer*, advocated: "Even a little dog can piss on a big building."

— ∞ —

What did activists talk about before we talked about social entrepreneurship? Answer: *Power.* Personal power. Political power. Institutional power. We asked ourselves: Whom should power serve? And, why do some of us have power, while others don't? And, what should we do to equalize, to democratize, power?

As social entrepreneurs pushing systemic change, you and I need to understand our power in relationship to the power structures that marginalize, degrade and dismiss people. We need a workable explanation of how we got into the mess we're in—a theory of the case (to borrow a legal concept).

My microfinance work at the nonprofit MCE Social Capital is one example. We finance small individual business loans so that women can earn some money to feed their kids, pay medical bills, buy clothes, etc. Widening my analysis, I don't ever forget that microloans are, in the first instance, necessary because the global banking system (money=power) fails, miserably and hurtfully, to serve impoverished women. Call it a market failure or call it gender discrimination. Call it chocolate soufflé if you like, but the larger context informs my selection of key performance indicators (KPIs) which invariably, for me, turn on reaching women at the deepest levels of economic isolation.

In our daily work, the victims of gender, racial and class oppression get the benefit of the doubt. To pick a stark example, instead of innocent until proven guilty, we don't need a judge and jury to condemn a sex trafficker; instead, we act immediately to rectify the injustice even if the perpetrator is never arrested. Whether or not a polluter is convicted and punished, my social entrepreneurship compels me to take corrective action to protect the environment. When unfair power dynamics are afoot, compassion and common sense put social entrepreneurs on the side of the underdog.

—∞—

Every action and every voice moving towards social justice invite an opposite (and sometimes unequal) reaction. If change is in our hearts, then glossing over the fractures and disagreements between what the defenders of the status quo think, and what you and I think, is dishonest. "It goes without saying that injustice is a commonplace. But one must never, in one's own life, accept these injustices, but must fight them with all one's strength. This fight begins in the heart," writes James Baldwin in *Notes of a Native Son.*

Throughout our lives, we are socialized (or more accurately, tranquilized) to soften our viewpoints, to sandpaper the sharp edges of our insights, to speak with ambiguity and tempering adverbs. We are socially-conditioned to avoid conflict. But who benefits when we are mealy-mouthed? Neither truth, nor justice, nor social change.

With good reason, the world associates raw, unchecked power with manipulation, avarice, aggrandizement, narcissism, conquest, domination, hegemony, tyranny and sociopathy. The power to compel. The power to crush. Guns, bombs, and violence are the imagery of power.

In the common parlance, power is understood in simplified, static dyads or polarities. You have it; I don't. Personal power versus institutional power. The franchised versus the disenfranchised. The haves versus the have-nots.

Moreover, in the day-to-day experience of power, we tend to think in hierarchical, institutional terms. Government, churches, the military, sports teams and corporations come to mind. But top-down organizational charts with lots of little boxes connected by solid or dotted lines only explain part of the power dynamic.

Consequently, the Founder of Share Our Strength, Bill Shore, in *The Light of Conscience* gives us the concept of 'moral entrepreneurs'. Without a moral compass, power is either pointless or dangerously pointed backwards. Conscience justifies power. Anything less debases us. No morality, no mission.

Conscience without power is like physics without math, music without rhythm or my car without wheels. If we are in a position of power (formally or informally; because we sought power or because our privileged birth bestowed it), let's be an ally to those without it. Stand by, and stand *with*, the overlooked voices in the room. Let's expand who's at the decision-making table. Let's finance social innovations for power-sharing.

Auspiciously, power – like learning and loving – is not a zero-sum game. Some power is exercised privately, like powerfully doing the right thing when no one is looking. Some power is exercised in community, like voting or working together to establish a public benefit. For you and me, as makers of social justice, the greatest feeling in the world is sharing our power the one person in the room who has none.

Take Two: Power

Alexandra McGee, 27, is the Community Power Organizer at MCE. Hometown: Middletown, CA. Favorite pastime: dreaming about homesteading. Guilty pleasure: boba tea.

"I struggle with the idea of power. Our society largely values power that is aggressive, which is a dangerously limited perspective. I understand that an activist can create the most impact by leveraging power (think: Robin Hood). However, as a nonviolent person, I fear that I'll be guilty by association if I use tools of power.

"The powerful have left a slimy trail of abuses and disgraces as they ooze through history and into modern day. It *is* tempting to avoid the shame associated with that legacy by identifying as 'powerless'.

"And herein lies the complexity of identity: as the mixed bilingual educated daughter of two cultures raised in rural California, the key to surviving this entanglement of power, privilege, and shame became the ability to switch between identities. If 'white' meant power, I made sure people knew of my Latino heritage. If 'urban' meant power, I'd wear my cowboy boots. If I could believe that I didn't benefit from systems of power, then I wouldn't be responsible for changing them.

"Turns out, hiding behind masks of marginalization is a slippery slope, a purity game where nobody wins. Eventually, I realized I could wield tools of power without them using me. Tools like local politics.

"I'll tell you a secret. You have local elected officials who *have to* listen to your concerns. After attending many Council meetings, I know firsthand that almost nobody takes advantage of the public comment period. This is your opportunity to speak truth to power. This is your opportunity to advocate for your vision of the future and possibly receive help in making it a reality.

"Vibrating your vocal chords with heartfelt opinion for 3 minutes is power. Rather than being ashamed of power, redefine it. *Empower yourself* with the courage to dive into the messy fabric of our shared society to take a stand for justice."

HEGEMONY

I'm a proselytizing missionary, preaching a gospel of progressive ideals about economic, environmental, racial, gender, and social justice.

Antigua, Guatemala is a picturesque UNESCO World Heritage Center. The charming central *zocalo*, chic garden restaurants, restored Spanish colonial architecture, trendy boutiques and quaint buildings in bright gold, blushing red and fading turquoise make it easy for tourists to forget that, just ten minutes' drive outside of town, the predominant reality isn't quite so picturesque. Life there includes loving families, laughter, home-cooked meals and bucolic scenery—but it also includes poverty, limited opportunity and entrenched patriarchy. As with most places in the world, life in Antigua is complex and convoluted.

One balmy summer, I was lucky enough to find myself in Antigua on a family holiday, staying in a private home complete with personal staff. Three times a day, the housekeeper-cook prepared a scrumptious meal while patiently allowing me to practice my Spanish.

As often happens in these situations, my housekeeper and I struck up a temporary 'friendship'. Seasoned social entrepreneurs often hear an acquaintance proclaim, "Oh, I was just in *such-and-such* country, and I loved the people." Commonly, a story ensues in which the visitor becomes 'good friends' with their tour guide, the innkeeper's family or the safari leader. When I am surrounded by waiters, maids, hotel clerks, translators and other service workers (who are paid to provide for my creature comforts), the truth is that nearly every person I come into contact with is incentivized to make me smile. Happy travelers tip better.

Hearing the rudiments of my housekeeper's daily routine triggered my sense of largesse and privilege. She was a single mom with a young child who, during the day, was left in the care of an aged grandmother. Walking an hour to work meant my housekeeper's day started before dawn and finished after dark. Apart from weekends, her only 'quality time' with her kid was while the little girl slept. Hearing this story about one of life's little inequities, I couldn't help but feel sad.

One day, while ambling about town, as a thank-you gift for my housekeeper, I purchased the sturdiest-looking bicycle I could find in the local bike shop. Instead of the one-hour trudge to and from work, my housekeeper could now breakfast with her daughter, cycle fifteen minutes to work, and arrive back home well before dark. Presenting it, we shared a moment of joy as I felt her gratitude.

Unfortunately, bicycles need servicing, replacement parts and the occasional new tire, none of which my housekeeper could afford. Within a year, the bike, rusting and inoperable, was discarded.

Seeking emotional relief from the glaring, chafing disparity between *my* family's holiday time contrasted with my house-keeper's daily absence from *her* family, and carried away with my self-styled Western capacity to problem-solve, I did what was obvious—not what was smart. And certainly without respecting my housekeeper's superior understanding of her own circumstances. All heart, no head.

If I had bothered to ask my housekeeper what she wanted, if I had honored her agency, or if I had been in-residence in her community (instead of just touristing through), perhaps she could have given *me* a gift: a clear understanding of how to better leverage my natural desire to help. Perhaps I would have learned that she coveted a sturdy pair of shoes. Maybe the sustainable solution was school fees to upgrade her earning power. When I paternalistically paid for a bicycle without paying attention to her agency, who knows what I didn't learn?

I don't regret what I did. I do regret the spontaneous foolishness with which I did it. I don't regret my generosity of spirit. I do regret the way that my generosity was wasted by *me*.

—∞—

Whenever and wherever I travel, I take myself with me. When I'm planning a new social venture, I think like myself. When confronted with a new idea, I filter it through my preconceived preferences, proclivities and phobias. What choice do I really have? "Be yourself. Everyone else is already taken," quipped Oscar Wilde.

When I arrive in a faraway township (or in an equally-unfamiliar, culturally-different, racially-segregated neighborhood a few blocks away from my house), I'm a captive of observer bias. "We don't see things as they are. We see things as we are," tartly noted the novelist Anaïs Nin. Healthcare professionals are likely to perceive a community's condition in terms of adequate or inadequate healthcare systems; engineers see a need for paved roads and irrigation pipes; internet geeks enthuse about apps and mobile money; economists thrive on economic opportunity plans.

Insofar as social entrepreneurs are committed to community-based, systemic change in this messed-up world, there's a better way. You and I can tap into local wisdom by asking, "Teach us how, or *if*, we might be helpful."

As it happens, I'm an American with an intellectual inheritance of Judeo-Christian moralities and Greco-Roman governance traditions—all nicely framed by a faithful confidence in scientific advancement. My life accomplishments fall under two main classifications: making money in the competitive, capitalist marketplace; and shaping public policy. When my mind is churning out cures for a societal malady, I have a tendency to mimic my life experiences.

As I drive with righteous determination towards my do-good destination, it's easy to concentrate on the road ahead, failing to remember the baggage stuffed in the trunk—the baggage I always carry with me. Wherever I go: I bring my culture, my core values, my management methodologies, my access to information and my global network of contacts. And, of course, I bring financial resources. I also bring the troubling backdrop of colonialism—the hegemonic context for American social entrepreneurship.

As an American social entrepreneur, a geographic accident of birth has awarded me a passport stamped with the power to spread my ideology of social change. Lest we forget: Western ascendancy has been largely won by force of arms, underwritten by a lucky abundance of natural resources, a wholesale land grab and genocide, superior industrial ability, slavery and an operational faith in white supremacy. The disturbing truth is that, under the guise of spreading civilization and commercialism to the peoples of the world, Westerners have exploited and terrorized just about everyone we've come in contact with. Plus, in modern times, American foreign policy has backed some brutally-effective dictators and despots. In many quarters of the world, that legacy leaves an understandable residue of suspicion.

Even if you and I try to respect local traditions, mindful of seen and unseen power structures, unavoidably we are a living, breathing Hawthorne effect (that is, the field agent's presence causes subjects to adjust their behavior). For example, if I ask an elder in an isolated, mountainous area to describe the barriers preventing him from sending girls to school, I might be communicating an entirely new idea—namely, that girls have untapped intellectual resources that merit educational opportunity. Inescapably, I'm spreading my contemporary, feminist ideas about gender equality.

"I am a white feminist. I want all people everywhere to be able to live lives free from oppression. This is what I, and other feminists, work towards..." writes Anne Theriault in 'The White Feminist Savior Complex'. "My intentions are good and my heart is, as they say, in the right place. Here in the West, we are taught to pity the women, those other women, living in other places, who do not enjoy the same rights that we do. We are taught to be thankful that we are not those women... When we take a closer look at these statements, however, their core message becomes clear: Our culture is better. We are more enlightened, more rational and more civilized."

When I say that you and I both have baggage, it's not a put-down. It's just the reality of the situation. We are all raised in a defining culture that frames our choices and constraints. It doesn't make us vile; nor does mean that our filters and perceptions are automatically wrong (or right). Nor does it mean that, as change agents, we can overlook, accept or condone the negative baggage of others.

As I go about my social change work, with the best of intentions, I judge cultural norms with my cosmopolitan, globalist, liberal, progressive, environmentalist, feminist, economic empowerment, human-dignifying, racially- and ethnically-inclusive values. I'm a mouthful of liberalities and prejudices which define the limits of my tolerance.

Equally, I am judged by others. Community residents, potential partners, clients, customers, local officialdom and merchants assess my intentions, my capabilities and my worth, both as a human being and as a change agent. From that basic and very natural starting point—people, communities and nations begin to build trust.

— ∞ —

Social entrepreneurs, by disposition and doctrine, prefer to honor indigenous traditions and promote community autonomy, authority and agency. We honor the differences and distinctions between peoples and cultures. We respect local leaders, local customs and local decision-making. We seek community buy-in.

Until we don't.

With disruption in my social entrepreneur's heart, I innovate myself into other people's business. Change and risk-taking, progress and innovation, all epitomize the ethos of the American change agent. In economic terms: creative destruction. Renewal. Redemption. Rebirth. Whatever you and I call our theory of social change, for the people being disrupted, we are constantly in danger of 'imposing' our values on them.

When social entrepreneurs enter a community, we presume a lot. After all, who asked me to show up, dragging along my newfangled ideas about clearing landmines with sniffing rats; fighting malaria with bednets; family planning for women? Clean-burning cookstoves to reduce indoor air pollution? Supply chains to reach consumers in advanced economies? By what right am I in someone else's community to 'fix things' in *my* image, reflecting *my* value system, employing *my* techno-charged innovations and using *my* turbo-charged management skills?

Even the tacit expectation that local community members should take time away from their jobs, businesses and families to engage with us to implement *our solutions* hinges on the hegemonic subtext of money, influence and power. What makes us think we're worth it? Is it because we're well-intentioned? Because we bring bags of money? Because we're smarter?

On the edge of what we think of as 'civilization', people live in their own version of civilized society, ordered in a way I may not be able to see or (if I do see it) respect. "Even exploitation and oppression still make society work and establish some kind of order," jabs the political theorist Hannah Arendt in *The Origins of Totalitarianism.*

Orderly or not, some locally-venerated practices and traditions *really suck.* After learning that slavery in Mauritania is part of the social fabric (not to mention an apparent economic linchpin), I'm still against it. After learning that Bangladeshi textile factories have significantly contributed to reducing the national poverty rate, I still push for worker safety standards. After learning that female genital mutilation is linked to religious practice in Egypt, I still oppose it. After learning that the American death penalty dates back to the founding of the country, I still think it's barbaric. No doubt, you have examples of your own.

The thing is: we are doers, not voyeurs. We're not passive about poverty or pollution. We are not going to stand idle in the face of fascism or unfairness. We are in the justice business, and justice demands our energetic allegiance. Either we take an active part in the world—or a part of who we are is lobotomized.

At the end of the day, social entrepreneurs practice *values hegemony.* We colonize with a righteous devotion to economic opportunity and ecological sanity. Our bible is the Universal Declaration of Human Rights. Our crusading sword is secular economics. Our votive candles burn on the altar of entrepreneurialism and innovation. I'm a proselytizing missionary, preaching a gospel of progressive ideas about economic, environmental, racial, gender and social justice.

— ∞ —

The paradigm challenge for us is captured by the Latin question *Quo warranto?* (By what authority?) By what authority are you, or I, or anyone, empowered to resolve the matter at hand? When differences of viewpoint (or complete disagreements) arise, the pivotal question is *Who decides?* When injustice, cruelty, economic deprivation, sexism, racism, environmental destruction or human indignity stand unchallenged in the town square, who decides what is best?

Consider this hypothetical from a make-believe village: A well-conducted needs assessment reveals a community consensus for both a religious sanctuary for *spiritual* refreshment and a saloon for *adult* refreshment. After much public discussion and debate, but no real controversy, community leaders confirm, without equivocation, the vital importance of both a better church and a bigger cantina. Or, maybe it's a bigger church and a better cantina. Whatever.

Predictably, our priorities might differ from the community's. Maybe you and I want to devote our time and money towards building a health clinic or school. Maybe our particular skill sets do not include purveying either prayer or booze. Maybe the government contract, foundation grant or donor dollars underwriting our social entrepreneurship are predicated on deploying farm irrigation systems to increase crop yields, distributing sanitary pads to keep girls in school, or paving roads to move goods to market.

Do we have the right to overrule local opinion? Sometimes? All the time? Never? What would you do? Do you pitch in to rebuild the church, take bartending lessons, or go home? Or, using the power of money, do you enforce your particular priorities and solutions?

In accepting responsibility for social entrepreneurship, you and I accept the inescapable tension between two very legitimate impulses: the impulse to respect a community, and the impulse to change it. Consequently, no matter what we decide our role is (whether that is throwing ourselves at a problem, or doing nothing whatsoever) someone is bound to conclude that it's the wrong thing to do, or that we are the wrong people to do it (or both).

Take, for instance, the base-of-the-pyramid consumer catalog company Copia (that I co-founded). As we worked to raise the all-important seed capital needed to beta test the idea in the peri-urban neighborhoods of Nairobi—numerous social impact investors and philanthropists refused to invest because they believed that the catalog should exclusively (or at least overwhelmingly) sell so-called pro-poor products, such as solar lights, healthcare items, water purifiers, clean-burning stoves, irrigation pumps and other consumer products deemed by Westerners as 'good for people'. *Say what?*

In an article entitled 'Product Paternalism', I made my position clear: "We might sleep better selling a screened product selection to the poor (that, hypocritically, we would never accept for ourselves), but it ignores the inconvenient fact that... product taxonomies require a flat, static and crimped view of the actual economic lives of the impoverished... In any event, a handy classification system is right in front us: Let the consumer – most probably a female making family purchasing decisions – choose. Yes, the Copia catalog sells solar lights, school supplies, and farm implements. It also sells nail polish, paper towels, diapers, detergent and toys. The consumer, not Copia, decides. Female consumers, businesswomen, mothers, daughters and wives in the developing world don't need a stack of smartass Westerners – most probably men like me – deciding what they should buy. They can handle that without our brilliance."

Of course, the frustration we feel is that there are no pat, easy-to-follow, hard-and-fast formulas for successfully navigating around our hegemony. Like so much of what we do in the field of social change, in the end you and I rely on our best intuition and open-hearted judgment. Put these six design notions in your pocket:

1. Step one is listening and learning. Every community, jam-packed with its various subcultures, is a hybrid mix of goodness and badness, a blend of the noble purpose and ignoble means, a mashup of the naïve and the sophisticated. "As an organizer, I start from where the world is, as it is, not as I would like it to be," notes Saul Alinsky in *Rules for Radicals*. "That we accept the world as it is does not, in any sense, weaken our desire to change it into what we believe it should be." This is a tough, but necessary, balance requiring clarity of conviction and flexibility of approach.

2. Simplistic thinking gets us nowhere. In our holy wars ('fighting' poverty and 'fighting' climate change) we teeter-totter between dueling, and diverging, stereotypes about the communities we care about. On the one hand, the 'noble savage' has a vibrant culture and basic dignity worthy of preservation at all costs. On the other, the 'primitive savage' has archaic rituals and customs that impede progress (whatever that means). Neither one accurately captures the richness, vibrancy and contradictions inherent in the real lives of the real people in the real places where life is lived whether we are there or not.

3. To work on systemic, not episodic, solutions, you and
   I need to immerse ourselves in a community problem
   set until we sufficiently understand its complexities,
   creases and crevices. Like wartime spies, social entrepreneurs operate subversively: blending in, taking notes
   and then taking action to reform systems that favor the
   few at the expense of the many. Like all 'spies', we need
   local partners, trusted collaborators and activist allies.

4. "Don't start by designing fancy solutions; identify
   underserved needs first," advises Root Capital CEO
   Willy Foote in 'The Value of Naiveté: Three Tips for
   Aspiring Entrepreneurs'. "The field of social enterprise
   is filled with talk of new innovations and disruptive
   business models. It seems that people are always
   looking for the next big thing. But often, the
   solutions are pretty straightforward."

5. For our own integrity of mind, it helps to have a little
   self-awareness. Otherwise, we look like imbeciles. In
   January 2015, when we added our American voices to
   the international outcry over the killing of five French
   journalists (plus seven others) by terrorists, and in
   the very same month virtually ignored the slaughter
   of hundreds (maybe thousands) of Nigerians by the
   terrorist group Boko Haram, we diminished our moral
   authority. Likewise, when we decry the humanitarian
   refugee crisis in the Middle East and Europe, while
   neglecting deportation and employment exploitation of
   Latinos and Southeast Asian immigrants inside the US
   (or presidential bigotry against Muslims), what fools we
   must seem.

6. For my part, I think we do more realistic social change
   work when we acknowledge that cultural intermixing
   and cross-border values-sharing are unstoppable. If
   you have any doubt on this point, come with me to
   the Maasai Mara National Reserve in Kenya where,

seven centuries ago, semi-nomadic tribes settled on the savannah. To Western tourists and economic development workers, the Maasai are renowned for their sacred relationship to cattle and for wearing bright red textiles and colorful beaded jewelry. Today, without any apparent concern for tribal cultural pollution, village elders strap on digital watches and hook cell phones to their belts. As agents of change, you and I wouldn't want it any other way. We want an interconnected world. Importantly, it's not our decision. It's theirs.

Jocelyn Wyatt, Executive Director at IDEO.org, offers humility, not hubris, to protect our good intentions from clumsy implementation:

"Be a learner, not a hero. Before heading abroad, check your intentions. Are you going because you believe you have ideas to share and solutions to introduce? Or are you going because you really want to listen and learn and immerse yourself in the complexity?

"Be a listener, not a giver of advice. Instead of landing with answers to the complex, intractable challenges, engage people on the ground in conversations. Visit their homes and their workplaces, ask them questions and share something about your life with them.

"Be a bridge, not a beacon. Share your creative ideas, but be open to an equal exchange with people who know their own context best. Seek to connect your world of resources to those living without. Work with community-based organizations to write grant proposals, raise money for their organizations or connect them with press opportunities. For many of us, our networks are the most important asset we can bring. Imagine how you can leverage your networks rather than thinking of yourself as a solution-creator."

Most of all, it seems reasonable to expect that people living without advantage (defined however you like) have a unique expertise about their own lives. It also seems reasonable to assume that social entrepreneurs, economic development experts and policy gurus have valid expertise. Start a conversation. Ask. Suggest. Listen. Learn. Ask again.

—∞—

Hegemony is a heavy word. At the very least, it connotes a differential in power, autonomy and agency. Like a boorish, unwelcome party crasher, it bespeaks an arrogant disregard for the rights, needs and wishes of others.

For a human-level example, in some cultures people believe that a photograph steals your soul. To my atheist way of thinking, this is superstition. Regardless, I certainly don't want to 'steal' anyone's soul. I have enough trouble with my own. Thus, when it comes to photographing people, I am the ethical anthropologist.

In contrast, when it comes to upsetting local health practices (also religiously- or superstitiously-based), I have no qualms. For instance, I have no reservations quarreling with the Catholic Church about women's reproductive rights or introducing (over the objections of the local shaman) vaccines and cures for measles, polio, diphtheria, meningitis, yellow fever and tuberculosis.

Honestly, I don't have a working hypothesis about why respecting one set of local customs or traditions, and not another, is defensible. At first blush, you or I might postulate that health care matters more than a silly photograph, but many would argue that a person's religion and soul matter even more. At this point in my social entrepreneurship career, the best I can say is: *I'm still learning.*

From the realm of personal friendships, perhaps there is a useful prototype for calibrating the scales of intended and unintended hegemony. A friendship is satisfying and productive, and indeed can only exist, when both parties offer mutual respect, mutual learning and mutual interest. Friendship is reciprocal, or dual, agency.

My agency and community agency, my agency and your agency, are of a piece. If my eternal remit is to be who and what I am, then surely it's fair-minded to promote the agency of all those around me so they, too, can be who and what they are. We might just call that the beginnings of community-minded social entrepreneurship.

Take Two: Hegemony

Rajasvini Bhansali, 42, is the Executive Director of Thousand
Currents and a passionate advocate for participatory grassroots-led
social change. Hometown: Bombay, India/Berkeley, CA. Favorite
pastime: hiking. Guilty pleasure: eating Thai food every day.

"When I was a young social entrepreneur with all kinds of ideas about how my training as a technologist and management consultant could help people in rural Kenya, I had many humbling experiences that challenged my ideas. I learned that my local colleagues were not only brilliant and resourceful under unimaginable pressures, they had very clear dreams and visions for their community as a whole. I learned that in order to raise funding from development agencies, they often had to hide their local innovations or disguise them in language that western agencies could understand.

"So much of their creativity and wisdom was lost in language of need and problems, painting themselves as victims just to please the donors. This only perpetuated the arrogance of development funders who thought it was fact, their minuscule aid doled out with the burden of a hundred reports.

"I know I must remain vigilant against the cultural imperialism inside me. That internalized tendency that erases the knowledge and insights not found in textbooks, conferences or otherwise sanctioned by powerful institutions. I must guard against claiming as mine that which must appropriately be recognized as the innovations, ideas, experiments of indigenous, small scale farmers, black, disabled, transgender and rural peoples: people whose knowledge and wisdom has been historically seized, colonized and derided.

"As we enter into a new era of political discourse based on mistrust, suspicion, insularity and supremacy in the United States, each social entrepreneur is being called to embody creative, connected, and culturally-competent ways to tackle the root causes of poverty and injustice. And we must start with our own learning behavior based on reflection, dialogue, and connection, adopting transformative practices that can dismantle injustice and inequity from its very roots."

WHITE

If we coddle racists or rationalize away their hate speech, then racists might, mistakenly, think that they are normal human beings.

I was born a white baby. To this day, I'm still white. I'm told that's pretty normal. As an adult, I've become a white social entrepreneur. That's also normal. Most American-born social entrepreneurs are white.

As social entrepreneurs, America's race problem is the inescapable context for our work. It affects how we think, what we do and who we do it with. It plagues every all-white social venture management team, every all-white non-profit board of directors, every all-white public policy panel and every all-white social sector audience.

As I write this essay, I am a community of one: one white person and zero diversity. Yet here we are, discussing a topic that, by its nature, requires the voices of hundreds, thousands, millions of people: people with disabilities, women, Native Americans, African Americans, Hispanics, Asians, Muslims, Jews, Mormons, the various gender identity communities and, also, Caucasian Americans. Each group – and each individual within each group – has their own story and history; issues and challenges; talents and contributions to add to the work of social entrepreneurship.

Fair warning: in this essay, we explore black-white relations as a kind of short-hand for all the cultural, ethnic and racial crosscurrents currently challenging American social entrepreneurship. Moreover, I wrote this essay expressly for *white* American changemakers. While everyone is invited to join the conversation, the intended audience for this essay is people who look a lot like me. Given my own life history and family upbringing, and my early awakening to civil rights work,

I felt that I could talk with some degree of authentically through these two lenses.

We humans like to sort ourselves in every way possible. By cultural background, racial identity, gender, ideology, financial resources, politics and so on. We are creatures of the herd. Everyone has their own version of a safe, predictable country club. Homogeneity is a treehouse, open only to the trusted, the tried and the true. Behind our barricades, we draw comfort from thinking: *We are the same. We belong. We are safe.*

In everyday conversation, white social entrepreneurs forget that racial identity applies to us too. White is a skin color. White is a race. Rembrandt painted white ethnic art. Taylor Swift and Frank Sinatra sing white music. Hot dogs are white ethnic food.

White racial identity (like any other) is learned in youth. From our earliest days in diapers, emergent systems (family, playmates, school, neighbors, town, etc.) imprint upon us. As a result, what we perceive in our emotional, psychic gut to be 'normal' and 'safe' is different than what *other people* feel is normal and safe. My tribal comfort food is different than your tribal comfort food.

Whether crossing borders or crossing the street, the *Other* exists all around us, and everyone is the *Other* to someone else. No one who thinks about this doubts it.

—∞—

I grew up in a stable, hard-working, blue-collar, two-parent family. My mother completed high school. My dad did not. In spite of his early promise as a straight-A student, he was yanked out of junior high school to work to support his relatives—a story he could never talk about without sobbing. We lived above my parents' small retail store on a nondescript San Francisco street. Having never outgrown his Depression-era fear of economic ruin, my father never took a day off. My mother worked alongside my dad in the store. She was a blatant racist with a particular distrust of African-Americans, and a pure hatred of Arabs.

When I was 16, my parents and I spent a summer exploring America by car. The year was 1964. In June, as we departed San Francisco, three civil rights workers were killed in Mississippi. Throughout the summer, race riots torched inner cities and (after a three-month filibuster) Congress passed the Civil Rights Act. Mohammed Ali, James Baldwin, Dr. Martin Luther King, Jr. and Malcolm X were regularly featured in the news. In South Africa, Nelson Mandela was sentenced to prison. Inside our cozy car laden with snacks and word games, oblivious to a country rioting for our attention, the Lewis family headed to the New York World's Fair.

Along the way, we routed through the Southern states. Above drinking faucets and on restroom doors, I saw signs saying *Whites* and *Colored*. In Florida, we drove past a street protest of black families surrounded by state troopers, police cars, barricades and floodlights. Even though we were a white family, ostensibly with nothing to fear, fear filled our car. The memory of it still stings, like a slow-healing paper cut.

When we finally arrived at the Fair, I was transported to yet another world that was not my own. I saw prototypes of unimaginable wonders: the first 'picture phone', IBM computers, the 'house of the future' and an early-model color TV. The Futurama and Progressland exhibits (by General Motors and General Electric) were shrines to the technologies that everyone assumed would transform the world's dystopian challenges into utopian realities.

On the whole, the Fair studiously sidestepped the gaping racial wounds hemorrhaging across America. That said, at the Illinois state pavilion, Walt Disney presented "Great Moments with Mr. Lincoln" featuring an animatronic President Lincoln delivering a composite of his speeches. Stirred by the words, I watched it twice: "The world has never had a good definition of the word liberty... Let reverence for the law be breathed by every American... let it become the political religion of the nation; and let the old and the young, the rich and the poor, the grave and the gay of all sexes and tongues and colors and conditions, sacrifice unceasingly at its altars."

I liked the naïvely idealistic assumption that *We the People* could be unified and equal in our universal respect for law, liberty and justice. Years later, around the time I was starting college, the National Advisory Commission on Civil Disorders made headlines, calling out our national fault line with prophetic accuracy: "Our nation is moving towards two societies; one black, one white; separate and unequal." I read every word with the ideals of a dead president in my heart.

Leaving New York that summer, on the long car trip back to San Francisco, in the rare moments when my father spoke about black people, he did so from two unresolved vantage points. As a shopkeeper coping with black teenage shoplifters, he feared black people. As a human being, he empathized with the humiliation of Jim Crow. Once, on a long stretch of Kansas highway, his eyes tearing up, he asked me to imagine what it must be like for a black family—out for a drive on a sweltering summer day; thirsty children crying in the back seat; unable to stop for a sip of water from a public drinking fountain.

When high school reconvened that fall, I started wearing a Congress of Racial Equality button. I attended a couple of inter-faith youth symposia about race relations. Yet with all the superficiality and naïveté of youth, I never wondered why my private all-boys school, all my friends, and all my youth groups were a blur of whiteness. It is an oversight that this essay will not repeat.

—∞—

Unless we are members of the American Nazi Party, the Ku Klux Klan or a Donald Trump voter, it's unlikely that either of us has done much to *intentionally* promote racism in the United States. In our personal lives, we are probably kind and considerate to people regardless of their skin color. In our social entrepreneurship, we probably support campaigns for social justice, civil liberties and human dignity.

Nevertheless, take a look around. If you're in a classroom, board meeting, planning session, conference or other event populated mostly by white-skinned people, then it's a good guess that everyone there has similar educational backgrounds, similar career expectations, similar cultural mores, similar financial opportunities and similar problem-solving approaches. Reality check: *someone's missing.*

When we turn our moral imaginations to our own profession, it becomes apparent that social entrepreneurship has a case of institutional racism. Throughout our sector, people of color are underrepresented. Considering that we are some of the most justice-minded people on the face of the planet, it's a sadly puzzling stain on our field.

Since most social entrepreneurs can count, the challenge is not our ability to perform a real-time diversity census. The challenge is that the white face of racism feels so comfortably ordinary, so safely normative, so blandly respectable. As a result, the question *Who is missing?* goes unasked. In that empty moment, I may not be aware of my isolation, but isolated I am.

— ∞ —

Racism is a core American competency. We're really good at it. It's part of our national social fabric—along with our innovative spirit, our technological advancement and our adoration of sports. American slavery lasted 246 years (1619 to 1865); legal segregation, in the form of Jim Crow, lasted 89 years (1865 to 1954); legacy racism continues with no end in sight—the stubborn and pervasive backdrop for American social entrepreneurship.

Skeptical? Take a test. Check out a one-minute video by Jane Elliott entitled 'A White Audience Is Left Speechless by a Brilliant Question about Race'. Elliot asks an all-white audience if anyone is willing to change places with an African American. Not a single hand is raised.

We both know why. The statistics about life in a racially-fractured society are grotesque, an appalling inequality of opportunity and lost talent. Consider these realities:

1. For the past 60 years, black unemployment has consistently been twice that of white unemployment. Incredibly, this opportunity gap even applies to college graduates. Media reports about black crime, black life, black opportunity, etc. 'black out' this contextual reality.

2. African-Americans live in an under-reported economic opportunity war zone. For one example, "In a classic 2003 experiment, economists... sent two sets of nearly identical résumés to employers, the only difference being the names at the top: Greg, Emily, Jamal and Lakisha. Greg and Emily received 50 per cent more callbacks than Jamal and Lakisha," reports Freada Kapor

Klein (Kapor Center for Social Impact) in 'Outsiders Can't Lean In If They're Locked Out'. A wine merchant rejecting half of all vintage wines based on the color of the labels would make as much sense as rejecting résumés based on (um...) the color of the ink.

3. In his *New Yorker* piece 'The Hidden Cost of Race', James Surowiecki reports: "At current growth rates, it would take black Americans 228 years to have as much wealth as white Americans have today." If, starting to-day, white America agreed not to accumulate any more wealth – not one penny – then I can't wait to celebrate wealth equality in the year 2245.

4. When I was a new father, no one needed to warn me about white health care versus black health care. Black babies in the United States are two and half times more likely to die within a year of birth than white babies. Black moms are three times more likely to die in childbirth than white moms. Blacks with a broken leg are prescribed pain medication less often than white patients.

5. When my teenage son stumbled into a scrape with the law, I did not fret about whether he was going to get white justice or black justice. Did you know that every 28 hours (roughly, once a day), an African-American father, brother, uncle or son is killed by a police officer? Just for a mathematical comparison, that means that every 13 years, the total number of black men shot by police equals the total number of black men lynched during 89 years of Jim Crow.

6. After electing the first African-American President in its 240-year history, the American people put a race-baiting bigot in the White House. Maybe some Trump voters thought that 'White House' was an ingredient label, like 'Vanilla Ice Cream'.

Freada Kapor Klein reflects: "For all its promise and opportunity, Silicon Valley has long been insular, clubby and steeped in the pernicious myth of the meritocracy. We are color-blind and gender-blind, the story goes, and we only hire the best talent available. But if we accept that on its face, are we to conclude that blacks, Latinos and women of all backgrounds are simply not as smart as white and Asian men, or that genius is disproportionately concentrated in race-based subsets of the population? Of course not."

As social entrepreneurs, you and I would think it strange if the founder of a successful social venture admitted to financial illiteracy, lack of domain expertise or ignorance about current events. So why are we comfortable with racial and ethnic illiteracy? One factor is the coma of ignorance. Skin color isolates us behind an invisible force field constructed, day by day, from our monochromatic life experiences. Consequently, it's too damn easy to develop a 'justice blind spot', to forget that, for many black social entrepreneurs, life is riddled with unfairness, unreasonable expectations and 'starting line' disadvantage.

—∞—

Personally, I'm sick and tired of hearing the wise and well-dressed, the sage and the smart, the talking heads of TV and radio call for the umpteenth national conversation about race. Been there, done that. As you and I pursue our social sector careers, at every step we have the opportunity to get our moral shit together. Whether on our own, on a committee, in a planning meeting, or in private conversation, let's raise these diversity questions:

1. Consider your social venture hiring practices. It's as if we have taken on the diverse challenges of the world without inventorying the diversity of people we need to get the job done. Typically, social sector job announcements are written by committees. Everyone adds their preferred qualification: one colleague thinks field practice is desirable; another adds language competency; a third wants five years minimum experience (no, wait, let's make that five years *plus* a Master's degree). It's

221

much easier to say 'yes' to each addition than to defend the simple truth that the more requirements, the less likely the most culturally-capable candidates will apply. Why? Because a low-income student, working her way through school in an unrewarding, unsexy, shit job might have missed out on those exotic summer internships, costly language immersion programs or social entrepreneurship competitions. Don't create barriers that might exclude the very person your organization needs to take it in new directions.

2. If you are a grant-maker or impact investor, don't be the hypocritical asshole who is paid a generous compensation package for your labors (and you are worth it, I'm sure), but who carps about the salaries and benefits paid by your grantees or social impact investments. Every funder who scrimps on general overhead support contributes to assuring that entry-level jobs with meager salaries are closed to students with large student loan balances, a bunch of whom are probably students of color from lower-income families.

3. This suggestion will get us in hot water, so let's keep it to ourselves: accept and endorse the principle that, in some cases, hiring a person of color is *the* defining job attribute. Why shouldn't my social enterprise specifically recruit Muslims, especially if my program or social mission works in Muslim communities? Why doesn't it make sense to hire an African-American teacher to teach in schools with a high percentage of African-American students? Why isn't being a native Spanish-speaker the first requirement for working south of the Rio Grande? Most of all, if my team is currently all-white, the meritocratic thing is acknowledging that the person with *the most* to contribute to my team's creative brainstorming is *not* going to be white.

4. Get comfortable with the widest variety of people, races, religions, socio-economic classes, etc. Not at the theoretical level, but at the practical shake-hands, look-people-in-the-eye level. 'Seeing things in black and white' is not merely a turn of phrase. Most Americans live in racially- or ethnically-separated neighborhoods. We hang out, for the most part, in self-segregated friendship circles. Fact: there is a three out of four chance that you have no black friends. Put another way: only 25 per cent of white Americans have a black American friend.

5. As white social entrepreneurs, let's agree to stop self-consciously whining about belonging to the dominant culture, and our implied baggage of privilege. It is what it is. Every time I walk into a room, I'm inescapably a symbol of the history that precedes me. It's not fair that we are forced to deal with legacy racism, but it's also not fair that people of color are forced to deal with it. Former Australian Prime Minister Kevin Rudd, in a Parliamentary speech acknowledging his country's maltreatment of indigenous peoples, hit the nail on the head: "We are the bearers of many blessings from our ancestors. Therefore, we must also be the bearer of their burdens as well."

6. While we're on the subject, let's skip the deflections, gaslighting and hectoring bullshit about black people pulling themselves up by their bootstraps, getting a better education or becoming more entrepreneurial. Systemic injustice requires systemic disruption, not victim-blaming. Social change work is a primal scream in protest against the sins we inherit, not an excuse to pick on people without the same power and privilege that we enjoy.

—∞—

White social entrepreneurs have a unique opportunity to dialogue with other white people. Whenever and wherever white people cluster, we (like any other racial, religious, gender and ethnic group) speak with a more relaxed familiarity. When white colleagues forget their better selves by doing or saying something racist, that's the perfect time to jump into the uncomfortably difficult race conversation.

An old canard about racist speech goes like this: Uncle Donald is at Thanksgiving dinner. Uncle Donald tells a racist joke, or says something intolerably racist, or reveals something racist that he did at work. An awkward silence ensues. A peacemaker at the table diplomatically changes the subject. Later, family members excuse Uncle Donald, saying something along the lines of 'he's a good person, he's not a racist in his heart, some of his best friends are African-Americans, that's just the way he was raised', etc. *Bullshit.*

Here's why. Let's assume that, unlike me, you are a lawful driver who never exceeds the speed limit. One day, in your brand-new, shiny red sports car, you exceed the speed limit. You are speeding. At that moment, you are a speeder. For obvious reasons, there's no 'not really a speeder' or 'he didn't mean to speed' excuses to exonerate you. Furthermore, if you or I total a car, killing a person or two, no one suggests that 'it doesn't really count because we are safe drivers most of the time', or because 'we are not a speeder at heart', 'some of our best friends are safe drivers', or any other nonsense. As we think about this analogy, we should pause to remind ourselves that racism, like speeding, has real-world implications and life-and-death consequences.

If we coddle racists or rationalize away their hate speech, then racists might, mistakenly, think that they are normal human beings. Racists need public approval, guilt-free membership in our clubs, invitations to our parties. Ostracism is chillingly hard for everyone, but the fact that people don't want to be called a racist is, in and of itself, a point of leverage. Publicly calling out a racist is a really hard thing to do. The backlash is nearly instantaneous. I'm sorry about that, but sometimes, in the life of a social entrepreneur, enemies are worth making.

Social entrepreneurs are not cardiac surgeons, ripping open chest cavities to figure out whose heart is decent and whose heart is defective. We are only interested in what people do and say, what their words reveal about them, whose side they take in the struggle for economic, environmental, gender, social and racial justice. Of course, occasionally we all say something inappropriate, tell a tasteless joke, use a stereotype, reveal our ignorance about a class or culture and so on—and, surely, everyone deserves the benefit of the doubt. However, you and I both know, instinctively and conclusively, the difference between a conversational mistake and racial animus.

At first glance, person-to-person dialogue might seem small and unimportant. Think again. "Even if you could fix something by magic, like wars or hunger, they wouldn't stay fixed. You'd have to fix people," the playwright Colin Teevan writes in *Doctor Faustus*. "And to fix them you have to fix their abilities to fuck things up. Which is sort of what makes us human. The best we can do is try to be decent to those around us, and then if the next person does that, and the next, and the next..." If we can't do it small, we can't do it large. At the most basic level, racial justice starts with confronting the racism in our everyday lives.

—∞—

It's one thing to opine about racism in the social sector. It's quite another to accept responsibility for doing something about it. "You're either part of the solution or part of the problem," Black Panther Co-Founder, social entrepreneur and author of *Soul on Ice* Eldridge Cleaver told white America in 1968. If you and I go along with the status quo, then we *are* the status quo.

Democratizing access to power is infuriatingly slow work. First: people with privilege generally don't appreciate being told they have it. Second: I can acknowledge my privilege, but it's human nature to resist change. Third: power is rarely gifted. Usually, it's purchased with social action. Fourth: overturning inbred societal injustices, especially ones rooted in cultural norms, is never quick, and never popular. Fifth: if we tackle too many issues simultaneously, our effectiveness dilutes and disappears.

Given this, perhaps we think that the best we can do is to lead a life of tolerance: Teach our children that everyone deserves equal opportunity. Donate to a few civil rights organizations. Attend a protest rally and carry a *Black Lives Matter* sign.

But combating racism in the field of social entrepreneurship, like institutional racism everywhere, is not about personal tolerance. Racism is structural. It's about money. Access and power. Fairness and justice.

Social entrepreneurs are all about systemic change. You and I, and all social activists, are best served by heeding this call-to-action from Nwamaka Agbo, the Innovation Fellow at the Movement Strategy Center: "True white allies must understand that they have a responsibility to address the structures of oppression that privilege them day after day. It is not enough to stand with oppressed communities at a protest. White people need to be walking up and down the halls of white supremacy to undo this nasty world that was created to uphold them as superior to everyone else. And that is because their privilege grants them access to spaces and people that I, as a black woman, will never be able to enter into." *Truth.*

America has had a white race problem for a long time. Ask any Native American. For the entire history of the United States, people of conscience have been pushing, cajoling and waiting for institutions controlled by white people – government, corporations, universities, hospitals, churches – to do something about racial injustice.

Our race problem was created of, by, and for, white people. No person of color invented slavery, unequal policing, racial profiling, housing, banking and employment discrimination, poll taxes or segregated schools. No black person thinks that 'white social entrepreneurship' is a splendid idea. For white social entrepreneurs like you and me, the gap between our principled commitment to inclusivity and our failure to live up to our principles is a self-inflicted, psychological stab wound to our profession and to our existential self-worth.

Unless white social entrepreneurs lean into the race issue, unless we get our house in order, social entrepreneurship will morph into just another industry – another profession, another educational establishment, another police department – in a long, long line of institutions that capitulate to America's racially-divided way of doing things. Our loss—and a loss for the cause of social justice.

Take Two: White

Lou Radja, 40, is a Congolese-American social entrepreneur and leadership speaker/trainer, and the Executive Director of EduCongo, Inc. Hometown: Portland, OR. Favorite pastime: Watching TED talks and playing with my two boys. Guilty pleasure: greasy food.

Dear white people,
I'm a black man. I'm African. I'm African-American. And like you, I'm a human being. We are the inheritors of an imperfect world. There isn't much we can really do about the genesis of our inheritance, history is not on trial here today, but there's an abundance in what we can do moving forward and away from the living legacy of racism right here in the US and around the world. With that as a backdrop here are some key ingredients I hope you will include in your 'social justice, equity and inclusion' recipe:

We [black people] need neither saviors nor saving: We are responsible for our lives. If it has to do with us, then we must be the leaders, not you.

We don't need 'allies': If you're fighting for social justice, don't do it as a favor, do it because of it impacts all of us as human beings.

You are not the standard for us to aspire to: Just about every statistic out there (employment, life expectancy, etc.) is always compared to whites. We are fighting for our right to pursue our own dreams. Don't make your standards our aspirations.

'White' privilege has never been the issue: Privilege is unearned advantage. The real opportunity is to leverage your 'white privilege' to make 'privilege' irrelevant for all.

Ubuntu: Human dignity can never be taken away from anyone whether they make $1 a day in rural Congo or $8 a day in East St. Louis. We are all interconnected. So if you see yourself in black people and black people in yourself; then we are truly human beings. Let's practice the true meaning of Ubuntu, our common humanity.

Your fellow human being,
Lou

GLOBALIZATION

Every social entrepreneur carries the globalization gene. Unabashedly, we are globe-trotting change agents. We love our passport stamps. They document our willingness to open our minds to new ideas.

Come with me on a typical (and hypothetical) speaking gig. I'll be giving a talk about the impoverished women who didn't get the memo about the benefits of globalization: the left out and the left behind, the beneficiaries of the microloans financed by MCE Social Capital.

After we arrive at the venue, you settle into a chair at the back of the room as I head off to find the event organizer. We are inside a hotel banquet room with mirrored walls and heavy drapery. Or possibly, even likely, we are at a private mansion in a sumptuous living room with a piece of showy art over the hearth.

To either side of you, the audience is dressed in the understated chic of the affluent. The vibe is convivial; assured; sophisticated. Everyone is obviously well-read and well-traveled. I'm the after-dinner floor show.

My well-rehearsed talk, delivered with conviction, is about poor women in the developing world who are exploited by predatory loan sharks. The microloans they get, thanks to MCE Social Capital, provide a heart-warming, optimistic story of grassroots economic opportunity. Not a panacea for ending poverty, but a proven model for doing our part.

As my speech concludes, you hear a muffled cough. A wine glass is refilled. A couple of polite questions – more casually curious than genuinely concerned – are asked. Someone from the back of the room (usually a woman) thanks me for my commitment to women's economic opportunity. People are starting to fidget, stealing glances at their cell phones and discretely slipping on their coats.

Then, another voice, half accusatory, asks: "Why aren't you offering microloans to poor people in *this* country? You know, we have lots of poverty here at home." That's when the twinkling moment of international empathy for women everywhere goes dark, shattered like a light bulb dropped on a concrete floor.

The question is a blunt challenge to the principal predicate of my remarks, to the notion that we live in a globalized world with globalized responsibilities. Instead, it's now a case of *us versus them.* By insinuation, I am on trial for unpatriotically caring about non-Americans. The audience morphs into a jury, ready to render a verdict on my answer. I'm guilty until proven innocent.

My defensiveness flares. I fight to hold my thermal indignation at bay. I answer calmly—looking for common ground, floundering to regain the audience's lost warmth.

"I'm glad you asked that. It's an excellent question," I fib. "MCE Social Capital focuses on developing countries because that's where impoverished mothers struggle to feed their children on only one dollar a day. That's where the need is greatest. Look around this room. The clothes that we wear, the food that we eat—it all comes to us from a globalized marketplace. Some of us drove here in imported cars. This building was probably constructed, at least in part, by foreign workers. Many of us have stock in multinational corporations. As global citizens, we have global responsibilities."

Of course had I allowed myself the luxury of showing how annoyed I was, I wouldn't have stopped there. I might have called out my prosecutor's blinkered and selfish perspective on America's place in the world. I might have unflinchingly challenged the audience, noting that most affluent Americans have the resources to generously do the right thing at home and abroad. I might have even quoted a popular internet meme: "If you keep your food in a refrigerator, your clothes in a closet, if you have a bed to sleep in and a roof over your head, you are richer than 75 per cent of the world's population."

I might have mentioned that, according to Oxfam, "Americans spend more on candy, lawn care, and soft drinks than the US Government spends on poverty-reducing foreign assistance." I might even have compared our military overspending to our wimpy foreign aid appropriations. I might have reminded the audience that the United States and Somalia are the only two countries in the world not to have ratified the International Convention on the Rights of the Child.

Of course, I don't actually say any of this out loud. After all, some Americans choose to define community differently than the way you or I do. Their generous hearts relate more fiercely to the social problems they see directly in front of them. To them, hands-on volunteering at the local hospital feels more meaningful than raising money to build a clinic in a country that's hard to find on a map. To them, working on a ballot initiative to fund a neighborhood park feels more achievable than working to save the Brazilian or Congolese rain forests. *Black Lives Matter* feels more urgently relevant than *African Lives Matter.*

As social entrepreneurs, we are public educators. It's part of the gig. At parties and public events, at family gatherings and in friendly conversations, in the oddest moments, we're called upon to justify why we do the work we do, not only as an act of compassion and justice, but in the larger context of global citizenship and the irresistible force of globalization.

—∞—

When it comes to globalization, I remain a mélange of major and minor hypocrisies, of double standards and unanswered questions. For most social entrepreneurs – perhaps for you too – unraveling or cherry-picking the constituent parts of globalization is an impossible and pointless task. Globalization and its kissing cousins – urbanization, mechanization, automation, computerization, consumerism, colonialism, capitalism, religion, airplanes, seaports, television, the internet – are welded together.

For example: I gag at discovering a Hard Rock Café in downtown Lima, Peru, but drool at the prospect of a Peruvian dinner in San Francisco, California. The glory of globalization is that, in both cities, I get a choice of cuisines. In both cities, I also owe it to my economic justice agenda to wonder whether the cooks and servers earn a livable wage.

When we dine out, we like our food grown on local organic farms. Ideally, our well-spoken and stylish server will know the precise pedigree of every item on the menu. However, when it comes to my cell phone, I have different expectations. No artisanal cell phones for me, thank you very much. We prefer our electronics assembled by robots operated by well-trained workers wherever they are in the world. Price and quality beat out 'buy locally'. Ask any PlayStation owner. Ask any Walmart shopper.

Globalization is a social entrepreneurship Rorschach test. When we're feeling hopeful, the inkblots reveal the humanizing poetry of Carl Sandburg:

> *There is only one man in the world*
> *and his name is All Men.*
> *There is only one woman in the world*
> *and her name is All Women.*
> *There is only one child in the world*
> *and the child's name is All Children.*

When we're feeling discouraged, those same inky images reveal dark forces plundering local autonomy, local traditions and local economies. We clamor in suspicious opposition to international trade agreements and fume concern over rapacious multinational corporations. Our paranoid conspiracy theories portray the World Bank, the International Monetary Fund and other multilateral institutions as enablers of exploitive, extractive, profiteering business practices.

—∞—

In Granada, Nicaragua, on the promenade called *La Calzada*, the advantages and disadvantages of globalization are on full display. With the city's colonial-era architecture still salvageable and undergoing restoration, Granada is actively cultivating tourism. Isolationism isn't an option.

In 2014, as I strolled *La Calzada*, the sun's glare stalked me, and the hot cement scorched through the bottoms of my canvas shoes. In search of shade, I stepped into *Soy Nica* (in Spanish, proudly, 'I am Nicaraguan'). Tucked between shops selling rough-hewn woodcarvings, traditional shawls and cheap ceramics, *Soy Nica* is a bustling, high-end leather workshop.

Luxuriating in the faint breeze from the slow-turning ceiling fans, I took my leisurely time checking out the shoulder bags, clutches, belts, key fobs, briefcases, backpacks, handbags and purses strewn everywhere. The enticingly sexy colors were fire engine red, margarita green, dark brown, lemony yellow, orangey orange, pink, purple and turquoise. The lush, flirtatious smell of new leather wafted around me, arousing my consumerism.

Soy Nica's imported Danish designs (it must be said) are competing with local craft traditions. The pricey designs are more Danish than indigenous. "All of our Danish-designed products are made in our workshop with 100% Nicaraguan leather by local craftsmen," proclaims the in-store advertising. Not a word about social responsibility, social purpose or fair trade. Still, as I watched the leatherworkers stack more and more, and then more, merchandise on the over-flowing hooks and shelves, local commerce was conspicuously on display. As I stepped back into the sunlight, laden with purchases, I had done my part for the gentrification and globalization affecting every aspect of life in Granada.

From skilled craftsperson to unskilled salesperson, with leather from every part of the cow, *Soy Nica* is creating jobs. *Soy Nica* epitomizes the type of economic development and globalization a social entrepreneur might happily endorse.

—∞—

As global citizens and as social entrepreneurs, we know that each time a human crosses a national border, it brightens our future in the same way that the stars brighten the darkest of night skies. The globalization of the world's populations and the migration of people (not the numbing, impersonal statistics—but real living, walking, eating, laughing, singing, dreaming, loving people) are a social entrepreneur's hope.

Immigrants are *the living* manifestation of our social entrepreneurial commitment to the unfettered flow of human capital and to the free exchange of ideas, traditions and knowledge. Newcomers, by definition, are cultural ambassadors—spreading new languages, new cuisines, new belief structures and new traditions from one community to another. The result is cultural diversity and (as a result) cultural strength and resilience. After all, let's remember that once long ago, German immigrants 'culturally imposed' hot dogs on America, and we are the better for it.

It's hardly a secret that some Americans are xenophobic. Even when I try my best to respectfully understand their frightened, shriveled, miserable viewpoint, I want to scream. Estranged from their ancestors' story of immigration and assimilation, they choose to forget that we live in a country that was settled by genocide. For more recent examples, they also forget the moral mistakes of World War II, when the United States blocked Jewish immigration and put Japanese-American citizens in internment camps. They implicitly disavow the words emblazoned on the Statute of Liberty:

> *Give me your tired, your poor,*
> *Your huddled masses yearning to breathe free,*
> *The wretched refuse of your teeming shore.*
> *Send these, the homeless, tempest-tost to me,*
> *I lift my lamp beside the golden door!*

Immigration is the human face of globalization. When an Indian software geek, a Mexican farmworker, a Filipino nurse or a single mom crosses an American border, our reservoir of human capital is replenished, refreshed and rejuvenated. As reported by *The Economist* in 2013, over 40 per cent of Fortune 500 companies were started by immigrants or their kids.

Every cosmopolitan nation has immigrants. According to UN statistics, 244 million people worldwide live somewhere other than their country of birth, including almost 20 million refugees. Over 43 million immigrants reside in the United States, comprising approximately 14 per cent of the population. Of that 43 million, 11 million people are without legal status—stigmatized and politically sterilized. For them, life without citizenship is an apartheid look-alike.

US industrial policy profits from northbound labor to make our beds, mow our lawns, pick our fruit, slaughter our meat, tend our children and cook in our kitchens. Simultaneously, American trade policy pimps American exports. Free trade and open borders for goods and capital. Unfree trade and closed borders for human capital.

If you believe in the basic oneness of humankind, then the people who scapegoat immigrants or demonize refugees test us. It's pretty damn obvious that a person who breaks the law to feed a hungry family, escape imminent personal danger or build a new life of opportunity is a fundamentally different kind of person than a criminal who violates the law with intent to hurt someone. Because we know this, we sign online petitions; vote against politicians spouting anti-immigrant bigotry; contribute humanitarian dollars to soothe our sadness over the latest refugee crisis; and support campaigns against human trafficking. It's the kind and decent thing to do.

In the end, all societies and all cultural traditions – no matter how storied or sacred – are a polyglot of influences, mythologies, cognates, cross-breedings and historical accidents. "Societies without change aren't authentic; they're just dead," concludes social philosopher Kwame Anthony Appiah in *The Case for Contamination*. Betting on cultural purity never works out because cultural purity doesn't really exist. It never did. And, it's not the social entrepreneurial way.

—∞—

As fair trade advocates remind us, our values are scanned at the checkout register. Embedded in every barcode is the story of globalization—of human creativity married to human industry, of labor's output crossing borders. In a globalized marketplace, we're privileged to be able to make ethical consumer choices—choices which can help or hurt, heighten or hinder, society's advance towards economic justice.

When you and I buy stuff (a box or a bowl, buttons or bananas) at a price that doesn't support a living wage for a worker, a farmer or a craftsperson: it's theft. We are stealing a person's labor. Thus, we become complicit in a system of exploitation, servitude and serfdom. It's true whether I walk on a rug made with child labor; eat a hot dog cooked by an underpaid kitchen worker; or buy a tomato harvested with poorly-paid migrant labor.

Exploiting a person's labor is so repugnant, so universally at odds with our common standards of decency, that we call it slavery or, in less extreme cases, paying slave wages. It can't be a coincidence that so many shit-wage jobs are primarily filled by immigrants, people of color, women and young people—the castaways of the American economic system.

As I sip my morning cup of fair trade coffee (shipped direct from Vega Coffee in Nicaragua), I'm aware that I've not escaped the gravitational force field of globalization and its best friend, capitalism. I'm consuming within the accepted norms of the marketplace—buying what I want, at the price I want, from the producers I want. It's another opportunity to act ethically.

We can't hide from the truth that we are often, albeit unwittingly, direct beneficiaries of a worker's misery and misfortune. Even if I don't have the time or the talent to personally organize a consumer boycott or lobby Congress, I can take a small step towards economic justice by buying fair trade certified products.

—∞—

For internationally-minded social entrepreneurs, the debate over outsourcing American jobs brings up one pivotal question: *is a worker in our country of lesser, equal or greater human value than a worker elsewhere?* Do you or I (as an American, a global citizen, and a human being) have a greater obligation to the unemployed in Detroit, Michigan versus the unemployed in Durban, South Africa?

Social entrepreneurs (and everyone else with a heartbeat and a conscience) are upset by globalization's collateral damage. The problems caused by historic and current colonialism, imperialism, mercantilism and corporate greed are well-documented.

It's wholly understandable that lots of people are pissed off by globalization. Caught in the riptides and undertows of globalization, there can be a panicky sense of drowning—both financially and culturally. Globalization is routinely, and wrongly, faulted for disappearing jobs (mainly caused by robotics, computerization or corporate consolidation) and wage stagnation (mainly caused by trickle-down economic policies that don't trickle).

As a result, the reality (and fear) of domestic job loss energizes opposition to international trade agreements and imported goods.

In noticeable contrast, shipyard workers who load and unload the merchandise we import and export; farmers and ranchers who sell food to the world; aircraft industry engineers and Big Pharma doctors and scientists are mysteriously disorganized and silent.

In the same way that assembly-line auto manufacturing disrupted bicycle makers; the printing press killed off jobs for scribes; and the steam engine reduced employment opportunities for horses—social entrepreneurs know that large-scale economic change creates winners and losers. Even if, in a utopian job market, every single worker worldwide had full-time employment with equal pay for equal productivity, a company that automated would eventually gain a competitive advantage. Sooner or later, workers somewhere would be laid off.

The 'Buy American' and 'Made in America' slogans are fundamentally and irrevocably at odds with our global citizenship—just another way to reinforce the *us versus them* paradigm. I don't shop for (or against) internationally-sourced products any more than I shop for (or against) American-made products. I shop for the best products. I hope you do too.

In any case, protectionist economic policies backfire. The macro-economic consequence of less trade is slower international development, which creates even more economic pressures for people in other countries to migrate to more robust job markets. Real-life people get hurt on both sides of the tariff walls that we build.

For most people, and for all social entrepreneurs, empathy makes no distinction between a crying child in Mississippi and a crying child in Malawi. If that's true for love of a child, why hide our compassion for a mother with children escaping starvation? For a hardscrabble farmer in a distant land? For a refugee escaping a war zone? Empathy makes global citizens of us all.

— ∞ —

Globalization – the interdependence of people and products, economies and markets, cultures and communications, artistic traditions and scientific knowledge – is unstoppable. The gods of globalization will have their way.

Unless you or I are card-carrying members of Hermits Anonymous, globalization is how we lead our lives. Before modern globalization, most Americans were unfamiliar with yoga, meditation or Indian food. Assemble-it-yourself furniture from the Swedish company IKEA depends on parts manufactured in Poland and China. The World Health Organization, the Boy and Girl Scouts and the Olympics are global institutions. So too is organized crime. And so is the American death industry (vomiting out handguns, assault weapons, missiles, jet fighters and battleships).

We breathe air from everywhere. When I did my bit for climate change, there was an 80 per cent chance that my new solar roof panels were manufactured outside the United States. Do I care? No. Should I care? No.

Globalization is both a fragmenting and a coalescing force for social justice. Even as globalization has lifted millions out of abject poverty, created a global middle class and put British mysteries in my TV lineup, it has also opened up a cavernous wealth gap between rich and poor countries. A paradoxical fact of globalization, and a reality we can't ignore, is that increased contact between peoples creates increased opportunities for greater understanding that are offset or undercut by more opportunities for greater misunderstanding. As we globalize, we homogenize and, as we homogenize, humans seem to have a psychological need to rediscover and deepen tribal identities.

Every social entrepreneur carries the globalization gene. Unabashedly, we love our passport stamps. They document our internationalism, our willingness to audaciously throw open our minds to new ways of doing things. Nonetheless, as we circumnavigate the globe, it's obvious that globalization is a mix of welcome mats and bolted doors.

You and I can reduce our carbon footprint. We can buy less. We can be energy efficient. We can purchase fair trade. We can oppose trade subsidies and tariff protections that hurt small farmers. We can fight for the rights of refugees. We can do lots of things.

What we cannot do is unhook ourselves from the global economy or the global marketplace of ideas. We cannot reverse the irreversible, but we can use our social entrepreneurship to soften and shape globalization so that it serves more than greed.

Take Two: Globalization

Saif Kamal, 33, is the Founder at Toru. Toru empowers and supports Bangladeshi youth to build and scale social innovations in education and health. Favorite pastime: cooking. Guilty pleasure: milk chocolate.

"Assuming that you consider yourself a global citizen, I would call on your empathy to add a dimension to Jonathan's impression of globalization. I would like you to ask: how is globalization experienced at the other end of the spectrum? By those who have the ideas to change the world but fall out on the margins of globalization?

"The obsession of seeing the developing world through the single story of 'beneficiaries' is one of the greater disparities of globalization. A question I ask again and again at international meetings, summits, and events is: is a social innovation that can improve lives doomed to fail just because it is not born in the developed world? I don't do it to guilt-trip or bait the well-meaning foreign donor. I ask because I honestly want to know the 'why' behind this disparity.

"Each year, hundreds of young people from developed countries parachute into developing nations through programs to volunteer and build community capacities or social enterprises. Their intentions are well-meaning, but it is seldom sustainable. In the long run, they don't dedicate themselves to the journey. While resources are channeled to accelerate the privileged changemakers' growth, local talents are unable to grow beyond the limits 'globalization' has created for them.

"By the sheer lottery of globalization and capitalism, is it acceptable that we, in the developing world, remain as 'beneficiaries', often blocked from becoming solution builders? Imagine if globalization had channeled the same resources and opportunities directly to the Nicaraguan who harvests the fair trade coffee you sip, the impact they could create would be incredibly powerful. Living in a globalized world comes with the responsibility to dignify the other's vision of a better world and not simply uplift them into our versions of a better world."

LIFEBLOOD

Social entrepreneurs do not exist without anchoring relationships. I am who I care about. I am who I fight for.

She and I first met in Bolivia. Because we were never formally introduced, I never learned her real name. In the secrecy of my mind, I called her *Musetta* – 'Little Muse' – for reasons you are about to learn. I thought of her the other day. Even after so many years, I count her close to my heart.

I had traveled fourteen hours by plane from San Francisco, California to La Paz, Bolivia. From the flat, agricultural delta of the Sacramento Valley at sea level to the world's highest capital city— a vertical climb of two and a half miles. After that, a day's journey overland awaited me.

She spoke Aymara, a pre-Inca language. At the time, I didn't even know that Aymara existed. Back then, I struggled to pronounce even a few phrases in Spanish. *Hola. Gracias. Buenas Noches.*

A further estrangement: altitude sickness. My first full day in La Paz was spent in a stark, unadorned hotel room. Under every available blanket, still fully-clothed and bundled in a parka, I shivered in bed. I drank coca tea by the bucketful. At one point, it occurred to me that, to save myself the trouble of getting out of bed so often, I should just pour the tea directly into the toilet. It was 24 hours before my body acclimated.

Even higher than La Paz is El Alto, a working-class city situated on the high plains, a study in peopled chaos and constant commotion. Colorless bleached buildings. Dirt and desperation. Debris blows in the fierce wind. Small shops cling to every available wall. Vendors and hawkers cater to every need—from produce to prostitutes.

El Alto is a city seemingly owned by feral dogs. They roam every median strip, scour every empty lot and gut uncollected black plastic garbage bags, leaving uneaten rubbish and waste in their wake.

As we cleared the city limits, El Alto became another faded mental snapshot. A vintage sepia photograph of a teeming mass of haggard faces in New York's Lower East Side or San Francisco's Barbary Coast. The sheer momentum of human survival captured in still-frame.

We traversed a bumpy, rocky road for long dusty hours until it withered into an imperceptible path, cutting through fields guarded by barking dogs and gaunt cows. We passed a young boy, maybe ten years old, and his younger sister tending a small herd of sheep, the lambs bleating. Otherwise, far above the tree line, it was deathly quiet. Desolate. Cold. No birds chirp. No insects buzz. You could hear the blood in your ears.

We approach an abandoned schoolhouse with broken windows. Dried goat shit covers the weedy school grounds. In an open field nearby, eleven women in traditional Bolivian garb huddle in a circle on the bare ground. Chill winds descend from distant snow-capped mountains; thick shawls cover sagging shoulders. Fingers fidget constantly. Hands dart into pockets deep inside heavily-layered skirts. One woman nurses a baby. Another uses the edge of her skirt to wipe a child's snotty nose. A third lifts a foot to expose a slipper shoe with holes. The women have haunting, furrowed faces. After years of living close to the sun, their crinkled eyes squint permanently. I guess an age range of 60 to 75; later I'm surprised to learn that the women are between 20 and 45 years old.

At the suggestion of the microfinance innovator Freedom from Hunger, I had come to Bolivia to learn about *Crédito con Educación Rural* (CRECER), a small business loan program for impoverished rural women. At the time, Dr. Muhammad Yunus had not yet won a Nobel Peace Prize for pioneering (and then popularizing) modern microfinance, but the economic development intelligentsia was already abuzz about grassroots 'village banking'.

By that time, CRECER was already successfully serving 68,000 women, each one eking out a hardscrabble life in remote Andean villages. With loans averaging $185, these women used skills hand- ed down by their mothers (farming, animal husbandry, sewing, selling, cooking) to start small enterprises to pay for food, health care and life's necessities. As part of the business loan package, the women automatically received social services (such as classes in financial literacy or business advice) plus health and wellness education. With a loan repayment rate of 99.6 per cent, CRECER was *an entirely self-financing nonprofit.*

The meeting begins. From within the women's pleated skirts, money emerges. The group leader, identified by the ledger on the dirt in front of her, uses her lap as a cash drawer, accepting repayments and making change for each woman. The loan officers and tellers for this mini-bank are the women themselves. Sisters-in-finance.

Each is watched carefully by the others and, when deemed necessary, the commentary is animated; focused; pointed. No danger of underhanded Wall Street accounting tricks; in this small community, non-repayment imposes huge social consequences.

Until she stands, *Musetta* is submerged in the circle. Like her peers, she wears the *pollera* (a colorful, pleated skirt) and a black felt bowler hat that, incongruously, was introduced in the 19th century by Europeans. *Musetta's* bowler hat is endearingly jaunty. She is short; rotund; compact.

She talks, slowly testing her words as they move off her tongue, and as she does, I could swear she grows a few inches taller. At first, her voice is nearly inaudible, but then it crescendos, resonating with authority.

My translator translates. *Musetta* reports that, for the first time, she is reliably feeding her children three times a day. Rapt, I study her body language, her intensity. I'm bewitched by the majesty of her movement. Empowerment embodied. Her eyes sparkle with maternal grit. My eyes water.

Banking done, the group unceremoniously dissolves. As women cluster in twos and threes to pursue private conversations and gossip, a lone woman breaks away to return home. Maybe to her children. Maybe to her husband. Certainly to her own business.

I wander back to the van, girding myself for the long trip back to San Francisco via El Alto, La Paz, and Miami—taking with me a memory, and a future.

Mentor or muse, anyone who brings out your life purpose is forever part of you. Over a decade later, this single, anonymous mother feeding her children informs and fuels my social justice work.

Confronted with a vexing decision about a social enterprise or impact investment, I pause to wonder what *Musetta* – or any parent suffering the heart-breaking sorrow of a hungry child – might advise me to do. Of course, I can never be sure what she might say, but just asking the question spurs a sense of urgency, and excites my unwavering belief that the work of social entrepreneurship matters.

—∞—

You and I share a sense of responsibility, kinship, and community that comes from recognizing that, to one degree or another, we are all implicated in the world's injustices. Global poverty is our problem. Ecological destruction is our problem. Racial, ethnic and gender discrimination is our problem. *Musetta's* children are our children.

Social entrepreneurs do not exist without anchoring relationships. I am who I care about. I am who I fight for.

People like *Musetta* inspire me to take sides. Social entrepreneurship is my pledge *to myself* to make social justice more than an ephemeral, take-it-or-leave-it part of my life.

You and I do this work because it's personal. At the grandest level, we yearn for justice, environmental sanity, racial and class equality. At the grittiest level, behind each of those ideals, there are real people—people that you and I know. People we think about. People we care about.

In the elegant phrasing of Rainer Maria Rilke in *Auguste Rodin*, you and I seek "the grace of great things". We make "common cause to find our souls". We pursue "dreams which become deeds, and deeds which pass away in dreams". We undertake "a task as great as the world itself—the task of centuries, limitless and without end. Like a rising sun, whose light rests everywhere."

Musetta, and so many men and women like her, remind me that transformative social entrepreneurship and disruptive social innovation are about creating hope, shifting human behavior, solving problems, creating opportunity and strengthening ourselves to furiously challenge the status quo. As United Farm Workers Founder Cesar Chavez used to say, "Every time a man or woman stands up for justice, the heavens sing and the world rejoices." In that respect, our social entrepreneurship is inspired and energized by the thunderous, irresistible social justice movements of history.

Justice is our lifeblood. Imagining a life without causes, convictions, or community is like imagining a life without hugs, smiles, laughter, hope, or love. A life without adventure, mystery, or wonder. I can't imagine it because it is unimaginable—like trying to visualize myself dead.

—∞—

Most people don't get to do what we do. Fighting for social justice is a special gift, conferred on us by our talents, our privilege, our moral code and our troubled times. As the American poet Clarissa Pinkola Estes describes: "We were made for these times. When a great ship is in harbor and moored, it is safe. But that is not what great ships are built for."

In my own life voyage, I feel most alive, most needed, most challenged – and most uncertain of myself – when I'm sailing far from home port, in choppy and foreboding seas, towards a lighthouse called justice. When I fail to claim a life sailing against the riptides and undercurrents of injustice, when I stay on shore like so much dried kelp—I fail who I am.

As a social entrepreneur: I'm an imperfect person, with imperfect answers, acting on imperfect information, with imperfect results. I need your vision, your virtues and your competencies to complete mine. The world needs all hands on deck. The ship of social justice does not sail itself.

Realistically, the world's woes are huge, and we are small. At best, our accomplishments are fragile. They can be wiped out by a war, a drought, a commodity price fluctuation, a bad president or an environmental disaster. The child we tutored yesterday could have a fatal accident tomorrow.

Secretly, inside our uncompromising selves, you and I know that our social entrepreneurship might not be transformative, radical or lasting. Indeed, we might not make any difference at all. This fear is the single most important truth that we consistently hide from critics and supporters alike.

Setbacks and reversals test us. "Activism is a daily, even hourly, experiment in dedication, moral courage, and resilience," notes Courtney Martin in *Do It Anyway: The New Generation of Activists*. Patience, persistence, endurance, guts and grit, personal and professional courage are the stuff from which we build our social justice careers.

Maybe now or in the past, you've felt dwarfed or discouraged by the enormity of the world's problems—the hate, the conflict, the gross disregard of human, economic and environmental injustice. By any reasonable calculus, you're entitled to a major case of issue fatigue. When my energy wanes or my spirits flag, when I am feeling selfish, or greedy, or lazy, I like the advice of Lick-Wilmerding High School's Rebecca Hong, speaking to its 2013 graduating class: "Move slowly. Mend things."

The Sisyphean truth of our social entrepreneurship is that we can't finish it, ever. The boulder we push is heavy, the problems intractable and the solutions uncharted. At the pinnacle, we re-discover, again and again, that justice is an inherently expanding, ever more inclusive, ever more elusive goal. Every step up the mountain of progress brings with it deeper understandings about community, as well as new resistance. When you decide not to give up—you're a social entrepreneur.

Muckraking Sixties journalist I. F. Stone said: "The only kinds of fights worth fighting are those you are going to lose because somebody has to fight them and lose and lose and lose. In order for somebody to win an important, major fight a hundred years hence, a lot of other people have got to be willing – for the sheer fun and joy of it – to go right ahead and fight, knowing you're going to lose. You mustn't feel like a martyr. You've got to enjoy it." Indeed.

At the point in our lives when we commit ourselves to a life of service, one truth ambushes us. Suddenly, seemingly without warning, we want a life that is worthy. A virtuous life that reflects and amplifies our best possible selves. A life that is challenging. Exciting. Uplifting. Laugh-out-loud joyful. We want a life in pursuit of social justice.

Social entrepreneurship is an existential statement about who we are. About my values. About your values. About our shared global citizenship. The world awaits.

CONFESSIONS

I confess. I have expectations of you. Now that you've read this book, I hope you kick injustice in the ass. More than once, and really hard.

I've told a few stories in this book. But the real story – the only story worth telling – is the one you will write for yourself.

After engorging ourselves on textbooks, magazines, lectures, blogs, newspapers, conferences, social media, policy papers, podcasts, memos and government findings—you and I want to do something, to complete our good consciences with good deeds. In the compelling phrase from Harvard economist and Nobel Laureate Amartya Sen in *Development as Freedom*, you and I have a case of 'constructive impatience'.

We are called to the big challenges of our time. Unquestionably, we're each privileged to answer that call differently, but we *are* called. In a world plagued by injustice, there's always plenty to do.

I confess. I have expectations of you. Now that you've read this book, I hope you kick injustice in the ass. More than once, and really hard.

Obviously, at this point, I'm assuming that you the think this book has value, and that other changemakers should know about it. As Miriam Kleynerman, a politics student at New York University wrote me: "While I can't imagine not making some kind of meaningful change, I'm not sure where to turn for help, or even what idea to pursue. I want equally-excited, passionate and caring people surrounding me to help me to think and plan my next steps. By opening up a dialogue, by *talking about your book* [emphasis mine], I can connect to other social entrepreneurs or even people who didn't realize they are social entrepreneurs."

I've crowdsourced a list of actionable, skill-building ideas for you to play around with, and included them here. Use the ones that fit your personality, interests and circumstances.

Also, let's agree, between us, to the following: On my side, I agree to apply book sale profits to causes that we both care about (and which, to my great shock, doesn't include the Jonathan C. Lewis Bahamas Retirement Fund). By now, you know my values. On your side, avoid promoting the book for its own sake. Instead, focus on the issues and questions inside the book.

If some of these ideas seem small or trivial, almost too easy, here's what I've finally figured out: each small thing we do builds career momentum. Every social action project hones our skills for when the stakes are higher, and harder. Social change work is also infectious. When you and I take action, it signals that social justice work is a thing—and that we are committed to it.

1. *Organize a community roundtable discussion.* Be sure to invite everyone, especially people who might not feel welcome because of the hue of their skin, their religious faith or their sexual orientation. Good venues include libraries, book clubs, campus centers, social impact hubs, social enterprise incubators and social venture training institutes. Use our free *Community Conversation Guide* (online at www.JonathanCLewis.com).

2. *Write a book review.* Potential outlets include your campus or local newspaper, online social change publications (too numerous to catalog, but easy to research), organizational newsletters or magazines. And, don't forget Amazon Customer Reviews because everyone, including their surprisingly-literate dogs and cats, reads them. After reading this book, if you think I'm full of shit—say so. Whatever you do, don't be silent. Silence is non-social entrepreneurship.

3. *Show your social entrepreneurial pride.* Wear *The Unfinished Social Entrepreneur* t-shirt, drink from our coffee mug, or carry the tote bag. We don't make or sell any of that stuff, so good luck.

4. *Become an expert.* Take any issue that you care about (or a question raised in the book) and learn more about it. Then (and this is the critical part), publish or share what you learn with others. Provoke others to think while you accumulate bylines and credits for your résumé. It's a devilishly fine way to spend an afternoon.

5. *Share the love.* Take a smiling, frowning or funny selfie with the book and post it on Facebook, Twitter or Instagram (tag it #UnFinSocEnt). If your friends don't even know the book exists, they can't decide for themselves whether or not to read it. Photo tip: Everyone looks smarter while eating a hot dog.

6. *Tweet it out.* I promise to read and react to your tweeted thoughts. My twitter handle: @SocentClinic. Follow me, and I will follow you so we can stay in touch.

7. *Shop fair trade.* Expand your personal market power by organizing a fair trade purchasing club. Go a step further and mount a community campaign to get local merchants to stock fair trade merchandise, eco-friendly goods, etc.

8. *Register to vote.* If your jurisdiction bans voting multiple times, then register your friends to vote. Throw a voter registration party. If that doesn't work, throw a fit.

9. *Be a guest.* Offer to be interviewed on a local radio, television or podcast show about whatever cause, campaign or project moves your heart. Lots of local

talk shows are looking for new voices. If you have a heartbeat, you may have a moment of hesitation or nervousness. I always do. Managing stage fright is a good skill to learn early in our changemaker careers.

10. *Be a listener.* Work on listening to the voices in your neighborhood that you normally don't hear (or see). Join a group outside your comfort zone. Prepare to be shocked at how many people live in the shadows.

11. *Reduce your carbon footprint.* Stuck for ideas on how? Wear a sweater. Watch less TV. Install energy efficient windows. Take public transportation. Read in the dark. Shower with a friend.

12. *Weaponize your talents.* While earning your MBA or accounting degree, volunteer to balance the books at a Planned Parenthood clinic. While studying the law, set up a legal clinic for undocumented workers. While majoring in agricultural sciences, help an inner-city community garden feed the homeless. While studying journalism, start muckraking. You get the idea.

13. *Invite me to speak.* Your campus or conference, a speakers' series or local bookstore, any podcast or radio show are all potential venues. Use the contact form at my website.

14. *Be a grunt worker.* Check out the local chapter of whatever national organization moves your soul. Volunteer, intern, go to meetings, join rallies, picket, protest, march for justice. Do whatever grunt work is needed because it is needed.

15. *Hug your local librarian.* Not everyone can afford to buy books, so ask your local library to stock *The Unfinished Social Entrepreneur.* If the librarian refuses, write a ranting press release to denounce socialized knowledge

paid for by over-taxed taxpayers who, if taxes were lower, would have more money in their pockets to buy more guns or gum. Don't actually send the press release. You don't want people to accidentally mistake you for a conservative.

—∞—

A single book, or even entire library of books, whether skimmed or studied, can only story-tell about the fulfilling joy of justice-making. Beyond the covers of *this* book, you and I can experience passion and purpose in our lives by the actual doing of it.

Moreover, nothing good happens in this world without persistence, dedication and extended commitment. A single blog post won't overturn racist, sexist, xenophobic, homophobic practices. A tweet, even a couple of retweets, won't rebalance society's unjust power dynamics. The environment is not nearly clean enough after one protest march. Start with small things. Aim for large ones.

You and I can't innovate social change or produce workable solutions alone. We need each other to build the world we want. We need each other to kick injustice in the ass.

The Unfinished Social Entrepreneur is finished. Our work is not.

CREDITS

Like social entrepreneurship, books are collaborations. My name is printed on the cover of this book, but the names of others are imprinted on me.

As this book became a reality, a loyal group of pro bono editorial advisors, friends, family members, business partners, fellow change agents and near-strangers read my chapters in their rawest stages of disorganization. When I doubted the book's worth (which was often), their margin notes, persistent commentary, loving support and relentless enthusiasm kept me going. Despite all evidence to the contrary, these colleagues and friends never stopped believing in the writer they thought I was: Karen Ansara, Lorene Arey, Gary Carrier, Darlene Daggett, Gary Ford, Michael Gordon, Jen Gurecki, Sara Hall, Amanda Hayden, Tracie Hudgins, Holly McKenna, Alexandra McGee, Chingwell Mutombu, Sally Osberg, Jan Piercy, Lissa Piercy, Clemens Pietzner, Ananya Roy, Rosalinda Sanquiche, David Sonnenberg, Tracey Turner, Akaya Windwood. With any luck, by now, they will have recovered from the experience. Then there are my wife Jeanette, and son Aaron who, by living their lives with decency, widen my moral vision.

If you are contemplating writing a book, an early measure of your connection to reality is the selection of an editor. My thought partner and editorial therapist has been the incomparable Katherine Knotts, Founder of Red Press. Some say that your toughest critic is yourself, but Katherine proved that bromide incorrect. She taught me to write a book and for that I am truly grateful.

In addition, the following registry records the people who offered a timely word of feedback, a helpful suggestion or a needed donation.

Some people will scratch their heads, wondering why they are listed at all. Others, who live in my heart, are entitled to wonder why the book is not dedicated to them. Someday, I hope you have the good fortune to spend time with the amazing people who have been my editorial allies, role models, voices of encouragement, inspirational confidants and collaborating critics.

To each one of you, thank you for your remarkable gifts of wisdom and wit, for caring about social justice and for caring about me:

Allison Aaronson, Mitra Adron, Amara Kyna Agbim, George Alcser, John Anner, Jen Astone, Mahabat Barantseva, Natasha Baimyrzaeva, Ted Barber, Andrew Barrer, Chris Benner, David Berge, Rajasvini Bhansali, Hilary Braseth, Karelli Cabral, Andrew Clark, Aaron Contorer, Mathias Craig, Monica Curca, Josephine D'Allant, Victor D'Allant, James Dailey, Sam Daley-Harris, Jim Davidson, Hannah Davis, Laura DeDominicis, Denny DeLeo, Sasha Dichter, Katie Drasser, Christopher Dunford, Jed Emerson, Christina Espinosa, Gloria Evans, Ellen Fish, Rick Foot, Jill Freeman, Jon Freeman, Elizabeth Funk, Saul Garlick, James Gaynor, Dan Geballe, Paola Gianturco, Debra Gittler, Yonatan Glaser, Patrick Gleeson, Natasha Goldstein, Michael Gordon, John Griffing, Mozart Guerrier, Sadhana Hall, Marie Haller, James Harrington, Cary and Gary Hart, Amy Hartzler, Kari Hayden Pendoley, Devin Hibbard, Rowland Hobbs, Tracie Hudgins, Shawn Humphrey, Pia Infante, Kathleen Janus, Christina Jennings, Mark Jordahl, Kimberley Jutze, Maggie Kaplan, Jeff Keenan, Noushin Ketabi, Miriam Kleynerman, Floris Koot, Mike Lapham, Tom Layton, Sumyee Sylvia Lee, David Lehr, Jennifer Lentfer, Wendy Leonard, Theodore Levinson, Chid Liberty, Linked Foundation, Jessica Loman, Emily Lutyens, Anand Madhvani, Annie Makela, Peter Maribei, Ramon Marmolejos, Ezra Mbogori, Ginger McNally, Forrest Metz, Bonny Meyer, John Meyers, Sara Minkara, Samantha Morshed, Tabitha Mpamira, Mark Muckerheide, Ashwini Narayanan, Lisa Nash, Charlotte Ntim, Tim O'Shea, Sara Olsen, Sachee Parikh, Babita Patel, Roshan Paul, Amy Paulson, Alison Pavia, Kristine Pearson, Robin Pendoley, Renato Orozco Pereira, Tiffany Persons, Clemens Pietzner, Sherri Pittman, Elena Pons, Ben Powell, Sasha Rabsey, Natalie Rekstad-Lynn, Carrie Rich, Gerald Richards, Amanda Rodriguez, Lynn and Larry Rolston, Taylor Rosty, George Scharffenberger, Beverly

Schwartz, Sujatha Sebastian, Ciru Segal, Jasmine Segall, Jessamyn Shams-Lau, Ritu Sharma, Chantal Sheehan, Bruce Sievers, Shawn Smith, David Sonnenberg, Doug Spencer, George Srour, Tom and Meg Stallard, Lori Steele, Gretchen Steidle, Ryan Steinbach, Keely Stevenson, Tanya Stevenson, Kiel Stroupe, Nancy Swanson, John Swift, Sonja Swift, Robert Terenzi, Triskeles Foundation, Two Parrot Productions, Sam Vaghar, Abhi Vallabhaneni, Jackie VanderBrug, Dana Vigran, Ayesha Wagle, Sandra Way, Bill Washburn, Anke Wessels, Emily West, Deb Wetherby, Whitman Institute, Rodger Widmann, Jorian Wilkins, Topher Wilkins, Emily Winslow, Britt Yamamoto, Yasmina Yusuf, Soushiant Zanganehpour, Teal Brown Zimring.

CPSIA information can be obtained
at www.ICGtesting.com
Printed in the USA
FSOW03n0046170617
35309FS